DOING DIFFERENCE DIFFERENTLY

Doing Difference Differently

Chinese International Students' Literacy Practices and Affordances

ZHAOZHE WANG

UTAH STATE UNIVERSITY PRESS
Logan

© 2024 by University Press of Colorado

Published by Utah State University Press
An imprint of University Press of Colorado
1580 North Logan Street, Suite 660
PMB 39883
Denver, Colorado 80203-1942

All rights reserved

 The University Press of Colorado is a proud member of Association of University Presses.

The University Press of Colorado is a cooperative publishing enterprise supported, in part, by Adams State University, Colorado State University, Fort Lewis College, Metropolitan State University of Denver, University of Alaska Fairbanks, University of Colorado, University of Denver, University of Northern Colorado, University of Wyoming, Utah State University, and Western Colorado University.

ISBN: 978-1-64642-642-3 (hardcover)
ISBN: 978-1-64642-643-0 (paperback)
ISBN: 978-1-64642-644-7 (ebook)
https://doi.org/10.7330/9781646426447

Library of Congress Cataloging-in-Publication Data

Names: Wang, Zhaozhe, author.
Title: Doing difference differently : Chinese international students' literacy practices and affordances / Zhaozhe Wang.
Description: Logan : Utah State University Press, [2024] | Includes bibliographical references and index.
Identifiers: LCCN 2024002448 (print) | LCCN 2024002449 (ebook) | ISBN 9781646426423 (hardcover) | ISBN 9781646426430 (paperback) | ISBN 9781646426447 (ebook)
Subjects: LCSH: English language—Rhetoric—Study and teaching (Higher)—Social aspects—United States—Case studies. | English language—Study and teaching (Higher)—Chinese speakers—Case studies. | College students' writings, Chinese—United States—Case studies. | Chinese students—United States—Attitudes—Case studies. | Generation Z—Education (Higher)—United States—Case studies. | Literacy—Social aspects—United States—Case studies. | Difference (Psychology)
Classification: LCC PE1405.U6 W36 2024 (print) | LCC PE1405.U6 (ebook) | DDC 808.042071—dc23/eng/20230311
LC record available at https://lccn.loc.gov/2024002448
LC ebook record available at https://lccn.loc.gov/2024002449

Cover art: "About Face," © Susan Chen, oil on canvas, 74" x 54", 2020.

Contents

List of Figures vii

Acknowledgments ix

Introduction 3

1. Discourse of Cultural Diversity and Ethnographic Case Study of Literacy Practices 19

2. Manna: From the Dance Floor to Writing Tutor's Table 35

3. Wentao: A Structuralist Poet in Disguise 61

4. Yang: A Translingual Gothic Musician in the Making 91

5. Bohan: A Cosmopolitan "Robot Master" 119

6. Doing Difference Differently 148

7. Networked Ecological Affordances 166

   Epilogue: Toward a New Understanding of Chinese International Students' Literacy Practices 182

Notes 187
References 189
Index 197

Figures

2.1. Manna meeting her dance club members 39
3.1. Course syllabus annotated by Wentao 64
3.2. Wentao's writing's room 69
3.3. Visual representation of "situational awareness" created by Wentao and his team 71
3.4. Promotional image created by Wentao 75
3.5. Wentao's WeChat status 87
4.1. 絵馬/えま/Ema, courtesy of DLKR (unsplash.com) 96
5.1. Bohan's writing's room 134
5.2. Bohan's WeChat status 143

Acknowledgments

I dedicate this book to my students, who invited me into their worlds and imbued what I do with new meanings and purposes. I am grateful to everyone who has provided intellectual, moral, and emotional support and helped me in various capacities to bring this project to fruition: Tony Silva, Margie Berns, Bud Weiser, Thomas Rickert, April Ginther, Rachael Levay, two anonymous reviewers/mentors, Ji-young Shin, Xiaoye You, Hadi Banat, Sweta Baniya, Xiaobo Wang, Kai Yang, Pat Burnes, Deborah Rogers, Dylan Dryer, Mark Blaauw-Hara, Sheila Batacharya, Michael Kaler, the team at Utah State University Press/University Press of Colorado, and many others. I am forever in your debt.

DOING DIFFERENCE DIFFERENTLY

Introduction

It was a chilly September morning in Cornville,[1] a small, quintessential US Midwestern college town home to approximately ten thousand international students who build their lives and dreams on the campus of Wabash University. The campus had just regained its hustle and bustle after a long, tranquil summer, as a new academic year began to unfold. As usual, I came to my office early in the morning to catch the first shaft of sunlight and get some grading done. A few weeks into the new semester, students in my writing classes, most of whom were from China, had not failed to regale me with their thoughtfully crafted literacy autobiographies that showcased the apotheosis of their rich, multifaceted literacy history. One student writer recounted how the hundreds of instructor-mandated weekly journal entries that she produced in high school led to a love-hate relationship with narrative writing, yet in the meantime cultivated in her an appreciation for the power of self-reflection. Another student writer reflected on how his experience with writing for a school newspaper helped him build confidence in writing papers for different courses in US high schools. Yet my eyes were locked on one piece, in which Yang, the writer, analyzed the lyrics of a Japanese song that was especially meaningful to her multilingual literacy.

In her literacy autobiography, Yang, coming from China, presented to her reader—me, her first-year writing instructor, also coming from China—the gateway to her then literacy world that revolved around Japanese pop culture. As I was appreciating her evolving understanding of the aesthetics of Japanese pop culture, as seen in the sentence "although [she] was never trained to understand what the definition of 'beauty' in Japanese culture is, [she] feels the resonance coming from this masterpiece [referring to lyrics by NaturaLe]" an email notification on my phone abruptly interrupted me. It was *Wabash Today*, a digital newsletter sent to Wabash University employees every workday morning. The headline in Wabash University's signature color read, "Rogers [pseudonym] Tapped to Communicate Wabash's Promise." Rogers, the former secretary of commerce for the state of Indiana and chief executive officer of the Indiana Economic Development Corporation, was named Wabash's executive vice president for communication and took on the responsibility of "enhancing Wabash University's visibility and growing reputation at home and around the world" ("Hasler Tapped," 2018). Specifically, Rogers would be in charge of brand marketing for the institution, strategic communications, media relations, and advertising.

This executive-level move didn't come as a surprise; as a matter of fact, it was in line with the university leadership's entrepreneurial vision of growing Wabash into a globally reputable brand that's capable of attracting qualified students, scholars, and sources of funding from around the world. Over the previous two years, several bold strategic moves have been carried out at Wabash toward the ultimate goal of global branding; some of them invited controversies, if not resistance. For example, in the spring of 2018, Wabash officially launched Wabash Global—Wabash's acquisition of the for-profit online college Lawson University. However, the marriage between the land-grant research university and the profit-driven corporation, unfortunately, was not a blessed one initially. The administrative rationale behind the deal, according to Wabash's president, was to position Wabash as a leader in the evolving online higher education (Douglas-Gabriel, 2017). Yet, before the Higher Learning Commission was scheduled to approve the deal in October 2017, more than 300 Wabash faculty members signed a petition opposing the deal. In the petition, faculty voiced their concerns with the administration's lack of transparency in negotiating the deal, the lack of faculty input in the decision-making process, and Lawson University's poor track record, which could potentially damage the university's reputation. Despite faculty pushback, the acquisition was greenlighted and the new Wabash-branded online university, Wabash Global, was up and running.

The university's ambition to increase the visibility and impact of its brand continues to yield inspiration for innovative marketing strategies. During its spring 2018 commencement ceremony, Wabash connected live to the International Space Station to award NASA astronaut and alumnus Andrew J. Feustel an honorary doctorate, which became a trendy topic on social media where tens of thousands of people circulated and reacted to the story. The story also endowed Chinese international students at Wabash with tremendous bragging rights on WeChat, the social media platform virtually all Chinese international students rely on to connect with each other and their family back home. More interestingly, Wabash has also become the birthplace of two Guinness World Records—one for the most train whistles blowing at the same time (more than 5,000 students participated) and the other for assembling the periodic table in 8 minutes 36 seconds (set by a chemical engineering professor).

Wabash University is certainly not the only institution that's caught up in the sweeping current of global expansion and a neoliberal political climate in higher education. Universities across North America, private and public alike, rushed to launch their marketing campaigns to earn a favorable position in fierce competitions for student enrollment, funding from the private and public sectors, and overall international reputation. According to the 2020 *Open Doors Report*, published annually by the Institute of International Education, the total enrollment of international students in US universities has well exceeded one million since the 2015/16 academic year. To attract more prospective international students from China, for example, around 50 prestigious universities, the majority of which are public institutions, participated in an annual college fair located in several major cities in China before the COVID-19 pandemic struck. A major contributing factor to this competition for international enrollment is an ongoing decline of state fiscal support for higher education. According to the *Grapevine Report* published by the State Higher Education Executive Officers Association (SHEEO), the year 2018, when the present study was conceived, witnessed the lowest annual percent increase in the 5 years preceding it in terms of state fiscal support, and almost all of the increase was accounted for by appropriations in only three relatively large states: California, Florida, and Georgia (Center for the Study of Education Policy, 2018). Worse yet, 19 states reported a decrease between 2017 and 2018 ranging from –0.1% in Ohio to –14.6% in North Dakota (2018).

Consequently, public institutions became increasingly dependent upon tuition instead of public funding for financial sustainability. International students are prioritized as the most valuable customer (and derogatorily dubbed "cash cows"), as their tuition is double or even triple that of their in-state counterparts, not to mention the job opportunities and commercial vibrancy they bring to the local service industry.

Another prevailing justification for universities' investments in the internationalization of their campuses comes into play, which lies in a discourse of cultural diversity. Over the past several decades since the Supreme Court regonized race inclusive admissions in its 1978 decision in *Regents of the University of California v. Bakke*, "diversity" as a term of art has gained prominence in university admissions. More recently, in the age of multiculturalism, "diversity" has been appropriated and institutionalized as a compelling argument to enroll students of various gender, racial, ethnic, cultural, sexual, and socioeconomic identities. Divisions of diversity and inclusion became ubiquitous in higher education institutions, and the term "diversity" has packed on a load of meanings; it has been subtly tied to notions of not only social justice but also student experience, excellence and success (Wang, 2022). For example, Wabash University's Division of Diversity and Inclusion (n.d.) claims that "a diverse, inclusive community is an integral part of the Wabash experience" and that "it is vital that we create and sustain a welcoming campus where all students can excel, and prepare all students to thrive in our diverse, global environment." In the same vein, a line goes as follows in another flagship public institution's statement of diversity and inclusion entitled "Inclusive Excellence: The *Relentless* Pursuit of Excellence through Diversity": "At the center of IE (inclusive excellence) is the recognition and acceptance of the talents, worldviews, perceptions, cultures and skills that diverse communities bring to the educational enterprise that can be *harnessed* [emphasis added] to prepare students for leading, living and working in a diverse world." These manifestations of the institutional discourse of cultural diversity are well aligned with, if not inspired by, the American Council on Education's and American Association of University Professors' claim that "diversity on campus provides educational benefits for all students" (2000, p. 3), which has been substantiated by statistical evidence (Gurin et al., 2002).

Revisiting Yang's rhetorical analysis of Japanese lyrics in her literacy autobiography, I couldn't help but wonder, Does this institutional discourse of cultural diversity[2] *really* represent the "differences" that international students embody and experience through their literacy practices every day? How might such discourse reduce and flatten our international students' "differences" that seem to only index institutionalized identity labels? What are the material consequences of a misalignment between institutional identity labels and students' situated and distributed practices of difference? Together, these questions suggest that we as a community of writing scholars have not done enough to complicate the notion of difference entangled with international students' multiliteracies and that we are readily receptive to the institutionalized discourse of cultural diversity that reifies and stabilizes differences.[3] Admittedly, many scholars in language, writing, and literacy studies have investigated how various institutional discourses of diversity mediate international students' practices of difference. In addition, there is an abundance of empirical accounts that shed light on how international and multilingual students who are institutionally labeled as "different" navigate the literate worlds that they deem different (see, for example, Canagarajah, 2013a, 2013b; De Costa et al., 2022; Fraiberg et al., 2017; Leki, 2007; Lorimer Leonard, 2013; You, 2016, 2018). However, we have yet to fully explore how these writers' literate worlds—networked ecologies a writer inhabits and makes meaning of—afford or constrain their practices of difference.

The years leading to 2020 can be characterized as a golden age for Generation Z[4] Chinese international students who sought higher education in western countries, particularly North America, as evidenced in the soaring enrollment statistics. They benefited from a booming Chinese domestic economy, a harmonious Sino-American diplomatic relation, relatively open international borders, a genuine interest in cultural exchange, and ever-greater transnational mobility. However, Chinese students enrolled in US colleges during the 2010s often ended up in a superdiverse cultural contact zone that was intertwined with a neoliberal institutional climate (Pratt, 1991; Vertovec, 2007). It has become increasingly challenging and sometimes confounding to navigate the complex material and discursive installations that purportedly embrace this group. Their "literacy practices of difference," the term I use to refer to the construction and negotiation of idiosyncratic positionality through activities that involve semiotic resources, are further complicated and afforded by their increasingly intimate relationship with the digitally networked environment and a heightened sense of bodies and social connections. Worse still, in recent years, Chinese international students are caught up in politically precarious situations thanks to the pervasive anti-Asian, anti-Chinese policies, rhetorics, and sentiments in relation to the deteriorating trade and diplomatic relations with China since before the COVID-19 pandemic struck.

The globalizing force along with the ubiquitous institutional discourse of cultural diversity finds its local iteration at Wabash University—a large public research university in the US state of Indiana. Wabash's internationally renowned engineering programs, echoing the current of globalization, helped the university to attract nearly one hundred thousand international students over the past decade. As a major contribution to campus diversity, international students comprised, at its peak in 2017, 21.9% of the total number of enrolled students (Office of International Students and Scholars [ISS], 2019). The total enrollment in 2017, sitting at 9,133, almost doubled compared with only a decade ago. International undergraduate students comprised 16% (4,964 in total in 2017) of the undergraduate body (ISS, 2019), a number large enough to characterize how the discourse of cultural diversity gets interpreted within this particular institutional context. Among the international undergraduate students enrolled at Wabash, the great majority (45.4% or 2,254) come from the People's Republic of China (ISS, 2019). These Chinese undergraduate students can be found in virtually all disciplinary majors.

Yet it is precisely the massive flow of bodies and financial and cultural capital that endorse the institutional discourse of cultural diversity, which in turn render individual voices muffled or marginalized. These Chinese international students are discursively profiled as profoundly different in toto from domestic white middle-class English-speaking families. The discursive profiling of the very identity category of international students, on the one hand, allows this evolving group to be seen and heard, yet on the other, conditions not only the public perception of the group but also each individual's social, bodily, and material experiences. For example, as the largest group identified by nationality within the international student body, students from China are highly visible on campus. They appear in small bands or individually in the libraries, dining halls, study and recreational areas, and classrooms across campus. They have assembled two large student/scholar organizations—the Wabash University Chinese Students and Scholars Association (WUCSSA), representing the entire Chinese community, and the Undergraduate Chinese Association (UCA), representing undergraduate students from China. Yet their dispersed presence on campus doesn't translate to their recognition as an integral and indispensable part of the "mainstream" college experience. These Chinese international students' individual struggles and efforts, achievements and failures, pains and happiness, talents and weaknesses often go unnoticed and, worse still, are characterized by the institutional discourse of cultural diversity simply as diverse cultural resources. In addition, their identity labels seem conveniently all-encompassing whenever the notion of difference appears in the official narrative. Their literate activities and experiences are reduced to those that only reflect their nationality or citizenship in the scholarship and public discourse (Canagarajah, 2017). Research in mobility studies, translingual practices, and cosmopolitan English suggests that literate activities can hardly be identified as bound to any particular language or modality that is solely attributed to a certain nationality or ethnicity. Rather, one's literate activities are always translingual and transmodal and are not always tied to static linguistic, cultural attributes in a modernist sense (Canagarajah, 2013a, 2019; Silva & Wang, 2021; You, 2016). Nonetheless, deafened by the tropes of resources and deficits, we have also been desensitized to differences other than nationality and citizenship, let alone students' own narratives and histories.

Critical applied linguists have long critiqued the neoliberal marketization of the notion of diversity and multilingualism by emphasizing the number of separate linguistic entities (Canagarajah, 2017; Makoni & Pennycook, 2006). The "exotic" cultures and languages that international students bring with them are seen as human capital linked directly to material profit. However, the institutional discourse of cultural diversity has yet to truly empower international students outside and beyond the more liberal educational sphere of first-year writing, as it puts students in a situation where they constantly juggle the resistance to prescribed labels of difference with their negotiated and performed difference. In other words, international students may feel valued and dismissed simultaneously as they navigate the discursive as well as physical space of a US university. Neglected or made invisible here are students' self-sponsored literate activities that may directly or indirectly shape the ways in which they perceive their differences and the ways in which they navigate literate worlds. This conflicting view is evidenced across most of our programmatic and pedagogical practices (Costino & Hyon, 2007; Matsuda et al., 2013; Silva, 1997). Students' agentive appropriation of their perceived differences remains in the blind spot of the institutional discourse of cultural diversity. As Chinese international students' literacy sponsors, we may be naïvely optimistic about our institutionally granted authority to intervene. Worse still, we may inadvertently contribute to reinforcing the myths about this cultural group that Qianqian Zhang-Wu identified in her ethnographic study. The most insidious ones are "(1) English is responsible for all the challenges facing Chinese international students, and (2) Chinese international students are well supported in American higher education, both linguistically and academically" (Zhang-Wu, 2022, p. 150).

To understand how Chinese international students inhabit their literate worlds and make meaning of their differences, I adopt an ethnographic case study approach and recount stories and counterstories of four individuals' (Manna, Wentao, Yang, and Bohan) ecologically situated and distributed literacy practices on and off the campus of Wabash University. Through analyzing extensive ethnographic data collected during the period from 2017 to 2019, including observations, semistructured and nondirective interviews, artifacts, and video recordings, I reconstruct the rich literate activities that the four students participate in—activities that are nonetheless consistently reduced to the myth of linguistic and cultural difference reified in institutional discourses of diversity.

Two questions guided me as I listened to the four individuals' stories and attempted to recount them:

1. How do Manna, Wentao, Yang, and Bohan, the four Generation Z Chinese international students in the study, *do difference* as they engage in everyday literacy practices?
2. How do Manna, Wentao, Yang, and Bohan leverage, resist, or counter the ecological forces that mediate their literacy practices of difference?

Granted, I did not expect to fully answer the guiding questions through my participation in the four students' literacy lives. The students' idiosyncratic orientations toward their own literacy practices of difference drove what I focused on. However, the two guiding questions inevitably prescribed a particular analytical lens through which I interpreted and made sense of the students' practices. While consciously aware of my privileged position as a researcher, I embraced this dynamic negotiation of our positionalities, knowing this is what we all engage in as we practice our differences.

I approached the protagonists of the book—Manna, Wentao, Yang, and Bohan—in the summer of 2018. Adopting a "typical case" approach to recruiting participants (Creswell, 2013; Miles & Huberman, 1994), I invited a total of 17 Chinese international students who had enrolled in the first-year writing course that I had taught between 2016 and 2018. Among them, four participants generously agreed to participate in my study. The four students, whose self-chosen pseudonyms for my study are Manna, Wentao, Yang, and Bohan, are all mainland Chinese in nationality and citizenship, and they speak and write Mandarin Chinese as their first or primary language.

Manna enrolled in my class in 2018. She would normally sit quietly in the back corner of the classroom, burying her head behind her laptop most of the time and occasionally raising her head to make eye contact with me. The writings she performed in class, however, revealed her otherwise-concealed personality traits—introspective, expressive, and adventurous. Born, raised, and educated in Beijing, the capital city and the political and educational hub of China, Manna appeared to be a free spirit with confidence and an open mind. Yet she rarely exuded an air of superiority—quite the opposite; she was down-to-earth, amiable, jovial, and always ready to connect with people and things around her.

Wentao didn't quite catch my attention until I read his literacy autobiography two weeks into the fall 2016 semester. Decorated with ornate expressions, his literacy autobiography took on the style of a seasoned columnist for *The New Yorker* as opposed to a recent transfer student from China. Born in southern China, Wentao spent most of his formative years in northeast China and one year of undergraduate studies at a prestigious university in Beijing before landing in the United States.

Rarely smiling, Yang didn't seem readily approachable. Peers around her easily noticed an unusual air of composure that meshed maturity and melancholy. Her composure rendered her emotional or cognitive engagement at any particular moment obscure and elusive. In a sense, most of the time, Yang appeared to be immersed in her own ironclad contemplation and indifferent to the happenings in her immediate surroundings. However, when I invited students to perform group activities or respond to my questions, Yang would instantly withdraw from her contemplation and engage with others. It was not until our first individual conference that she apologetically revealed to me that her train of thought would sometimes go off on a tangent when the class discussions seemed easy to grasp. And it was not until I read her writer's literacy autobiography that I learned that her train of thought went off on a tangent to brainstorm the theme of her next lyrical project.

At first sight, Bohan seemed reserved, collected, and somewhat nerdy. Growing up in Shanghai, the financial capital of China and a megacity with a population of almost 25 million, Bohan did not carry with him the cynicism, frivolousness, and condescension that urban citizens from metropolitan areas in China are stereotypically associated with. Rather, Bohan would put on his signature laid-back smile whenever I saw him and cheerfully greet me in English: "How are you, Mr. Wang?" As the conversation went on, Bohan would gradually retreat to his comfort zone and answer most of the questions with a simple yes or no and only occasionally a brief elaboration. Though brief, Bohan's responses never failed to put me, and perhaps anyone who interacted with him, at ease.

My observation of and interview conversations with these four individuals took place in multiple spaces across and around the Wabash campus: class buildings, residential halls, dining halls, student union, libraries, theaters, cafés and bubble tea shops, among others. Importantly, the notion of a research site here is both a geographical and a discursive formation, as oftentimes a mere description of the site's geographic formation fails to account for the meaningful interaction between the participants and the physical space. For example, Wentao ritualized an on-campus tea shop as his prewriting warmup place, which, according to him, offered him inspirations and motivation. Data collection assumes not only a holistic (Fetterman, 2010; Hammersley & Atkinson, 1995; Spradley, 1980) but also a dynamic approach; that is, documenting indiscriminately every observable occurrence as it emerges and doing so on the move without precategorizing the documented. My participants' literate activities are not always accessible. For example, Wentao and Bohan usually compose papers for course assignments in their dormitory rooms. In such cases, I needed to be adaptable and employ a variety of methods to trace meaningful literacy practices without the intrusive presence of the researcher. For example, with their permission, I asked the four participants to tape-record moments of their writing processes and then-ecologies through their own lenses with the aid of a digital camera. In short, the data-collection process was purposefully unstructured so that it could be maximally generative and unobtrusive.

For observations, I assumed different roles at different stages: during the semester when they were enrolled in the writing course I was teaching, I assumed the role of a participant observer; after I recruited them back as my research participants, I assumed the role of a nonparticipant observer or nonpresent observer (or I would like to call asynchronous observer, as I was observing through their self-recorded video clips). I conducted observations at a range of strictly or loosely bounded sites, including classrooms, libraries, milk tea shops, an auditorium, the recreation center, and restaurants. I participated in some of their activities, but more often I observed the activities from a distance.

In addition to observations, I also conducted biweekly interviews with the four students. The interviews were loosely structured or completely participant-led, and typically ran from 30 minutes to 1 hour. The rapport established between Manna, Wentao, Yang, Bohan, and myself enabled participant-led interview sessions; that is, I would initiate the conversation with open-ended questions such as "Could you recall any memorable activities that you participated in over the past two weeks?" and prompt the participants to decide where they would like to take the conversation. My rationale for doing so is that I believe only by restricting researcher interventions during interactions would I obtain responses that more truly reflect what participants care about. The interview questions revolved around participants' literate activities and their reflections. I encouraged the four multilingual students to mesh whatever language resources were at their disposal during the interviews. Not surprisingly, they all opted for Mandarin Chinese—their native/first language—while more than occasionally meshing English phrases into the conversations. The linguistic safe (and comfort) zone that I consciously created helped us more effectively build rapport and capture expressions that were as intimately reflective of participants' literate world as possible. I audio-recorded the sessions, selectively transcribed the recordings, and translated the transcript into English. I also participated in several extracurricular activities upon participants' invitations, such as Manna's dance competition, to better understand how they projected their persona in social engagements.

Multimodal artifacts include the four students' writings for different purposes, including: class assignments such as collaborative projects, reflections, song lyrics, and email exchanges; course materials such as syllabi and assignment prompts; and social media posts such as pictures and videos of participants and their surroundings or ones posted on social media sites. My collection of these artifacts was ongoing during the research period. Some artifacts were used to help the four students create retrospective accounts of their engagement with a particular literate activity during stimulated elicitation (Prior, 2004; Prior & Shipka, 2003; Roozen, 2010).

This multifaceted and triangulated collection of Manna, Wentao, Yang, and Bohan's literacy practices has bestowed on me, an important sponsor and documentarian of their literacy, the privilege to coconstruct and reconstruct their meaningfully different literate worlds, bringing to the forefront their uniquely afforded meaning-making practices that shape their emerging differences. In fact, their idiosyncratic emerging differences, which altogether rewrite the institutionalized differences, are profoundly situated and distributed, so much so that only by rhetorically listening to stories recounted in their entirety and on their own terms, and by negotiating meaning with them through thick descriptions, can one begin to appreciate the four Chinese international students' effort in doing difference differently. And only by appreciating their effort in doing difference differently can one begin to reexamine the contradictory coupling of an institutionalized discourse of cultural diversity and a deficit discourse of international students' language performance and question the inequitable institutional structures that marginalize this cultural group.

The notion of "doing difference" finds its intellectual roots in Candace West and Don H. Zimmerman's (1987) landmark theorization of "doing gender" and subsequently, West and Sarah Fenstermaker's (1995) notion of "doing difference." Countering the conception of gender as an innate, essentialized property of individuals, West and Zimmerman (1987) reconceptualize gender as a "doing"—an emergent, socially constructed performance through human interactions. As such, individuals "organize their various and manifold activities to reflect or express gender, and they are disposed to perceive the behavior of others in a similar light" (West & Zimmerman, 1987, p. 127). In other words, West and Zimmerman argue that gender is created by individuals through everyday interactions and in accordance with socially accepted gender expectations. West and Zimmerman acknowledge, however, that "doing gender" prioritizes individual accountability for gender performance at the expense of questioning the inequitable social structures based on the gender dichotomy. The consequence of such prioritization is the neglect of acts of resistance in the face of inequitable social structures, as critics rightfully point out. Later on, West and Fenstermaker (1995) proposed a new understanding of "difference" as a "doing" by extending the notion of gender as an emergent, interactional performance into the areas of race and class, asserting that the intersection of the three social categories constitutes mechanisms for producing social inequality. "Doing difference" interrogates the idea that difference—if understood as socially constructed attributes or identity categories—can and should be used to predict an individual's behavior or aptitude and structure their experiences.

A reified "difference" that predominantly structures international students' bodily and material experiences of studying in a North American higher education institution is arguably "language," or more precisely, their multilingual status and perceived lack of English proficiency. Relatedly, "culture" often appears alongside "language" in institutional discourses on international students' campus presence, surreptitiously dictating how their presence is viewed and valued. In the four protagonists' cases, other such reified differences intersect as well, for example, Asian or Chinese identity, or engineering major. These differences are not constructed and reified free of axiological bias: differences matter; certain differences matter more than others. The differences, once reified, aggregated, and institutionalized as default demographic identifiers that appear in discourses about international students, possess immense constitutive power: they constitute who these group-affiliated individuals are supposed to be, what they are supposed to pursue, how they are supposed to interact with others, and ultimately, what differences are valued. As such, international students' experiences are institutionally structured through the dominant discourse's frame of reference (which is often ambiguous and contradictory in and of itself), rendering their agential "doing difference" invisible.

For example, the conflicting institutional discourses of embracing international students' linguistic and cultural diversity and upholding academic excellence profoundly frame Manna, Wentao, Yang, and Bohan's ambivalent positionality as they engage in literacy practices. On the one hand, the four individuals not only demonstrate an acute linguistic and cultural awareness but also, in their own ingenious ways, perform linguistic and cultural differences to achieve their academic, social, and rhetorical goals. They have seemingly, to different degrees, internalized the institutional discourse of cultural diversity that highlights the neoliberal value of their linguistic and cultural resources and cracked the code of leveraging the resources to their own advantage. On the other hand, however, they share a collective sense of insecurity and befuddlement about their precarious positionality in relation to the dominant structuring forces, even if these forces are most likely discursively invisible; for example, disciplinary writing conventions, standardized written English, student organizational cultures, and Western rhetorical traditions. Although the four Chinese international students tend to frame their "doing difference" through dominant discourses and traditions, they nonetheless consciously, actively, and confidently "transgress" the institutional discourses, written or unwritten linguistic, cultural, and social norms, through their everyday literate activities.

Manna does difference by defying the tacit tradition that a writing consultant position in a university writing center is a privilege reserved exclusively for English native speakers who are advanced students in the humanities; yet meanwhile, when she, as a Chinese international student from mechanical engineering, attempts to get through the training course in preparation for her active service in the writing center, Manna struggles with her self-perceived vulnerable position and a lack of legitimacy. In the competitive community of Chinese international students, academic achievements and cultural assimilation to the host country usually carry important social capital. Manna does difference by cultivating her kinesthetic capacity and choreographic creativity and by participating in and shaping the multicultural dance community on campus. Yet she also wonders what material benefits the cultural practice of hip-hop dancing would bring to her in the "mainstream" academic community. Wentao's approach to doing difference differs from Manna's, as he resists the pervasive English-only cultural assumption and attitude on campus by tapping into his multilingual competence in multiple academic and organizational spaces. He takes advantage of his craftsmanship in composing English essays to assist friends in the Chinese international student community, which earns him a decent reputation and helps him to gain social capital. In turn, Wentao leverages his social capital in the community to seek reliable collaborators for his class projects. With a more nuanced and refined understanding of the creative potential of languages, Wentao channels his experiences of learning Chinese as well as English into learning how to compose a descriptive essay in Japanese and into crafting a deliberate social media persona. Yang pushes her translingual capability to a new creative level as she takes charge of composing, performing, producing, and disseminating Japanese pop songs, all the while documenting an insightful account of how the music industries operate in different sociocultural contexts. Yang's "difference" has little to do with her institutionalized identity label of "Chinese international student"; she fuses rhetorical and poetic energies from a cosmopolitan palette of cultural elements in her music creation, far beyond what the identity label is capable of describing. Rather, Yang's difference is an everyday doing of her translingual creativity, lyrical sensibility, business acumen, and cultural openness, an act of renegotiating the imaginary boundaries of the so-called Chinese international students' literacy practices. Bohan, akin to Manna, Wentao, and Yang, consciously constructs a cosmopolitan public persona, albeit oftentimes with a neoliberal twist, yet unlike the other three individuals, feels subtle contempt for an institutional discourse of cultural awareness. Rhetorically sensitive as Bohan is, he employs "rhetorical absence"—strategically displaying rhetorical unavailability and disengagement in order to secure the ultimate win—in responding to the university's intercultural competence education and in curating his social media presence. Bohan's doing difference also manifests in pragmatically renegotiating his representation and cultural value in a robotics student organization, as he marshals social and rhetorical resources to help recruit new members from the Chinese student community.

As the stories of Manna, Wentao, Yang, and Bohan continue to unfold throughout the book, the theme of doing difference differently also becomes more salient and packs on more nuanced meaning. With the unintended alliteration, "doing difference differently" seems tautological, if not meaninglessly circular; after all, "doing difference" already implies performative invention of one's unique identities in relation to other human and nonhuman agents. The addition of the adverb "differently," however, is intended to underline the inherent teleological uncertainty of doing difference; namely, the impossibility of negotiating the four Chinese students' purposes for doing difference without anchoring the negotiation in their immediate literacy and rhetorical ecology. The four individuals do differences in different ecologies at different times through interactions with different agents for different purposes with different affordances; it's unproductive to aim to generate a grand theory that accounts for their doing difference. Rather, accounting for each individual's doing difference calls for situated thick descriptions and an openness toward divergent interpretations of such descriptions. The addition of the adverb "differently" is also intended to draw our attention to the question of "how," that is—recalling the first question I posed—how do the four Chinese international students do difference as they engage in everyday literacy practices?

While investigating how Manna, Wentao, Yang, and Bohan do difference assumes literacy and rhetorical agency, I'm also consciously aware of the ecological forces that condition and mediate the four individuals' literacy and rhetorical practices: material surroundings, technological tools, literacy sponsors, social communities, prior experiences, expressive bodies, emotions, motivations, languages, social norms and conventions, institutional policies, among many others. These ecological forces motivate them to engage in various literate activities, support them with different strategies, empower them to tap into their cultural repertoires, and ultimately play a crucial role in shaping their emerging cultural identities and socioacademic communities. In a sense, doing difference is a rhetorical manifestation of the four individuals' constant attempt to make sense of and negotiate these mediational ecological forces. As such, unpacking these ecological forces is essential to renewing our understanding of the doing of difference. To do so, I documented via research memo comprehensive key ecological data during fieldwork along with observation and interview data about the literate activities the four students were engaged in. During data analysis, I examined the ecological data that reveal the literacy affordances through six analytical lenses: structural, semiotic, experiential, social, bodily, and material. Unpacking the ecological forces through these lenses allows me to trace, document, deconstruct, and reconstruct the four Chinese students' doing difference as a purposeful, performative, and dynamic shift of social and material relations that is always afforded or constrained by structures, discourses, bodies, materials, and histories that constitute the students' literate worlds. Doing difference is an act of agency, yet the agency is always mediated by ecological affordances. As I recount the stories of Manna, Wentao, Yang, and Bohan and reconstruct their literate worlds, I attempt to fully unpack their convoluted ecological affordances.

In Chapter 1, I describe the contemporary globalized neoliberal climate that conditions institutional culture in higher education and how this climate dictates our perceptions of Chinese international students and approaches to supporting them. Following the description of global and institutional cultures, I describe the ecological forces at greater length. In the next four chapters, I recount "doing difference" stories of Manna, Wentao, Yang, and Bohan, respectively, highlighting their ecological affordances. In the final chapters, I critically read the four students' stories through the lens of doing difference and affordance and explore how these stories may help educators, educational administrators, policy makers, and the public to meaningfully and ethically communicate with this growing population that we reductively call "Chinese international students."

The four stories critically engage with two broad and interconnected concepts that are essential to educators' collective understanding of not only Generation Z Chinese international students but also students brought up in cultural and educational contexts outside of the Euro-American sphere. These two concepts are difference and affordance. For example, the stories interrogate the deep-seated deficit model in writing education that flattens students' richly different literacy practices as issues to be fixed and demonstrate that students' differences as embodied in their literacy and rhetorical "doings" are emergent, relational, and material (Wang, 2019). In addition, the stories provide a microscopic view of the structural, semiotic, experiential, social, bodily, and material affordances that enable and empower the four individuals to make meaning of and leverage their differences. Storytelling in these students' own terms is a particularly valuable and effective technique in combating global COVID-induced anti-Chinese sentiments that significantly impact Chinese international students' well-being. Ultimately, a new understanding of these Generation Z Chinese international students' afforded literacy practices of difference will inform not only writing, literacy, or language teachers but also educators of all disciplines as they interact with this particular population, design curriculum for them, support them, and, most importantly, advocate for them.

1
Discourse of Cultural Diversity and Ethnographic Case Study of Literacy Practices

We are rushing into a post- and trans-world from a multi- and pluri-world. Not too long ago, the zeitgeist was characterized by modernism, multiculturalism, multilingualism, and multinationalism. Today, our collective discourse seeks answers to our fundamental questions from postmodernism, post-multiculturalism, translingualism, and transnationalism. Thanks to the flows of peoples, capital, materials, and cultures brought about by the force of globalization, we are discursively reconstructing the world that we bodily, cognitively, psychologically, and emotionally inhabit; and we do so in ways that recognize the temporality, spatiality, fluidity, and transformativity of the social and political structures that were traditionally conceived to operate in multiple neatly bounded and static silos (Ang, 2001; Appadurai, 1996, 2013; Miyoshi, 2000). Technological advancement, including modern-day means of transportation (such as flights, high-speed rail, and highway systems) and telecommunications infrastructure (such as the Internet and cellular network) has catalyzed the global flows of peoples, capital, materials, and cultures that collectively reconfigure our social and material surroundings in dramatic and subtle ways, shortened the distance between people and peoples and the homogenizing forces and prompted rearticulation of what it means to be "different." In other words, as a consequence of the increasing geographical and social mobility enabled by technology, we now live in a complexly networked world where boundaries that divided the "old world"—national, racial, cultural, linguistic, socioeconomic—are blurred and we gradually became *indifferent* to what we used to perceive as different.

Let me piece together my fragmented childhood memories to illustrate what this conceptual shift entails. I was born at the dawn of the eventful 1990s, a year after the student protest at Tiananmen Square (and the subsequent military suppression) in Beijing—the climax of the Chinese democratic movement—and the fall of the Berlin Wall, and months before the beginning of the Gulf War and the resignation of Mikhail Gorbachev, the last leader of the Soviet Union. Of course, none of these world-shaking historical moments were brought to my infantile attention until later when I read about them in history books. Before I started middle school in the early 2000s, the 21-inch-screen CRT TV—which I nicknamed the "big colorful box"—placed in our living room was a window through which I explored the wild world out there. I remember spending hours and hours during summer breaks watching old black-and-white or early color movies on a movie channel, such as *Tunnel War*, a classic Chinese war film set against the backdrop of the anti-Japanese war, Bruce Lee's *Fist of Fury* and *Game of Death*, and Charlie Chaplin's *Modern Times*. During a time period when the Internet was unheard of in a secluded town in the far west region of China and when traveling or studying abroad represented the luxury of the wealthiest of the wealthy, the big colorful box that put on stringently censored and propagandist TV programs was the only way for me to observe people that looked, spoke, and behaved differently than I did. Thanks to the dramatized depiction of those "heinous" Japanese soldiers and "barbarian" Westerners that we used to call *yangguizi* (foreign devil), I regarded all non-Chinese people as ugly and greedy imperialistic bullies trying to destroy the stoic yet peaceful lifestyle of the Chinese people. Fast forward to summer 2018: I was sitting in a comfortable seat on a train that was traveling from Cambridge to London Gatwick Airport, sending text messages to my US-green-card-holding Palestinian colleague about our upcoming conference trip to Vancouver. In merely 20 years, I transitioned from watching "foreign devils" in the big colorful box to working with them in the same institution and living with them in the same neighborhood; and my perception of their differences (and my own differences) has taken on more subtle connotations.

Arjun Appadurai (1996), in his seminal work entitled *Modernity at Large: Cultural Dimensions of Globalization*, characterizes this fluid and in-flux sense of global and local community created by media as "no sense of place." He argues:

> The world we live in now seems rhizomatic (Deleuze & Guattari, 1987), even schizophrenic, calling for theories of rootlessness, alienation, and psychological distance between individuals and groups on the one hand, and fantasies (or nightmares) of electronic propinquity on the other. (Appadurai, 1996, p. 29)

Technology- and media-empowered mobility and communication profoundly invalidate yet at the same time intensify the debate around "us versus them." As people migrate in cyber/virtual as well as physical spaces—travel, resettle, seek shelter, study, work, marry elsewhere, and connect with others on the Internet—more efficiently and frequently than ever before, it's increasingly difficult to hold on to a complete and coherent sense of self while constructing an image of others. We are all caught up in the flows (connectivity and circulation) of cultural objects and cultural forms (Appadurai, 2013) and in what postcolonial scholar Homi Bhabha (1990a) terms the "third space of hybridity." To borrow Edward Said's (1999) words, we are "always out of place" (p. 3).

Cultural studies scholar Ien Ang's (2001) autobiographical account captures this tension of "in-between-ness" (Gilroy, 1993) with critical intimacy. As a person of Chinese descent born in Indonesia and raised in the Netherlands, Ang (2001) found herself perpetually entrenched in an in-between space: "It was the beginning of an almost decade-long engagement with the predicaments of 'Chineseness' in diaspora. In Taiwan I was different because I couldn't speak Chinese; in the West I was different because I looked Chinese" (p. vii). Upon reflecting on her one-day trip with a group of Western travelers to mainland China, she says, "I felt like wanting to protect China from too harsh judgments which I imagined my fellow travelers would pass on it, but at the same time I felt a rather irrational anger towards China itself—at its 'backwardness,' its unworldliness, and seemingly naïve way in which it tried to woo Western tourists" (Ang, 2001, p. 23).

In another fascinating autoethnography, however, Juria Choi (2013), through examining artifacts that were key to her literacy and linguistic trajectory, explored the "anxiety, confusion and frustration on issues of authenticity and legitimacy in relation to language and identity," and how her own bodily experiences of anxiety, confusion, and frustration challenge what the postcolonial literature legitimizes as dissolving essentialist ideas of race, nationality, cultural practices, and linguistic identities. Choi, too, is caught up in the transnational and diasporic flow: she was born in New York to a newly immigrated Korean family, spent her teenage years and young adulthood in Japan, South Korea, China, and Australia, while constantly juggling her sense of self, nationality, heritage, and symbolic capital. Contrary to Ang's take on hybridity that dismisses the notion of boundedness, Choi insists on the cultural importance of boundaries. As she observes, "we are all shifting in and out of, entangled in, and influenced by our many different voices" (Choi, 2013, p. 9).

Both accounts speak to the impossibility of constructing a singular stabilized subjectivity that neatly identifies with a named nation-state, ideology, language, and culture; subjectivities always simultaneously occupy multiple national, ideological, linguistic, and cultural spaces. To chart the globalizing flows and articulate the multiplicity, fluidity, and hybridity of human subjectivities in a more critical and generative manner, language and literacy scholars have begun to rewrite the dominant discourse with a "post-" or "trans-" prefix. For example, Makoni and Pennycook (2006) criticize multilingualism's "romanticized plurality" that is based on "putative language counts" and point out that one's complex semiotic resources are not discrete and conveniently countable. Horner, Lu, and Canagarajah, among others, theorize a translingual disposition (Horner et al., 2011) and translingual literacy/practice (Canagarajah, 2013a, 2013b) that view language differences as resources rather than deficiencies. In addition, Barlow (2016) calls for the cultivation of "postmulticulturalist sensibilities" that add critical dimension to the celebration of institutional diversity that seeks to categorize people based on their discrete physical attributes. These are scholarly attempts at capturing the complicated entanglement of peoples, cultures, and languages as opposed to approaching them in isolation. As the borders that used to demarcate and separate become more symbolic and less functional, this line of scholarly inquiry is timely in helping us to rethink what the notion of difference means and what consequences it entails.

However, this acknowledgment of mobility and fluidity and skepticism toward, if not dismissal of, boundedness in the scholarship are not without conceptual limitations. To start with, minority scholars who are informed by critical theories voiced their concern over the loss of the critical status of difference and the flattening of differences in institutional practices. For example, Keith Gilyard (2016) rightfully cautions that translingualism as a philosophical and pedagogical orientation toward language may become "an alienating theory for some scholars of color," as it may contribute to the flattening of language differences (p. 284). According to Gilyard (2016), the "difference as the norm" argument prevalent in translingual scholarship may tacitly dismiss the suffering of the linguistically marginalized writers have undergone and the effort they have contributed to the linguistic rights of minorities. Along the same line, Alexander and Rhodes (2014) identify the underlying homogenizing force that drives current practices of uncritical multicultural pedagogy:

> Our experiences as multicultural pedagogues for nearly two decades have shown us that the "reconstructed language" often taught—and modeled curricula and textbooks—is rather bland, emphasizing commonalities that prevent us from perceiving and analyzing critical differences. We call such emphases on "shared humanity" the *flattening effect* [original emphasis], or the subtle (and sometimes not-so-subtle) erasures of difference that occur when narrating stories of the "other." (p. 431)

This uncritical celebration of the plurality of cultures in dominant discourses, as well as the uncritical treatment of difference as the norm, could be best characterized by Bhabha's (1990b) notion of simultaneous encouragement and containment of cultural diversity. Indifference to difference or difference blindness may undermine what cultural workers have fought for and muffle the voice of writers discursively portrayed as writers of difference.

It is also unfortunate that the post-/trans- scholarly discourse has not effectively addressed the disparity between the institutional portrayal of our international students' transcultural/transnational experiences and the reality of their literate worlds under the contemporary political economy of North American higher education. In the next section, I will go into detail on the ways in which universities respond, or fail to respond, to the flows of globalization and the ways in which an institutional discourse of difference may condition international students' literacy experiences.

An Institutional Discourse of Cultural Diversity

People migrate for a range of purposes: to escape from political and economic instability and seek shelter, to receive education, to work and do business, to reunite with family, to enjoy vacations, and for other individual purposes. For Generation Z Chinese young adults in the United States, receiving education has been the primary, if not *the*, purpose of migration. According to *Report of the Visa Office 2021* (United States Department of State-Bureau of Consular Affairs, 2021), among nearly three million nonimmigrant US visas issued to international travelers in 2021,[1] 377,659 were F student visas. More than half of the F visas were issued in Asia—China, India, and South Korea being the top three countries. Institutions of different types ranging from private as well as public schools, doctorate-granting research universities, liberal arts schools, community colleges, special-focus institutions, and language-training schools openly embrace students from abroad. It's no exaggeration to claim that we encounter international students in virtually every corner of any campus.

As a salient manifestation of the globalizing force, the influx of international students, the majority of whom are multilingual or English as a second language (ESL) speakers and writers, is viewed by institutions simultaneously as an economic and cultural resource and a logistical challenge. On the one hand, institutions of all types across the US, especially public schools, continue to increase international enrollment and out-of-state tuition to compensate for the decreasing state funding, while marketing the benefits of a culturally and linguistically diverse student body. On the other hand, a variety of innovative support and service programs on campus constantly remind these international students that they are different from their domestic classmates and in need of special accommodation. To be sure, these support and service programs are well-intentioned; they embody the institution's investment in the academic and social well-being of its international student body. Nonetheless, such programs that are oftentimes remedial in nature inadvertently send the message that international students simultaneously face challenges from and pose challenges to the institution. International students, especially those whose previous cultural and linguistic experiences are deemed different from their domestic counterparts, usually find themselves positioned in these conflicting discourses, navigating the university with institutional support yet navigating their own subjectivities with ambivalence. Their experiences are conditioned and mediated largely by an institutional discourse of cultural diversity fermented in a neoliberal political economy.

An institutional discourse of cultural diversity has become ubiquitous in higher education in the US, marking the institutions as "equity, diversity, and inclusion"—ready to enroll students who would check boxes of predefined demographic labels. Here, I define an *institutional discourse of cultural diversity* as a set of typified tropes associated with and often used to characterize socially and institutionally constructed identity attributes. An awareness of this discursive construction allows us to critically examine how institutions reify diversity. An institutional discourse of cultural diversity has been appropriated to constitute knowledge, form subjectivities and power relations, and structure ways of intervening in current institutional practices (Weedon, 1987). In other words, as the discourse circulates and sediments in different institutional contexts, it becomes rhetorically powerful in shaping collective understandings and values of "difference."

There are generally two widely circulated tropes undergirding the prevailing discourse of cultural diversity in US higher education institutions: rights and resources. The trope of rights—access, equity, and representation—appeals to historically underprivileged or minority groups, assuring them of inclusive educational experiences. For example, the Office of Institutional Diversity and Inclusion at Northwestern University states on its website that their vision is to "realize an ideal Northwestern University where community members are challenged to engage differences as strengths in an environment that ensures equality of access, opportunity, representation and participation" (Office of Institutional Diversity and Inclusion, n.d.). In this statement, the rights of the diverse student body are embodied in their equal access to educational resources. The trope of resources, on the other hand, is reflective of the current neoliberal political climate that conditions the operation of institutions. It could be easily appropriated as a marketing strategy used by corporatized institutions to gain traction in a competitive educational market, and it responds well to the discourse of globalization. For this reason, the trope of resources in the discourse of cultural diversity merits further contextualization.

Neoliberalism is understood as political and economic practices that favor individual entrepreneurial freedoms and free markets in all areas of life—civic and institutional (Harvey, 2005). The discourse of cultural diversity views individuals' differences as capitalizable "authoritative resources" (organization of social time/space, chance for self-development, relationships between people; Giddens, 1984), which is aligned with the neoliberal ideology of pursuing "distinction" that adds value to the marketed products. As Margaret Willard-Traub (2018) cautions us, "All kinds of pedagogies and programming are at risk of becoming complicit with neoliberal practices characterizing universities' own movement into a fiercely competitive, globalized marketplace" (p. 57). The premise upon which a corporatized and profit-driven institution gets a head start in free-market competition is the creation of an inclusive discourse that connects with the peripheral student consumers. The discourse of cultural diversity, despite its administrative and legal necessity, has been appropriated as an inclusive discourse that aims to cater to consumers that represent institutionalized differences. The ways in which the discourse of cultural diversity is appropriated to meet the neoliberal agenda of marketization is by weaving it into the discourse of excellence upon which modern universities are constructed (Readings, 1996). For example, Wabash University's

Division of Diversity and Inclusion claims that "a diverse, inclusive community is an integral part of the Wabash experience" and that "it is vital that we create and sustain a welcoming campus where all students can excel, and prepare all students to thrive in our diverse, global environment." Terms such as "experience," "excel," and "thrive" are all inextricably intertwined with a discourse of consumerism and excellence.

In such discourses, diversity becomes an authoritative resource that affords consumers a better experience and better preparation for success. This market-oriented appropriation of the social construct of diversity reflects a common phenomenon in neoliberal economics; that is, tertiarization—"while production based on raw materials and its conversion into synthetic products were the first and second stages of industrialization, it is symbolic production relating to product development, marketing, and networking that are more important in the current tertiary stage" (Canagarajah, 2017, pp. 13–14). Granted, we are not dealing with manufactured commercial goods here; educational service is itself a tertiary product. However, the way educational service is branded is characteristic of the practice of tertiarization.

The marketization of diversity can also be partially ascribed to globalization's impact on academia, a trend commonly known as global corporatization in academia (Giroux, 2002). The intensified flows of goods, capital, labor, and materials transcending national borders give rise to the privatization of the public sector, which then leads to increasingly fierce competition, opportunism, and eventually the fragmentation and atomization of society (Miyoshi, 2000). Universities, especially ones in the US, were not able to evade the transformative power of this global socioeconomic climate and began to seek partnerships with corporate business. Masao Miyoshi (2000), in his provocative critique of corporatized universities, pessimistically predicts:

> At least for the foreseeable future, the academic head is a corporate manager who is expected to expand the institutional and corporate base and alliance, build intellectual property, raise funds and endowments, increase labor productivity, finesse the public relations with external organizations, including various governmental agencies, and run the machinery with dexterity. The university-corporation identification cannot be much closer. (p. 24)

The corporatization of universities reinforces the marketization and even commodification of diversity by integrating a discourse of cultural diversity into their marketing strategies—"Diversity is integral to every student's success. Diversity makes our program stronger. We welcome diversity." The discourse of cultural diversity, it seems, is reified as the appropriation of identity politics in the name of self-promotion. And international students as a cultural minority are co-opted to serve institutional needs (Daniel et al., 2022).

For newly arrived international students, navigating the complex curriculum and assessment ecology within a culturally and linguistically alien educational context is already a formidable task; reconstructing identities as culturally different and visible university citizens is all the more daunting as they practice differences through literacy under the impact of the confounding institutional discourse of cultural diversity.

Ecological Affordance

Caught up in a confounding and contentious space between the institutional discourse of cultural diversity and discourse of deficit, international students tend to develop a heightened sensitivity to conflicting representations and asymmetrical power dynamics resulting from such representations. However, their experiences of conflicting representations and asymmetrical power dynamics may, in turn, empower them and afford their construction and negotiation of meaning in the superdiverse and oftentimes marginalizing world. As Lorimer Leonard (2013) articulates, "As multilingual writers use and create their literate resources in everyday practice, they develop an ear for difference, a practiced negotiation of meaning for effect, or what we might call 'rhetorical attunement'—a way of acting with language that assumes linguistic multiplicity and invites the negotiation of meaning to accomplish communicative ends" (p. 163). In other words, writers develop a rhetorical sensibility (Guerra, 2016b) toward difference through engaging in everyday literate activities and perceive, perform, and transform their difference to better position themselves between divergent interpretations of diversity within the institutions.

These international students' differences as embedded in their lived linguistic and cultural experiences mediate and are mediated by their literate activities. To understand the intertwined relationships between literacy—meaning making through semiotic resources—and practices of difference and the complex processes of mediation and remediation, I made special descriptive and analytical efforts to capture the networked ecological forces that afford or constrain writers' literacy practices. This has proven to be a challenging endeavor, given how complex, multifaceted, ephemeral, and intricately networked these ecological forces are. I was aware that any attempt to tease out the ecological forces would inevitably risk oversimplifying the emergent relationality that fundamentally define them. Nevertheless, for analytical expediency, I invoke the concept of *affordance* that manifests in multiple interconnected ecological dimensions to paint a holistic yet nuanced picture of the four international students' situated and mediated literacy practices. Particularly, I highlight the structural, semiotic, experiential, social, bodily, and material dimensions of affordance that collectively offer a holistic analytical heuristic.

Originally introduced in Gibson's (1979) influential book *The Ecological Approach to Visual Perception*, "affordance" refers to "what it [environment] offers the animal, what it provides or furnishes, either for good or ill. . . . It implies the complementarity of the animal and the environment" (p. 127). Later on, in the context of language learning, van Lier (2004) defines the notion of affordance as "relationships that provide a 'match' between something in the environment . . . and the learner" (p. 96) or "what is available to the person to do something with" (p. 91). These definitions highlight the external forces and material conditions in the environment that enable and make do. I expand the original notion of affordance, which now entails not only the external but also internal, not only the material but also structural and semiotic, and not only the present but also the historical. Affordances do not mediate a literacy and rhetorical agent's practices in isolation; rather, they are intricately connected and constantly shifting, altering the differential relations between the agent and their material and social environment.

There are as many analytical dimensions of affordance as there are researchers; after all, the concept of affordance is a phenomenological tool that helps researchers make sense of the ecological forces at work rather than an observable, measurable, empirical reality with positivist certainty. As such, after I sifted through the data through the lens of affordance, the following analytical dimensions emerged as salient: structural, semiotic, experiential, social, bodily, and material. Structural affordance refers to socially, culturally, politically, and institutionally constructed relations that serve to organize and regulate practices and activities. These relations could be written and prescriptive or unwritten but internalized by a certain community. Examples range from cultural and linguistic norms, social expectations, and institutional identity markers to course syllabi, assignment deadlines, instructor feedback, and the APA formatting style, among others. Semiotic affordance refers to signs, symbols, texts, and other multimodal communicative discourses. Examples include idiosyncratic linguistic repertoire,

Internet search engines, books, lectures, and so on. Experiential affordance refers to abstractified cognitive personal histories that tacitly shape how the agent makes sense of and engages in future literacy practices. Social affordance refers to interpersonal connections established with fellow community members, including, for example, classmates and colleagues, friends, roommates, co-dancers, course instructors, academic advisers, or anyone who comes in social contact with the agent through meaningful communication. Bodily affordance, broadly defined, refers to any condition, relation, or movement that involves human body, such as skin color, health condition, fatigue, emotion, desire, dispositions (Bourdieu, 1977). Note that it also encompasses affective dimensions, as affects are fundamentally bodily sensations (Papacharissi, 2015). Material affordance refers to things in the environment, such as tools, technology, and writing's rooms (Rule, 2018). As affordance, these "vital things" (Bennett, 2010) are conceptualized as rhetorical agents, following a new materialist critique of the Cartesian dualism that separates subjectivity and objectivity (Alexis, 2017; Bennett, 2010; Gries, 2015; Latour, 1993; Micciche, 2014; Rickert, 2013).

Evidently, the six dimensions of affordance are not mutually exclusive and can by no means be neatly categorized as they may appear to be. They overlap and intertwine with one another. For example, one's social connections are necessarily an essential part of their experiential affordance, while material affordance also structurally empowers one's literacy practices. To account for the "messiness" and interdependence of the ecological forces, I turn to literature on ecological approaches in rhetoric and writing studies and language studies. Marilyn Cooper (1986) proposed "an ecological model of writing" as early as 30 years ago at the dawn of the "social turn" in writing studies, stating its fundamental tenet as follows: "Writing is an activity through which a person is continually engaged with a variety of socially constituted systems" (p. 367). This is a powerful critique of the then prevailing methodological approach of writing process that focused almost exclusively on individual cognitive behaviors. Writers don't write alone; rather, they interact with other people and materials within a constantly changing but structured system.

Later on, Margaret Syverson (1999) fully unfolds the ecological system of writing and lays out the implications of this conceptualization. She defines ecology as "a kind of meta-complex system composed of interrelated and interdependent complex systems and their environmental structures and processes" (Syverson, 1999, p. 5). Built upon Cooper's (1986) initial theorization of the writing ecology, Syverson's (1999) notion of writing ecology encompasses more complex relations than social relations highlighted in Cooper's account. She explains, "Writers, readers, and texts, together with their environments, constitute one kind of ecological system" (Syverson, 1999, p. xv), and "in a complex system, a network of independent agents—people, atoms, neurons, or molecules, for instance—act and interact in parallel with each other, simultaneously reacting to and co-constructing their own environment" (p. 3). Here, the constituting force is bidirectional: the ecology conditions writers' activities, while meanwhile, writers' interactions with other ecological elements in turn constitute the ecology. As Syverson (1999) succinctly puts it, "we are embedded in and co-evolving with our environments, which include other people as well as social and physical structures and processes" (p. xv).

Although Syverson's (1999) writing ecology recognizes—or, more precisely, implies—the meditational power of physical structures, human agents are still unapologetically positioned at the center. Around the same time, however, new materialism in sociology began to enter the scholarship in rhetoric and writing studies that would later challenge not only anthropocentrism but also the binary view of human versus nonhuman. I would like to quote Micciche (2014) for a concise characterization of the central concern of new materialism: "New materialism is a transdisciplinary effort to reshape materialist critiques in order to acknowledge and reckon with a much-expanded notion of agency, one that includes humans, nonhumans, and the environmental surround" (p. 489). New materialism is disciplinarily rooted in "René Descartes's view of matter as corporeal, Gilles Deleuze and Félix Guattari's assemblage concept, Bruno Latour's view of commingling human and nonhuman actants, and various versions of chaos and complexity theory" (Micciche, 2014, p. 490). Agency, the anchoring notion of new materialism, is considered "an act of change that arises from an entanglement of human and nonhuman entities and other environmental factors" (Gries, 2015, p. 68) and "distributed across things and people and structures" (Micciche, 2014, p. 490)—the aggregate of which is called "assemblage" by Deleuze and Guattari (1987) or "collective" by Latour (1993). In other words, humans don't "possess" agency by default; rather, agency is a particular "doing" co-produced by humans and their material surroundings.

An ecological approach and new materialist theories are wedded in Thomas Rickert's (2013) theorization of ambient rhetoric, where he argues for "an ecological shift in what it means for rhetorical agents to inhabit and interact in an environment" (p. xv). With the notion of ambient rhetoric, Rickert (2013) rejects the valorization of language characterizing the "social turn," claiming that "language does not grant things their being. Rather, language stems from world, understood as a composite of meaning and matter" (p. 102). He continues to argue that "Language is ambient, occasioned by the world as well as by human being since the material world comes forward to take part in what language discloses" (Rickert, 2013, p. 103). Put simply, the material turn shifts our attention away from the human versus environment duality and helps us see the ecology humans inhabit as a meaningful whole. Meaning making is not solely semiotic but, as Canagarajah (2013c) puts it, "embedded in a social and physical environment, aligning with contextual features such as participants, objects, the human body, and the setting" (p. 7). Or, as Jay Jordan (2015) suggests in his discussion of a material-rhetorical ecology and translingualism: language work ought to "diffuse attention beyond 'language' and 'languaging' to include attention to the air, sweat, plastic, memories, twitchiness, cheeses, skin, color that are materially co-present, co-evolving with language" (p. 380).

An ecological approach also finds its scholarly presence in language studies. A recent attempt at synthesizing theories on ecological affordances in language learning comes from Atkinson et al. (2018). The synthesis is premised upon the fundamental theory that human beings are "evolutionarily adapted to adapt" (Atkinson et al., 2018, p. 472). It evolves from Atkinson's sociocognitive approach that holds that "social, the cognitive, the embodied, and the material are fundamentally integrated in human activity" (Atkinson et al., 2018, p. 471) and introduces Bateson's (1972) notion of "organism-plus-environment" and Atkinson's (2014) concept of "mindbodyworld." Although Atkinson et al. (2018) do not focus on agency per se, their invocation of the notion of "dwelling" (Streeck, 2015) and deconstruction of environmental affordances imply that agency, to them, is manifest in the alignment between the mental, bodily, and ecological. Ecological affordances are, in Atkinson et al.'s (2018) words, "relational and dynamic," and "they are the adaptive support structures environments grant to species evolutionarily designed/positioned to utilize them" (pp. 473–474).

Ethnographic Case Study

Language educationist and ethnographer Brian Street (1993) proposed that we rethink "culture" as a verb rather than a noun, and see culture as unbounded, kaleidoscopic, and dynamic. Writers "culture" their literate lives within and across vastly different yet interconnected affordances, and at the same time "culture" their literate identities and subjectivities. As a crucial ethnographic research instrument, I, the sole researcher, need to "culture" myself with my participants as they see, think, learn, and grow and unpack how my participants shape and are shaped by their emerging and shifting affordance. Here, to me, the term "culture," if used as a verb, means to align oneself bodily, mentally, and ideologically with the dispositions, expectations, discourses, bodies, and material surroundings of a social group. Applied linguists in the sociocognitive orientation championed by Dwight Atkinson have also theorized the notion of "alignment," which they define as "the means by which human actors dynamically adapt to—that is, flexibly depend on, integrate with, and construct—the ever-changing mind-body-world environments" (Atkinson et al., 2007, p. 171). However, I adopt Street's (1993) concept of "culture" as a verb to suggest a "flat ontology" (Marston et al., 2005), which assumes that agency manifests not exclusively in human actors but in other material artifacts as well. Therefore, maintaining an open mind and being willing to culture and be cultured are crucial to thoroughly understanding not only the human agents but also the spatiotemporal ecologies that condition them.

A disposition toward embracing uncertainties and commitment to culturing the researcher themself as the participants relive or represent their cultural experiences are essential prerequisites for aligning oneself with a particular methodological approach. I use the phrase "aligning oneself with" as opposed to "adopt," as I intend to challenge the idea that research methodologies are neatly categorized and shelved entities out there for researchers to pick up just as a mechanic picks up tools to fix a malfunctioning car. Research methodologies are ideologically and culturally conditioned, loosely bounded, and emergent and dynamic. It would be at best irresponsible of a researcher to uncritically and unreflectively "adopt" a certain methodology based simply on factors such as the researcher's preference or expertise, the purpose and objective of the research, the research site, or the scholarly community where the findings will circulate. Worse yet, it would be potentially perilous to dismiss certain methodology simply because it does not conform to the researcher's beliefs or because other methodologies are more popular. Rather, the researcher needs to actively seek alignment between his/her philosophical and ideological dispositions and the factors mentioned above, since regardless of the methods and instruments chosen or developed, the researcher is the ultimate research instrument that actively adapts (Heath & Street, 2008).

I aligned myself with the methodological approach of ethnographic case study. First, informed by new materialist theories, I place the focal point of this research on not only human subjects who act and react but also their ecological surroundings, which may be nonhuman or material, as they agentially act and react as well. In other words, I intend to capture the interactions between and among human agents, in this case, Chinese international students at Wabash University, and what they live with and live by every day. An ethnographic approach meets the purpose optimally, as the goal of ethnography is, according to Heath (1982), "to describe the ways of living of a social group, a group in which there is in-group recognition of the individuals living and working together as a social unit" (p. 34), and "to identify specific cultural patterns and structural regularities within the processes of both continuity and change" (p. 35). Note, however, an ethnographic approach should be distinguished from a traditional full-scale ethnography in terms of relative scope, stance, focus, and problem-orientation (Heath, 1982; Ramanathan & Atkinson, 1999). Although criticisms abound regarding nontraditional ethnographic approaches as they may not realize the full potential of ethnography, I characterize the current research methodology as a pragmatic ethnographic approach rather than an ethnography because my purpose is not to provide a thick description of the "culture" per se, but to understand the ways in which several participants experience the "culture" and to learn the patterns of values, behaviors, and beliefs (Creswell, 2013; Harris, 1968).

Further, the rich literacy history and ongoing literate activities of the four key informants determine that I need to articulate the boundaries of my descriptions and analyses of these participants' ways of living. A case study approach best complements the ethnographic approach I argued for, as it helps to clearly, though not definitively, frame what *it* is that I investigate, as opposed to entering a research field completely open to any possibilities and directions. An articulation of the "it" here is the case to be studied, which may not be narrowly understood as a particular person, object, event, or phenomenon. Rather, a case can also refer to a relationship or a set of relationships, or an assemblage, a collective. Case study, Robert Stake (2000) claims, "is not a methodological choice but a choice of what is to be studied" (p. 435). The case I chose to look into for the present study is the four multilingual writers' perceptions and practices of difference embedded in and afforded by their literacy practices and literate activities. Synthesized with an ethnographic approach, a case study approach allowed me to build rapport with the participants and participate in their cultural activities, document their ways of living and interacting with people and their material surroundings in thick descriptive accounts with critical reflection, while still maintaining the focus on the predefined problem.

An important aspect of the approach of ethnographic case study that merits discussion is its critical dimension (Madison, 2005). My belief has been that no research is ideologically neutral (this very belief is a testament)—the researcher's disposition, philosophical and ideological stance, and bias are embedded in and intertwined with the very first decision they make, such as what to research about. A researcher's position then affords or constrains every step of the research, including ways to enter the field, collect and analyze data, report findings, and make arguments. The modernistic notion of "objectivist ethnographer" (Philipsen, 1991) that views ethnographic work as apolitical has lost its epistemological ground in a postcolonial and postmodern academic climate. As James West (1993) points out, "Ethnographers do more than just observe the lives of Others. They participate in a series of multivocal reflexive interactions that are saturated with power relations and struggles over the meaning of cultural identity" (p. 209). In light of this line of critique in the ethnographic tradition, I wouldn't go so far as to deny that I'm free from researchers' bias. As a matter of fact, quite the opposite. I acknowledge that my research agenda was constructed with a critical bent, as my ultimate goal is to amplify the muffled voices from the stereotypically silent (note: may not be silenced) multilingual writers. However, the current research is by no means *driven by* a critical agenda, nor is it a full-scale critical ethnography (Thomas, 1993). Rather, as a teacher-researcher whose research agenda grew out of fieldwork and whose teaching focuses on equipping students with a critical pair of eyes to examine textual authority and power and cultural representation, I hope my research will provide insights and evidence for collaborators engaged in critical praxis. As Chiseri-Strater (2012) argues when she critiques the ethical turn in the composition research community, "More than a methodology, a pedagogy, or an experimental genre, ethnography offers a way of seeing and being in the world with others that enlarges our vision of both ourselves and 'others'" (p. 210). All ethnographic research is critical in nature not because it necessarily aims to challenge the status quo but because it changes the ways in which we are positioned in the social, cultural, and political world.

Thus begin the stories.

2
Manna

From the Dance Floor to Writing Tutor's Table

Manna always knew she would come to the US to pursue her undergraduate studies. Having studied in an international high school in Beijing, she had received intensive training in general English communication skills along with other core subjects before setting foot in Cornville. Yet Manna admitted that she struggled quite a bit with English, especially writing, in high school, because she "had a tough time with grammar," as she wrote in her writer's literacy autobiography.[1] Although she knew she would study in the US and that she did not resist the idea, it wasn't entirely her agentive decision to do so. Her international high school placed students into two tracks: regular (domestic) and international. The regular track required higher test scores, which Manna barely achieved. To make a safe bet, Manna eventually landed herself in an international class that prepared students to seek undergraduate studies abroad.

Although Manna initially chose the natural science major of physics/mathematics, she quickly opted for the applied science major of mechanical engineering, partly in response to her parents' incessant advice and encouragement. As Manna bittersweetly recalled, her parents, who are both successful mechanical engineers in China, would take every opportunity to inculcate in her the importance of applying what she learns to creating new things and

https://doi.org/10.7330/9781646426447.c002

the profitability of doing so. Swayed by her parents' pragmatistic indoctrination, Manna transferred to the mechanical engineering department and began to settle down in this male-dominated disciplinary treasure island, all the while continuing to explore other facets of college life through bodily and literate activities.

One such activity that Manna has been fervently engaged in since she was little is dancing. Breakdancing, popping, locking, robot dance . . . Manna is not only a "jack of all trades," but also a master of all. "Practicing is an essential ingredient of my life, just like breathing, eating, and sleeping. I can't get by without practicing whenever and wherever I want to. I dance when I feel happy; I dance when I feel sad or upset. There's no better way to express myself other than moving my body." Manna's eyes lit up when she was reflecting on her dancer-self. To justify her enthusiasm for dancing to her parents as well as her social circle, Manna decided to officially minor in dance in the School of Design, Art, and Performance, legitimizing dancing as her academic pursuit rather than a mere hobby. Outside the mandated curriculum, she also joined two dance clubs on campus to situate herself more deeply in the cultural community of street dancing.

Mindfully seeking social and cultural capital beyond taking mechanical engineering courses, Manna also attempted to embark on a unique journey that her peers in her department had rarely considered: enrolling in a training course to become a writing consultant at the university's writing center. Admittedly, every enrolled student, undergraduate and graduate alike, is eligible to register for a practicum course and potentially work in the writing center as a consultant. Yet historically, these positions are predominantly occupied by domestic students from the humanities. Manna, despite her disciplinary and linguistic "differences," courageously broke into a realm of the unknown and exposed herself to a different set of challenges while at the same time rewriting the institutionalized discourse of difference that defined her boundaries in the first place.

Extending the Kinesphere: Articulating Rhetorical Difference through Dancing

"Kinesphere" was the first term Manna brought up, a term that emerged in the study of dance and refers to "the sphere around the body whose periphery can be reached by easily extended limbs without stepping away from that place which is the point of support when standing on one foot" (Laban, 1966,

p. 10). An average person who has not received training in effectively manipulating their muscle contractions may create a small and restricted kinesphere, whereas a professional dancer may reach farther and thus create a bigger kinesphere. In a sense, the notion of kinesphere denotes our anatomical possibilities and limitations. As a dance minor and enthusiast, Manna firmly believed in the bodily possibility of extending the kinesphere and making better use of her bodily and spatial affordances in her artistic expression. Yet not only did Manna believe in breaking her bodily limitations but she also enacted her belief of breaking limitations in performing herself in other rhetorical ecologies; for example, her literate stage where she needed to perform the manifestation of her mind.

It's no exaggeration to say that all of Manna's extracurricular activities were directly or indirectly associated with dancing. She was a member of two campus dance organizations, practiced multiple dance styles on a daily basis, and participated in dance competitions and performances as frequently as she could handle. Not too long after I entered her literate world through data collection, Manna informed me that she was preparing for a campus-wide dance competition that would take place in a month. The dance competition was organized and sponsored by the breaking dance club she was a member of at the time and was open to the entire student body. Manna jumped on board without hesitation.

> I always try to take advantage of opportunities like this to perform. For one, for selfish reasons, it helps me to overcome my stage fear. Here in America, there are just so many platforms for you to perform in public; for example, a lot of my classes asked us to do a presentation at the end of the semester. Although dancing is different than speaking or singing, the stage fear is always there. On the other hand, dancing is just like writing; unless you are writing a diary, you want your writing to be read by others, even if it would invite criticism. Unless I'm practicing, I want to dance in front of my audience and hope I could entertain them or evoke their emotions. Plus, it's a competition, you get to use your dance moves to meet new friends in the small circle, and you'd feel great if you go home with a prize!

To qualify to participate, Manna needed to select the music and choreograph the moves all by herself. It was no easy task for her despite having taken courses on choreography and choreographing several dances over the past 2 years for other competitions and shows. Writing as a simile surfaced again when Manna was describing her behind-the-scenes thought process when selecting the music, perhaps as she was co-constructing this lived experience with me, her former writing instructor.

> I still remember the days in our writing class when I had to do research and find different sources to support my argument that we need to dig deeper into the rationale for eating or avoiding eating dog meat. Picking a song for my dance is just like finding sources for your argument. I had this idea of creating a dance that would highlight the theme of ghost spirit, since the competition will fall around Halloween. I went over all of my music collections on my iTunes, shortlisted five songs, and then consulted my friend/co-dancer Daniel. Finally, we decided on a Japanese song that we believed would do a great job 烘托气氛 [heighten the atmosphere].

Dwelling on the music and listening to it over and over again and letting it sink in, breaking through the wall between her short-term memory and psyche until it draws out her intense emotional reactions is only the initial step of choreographing a dance, according to Manna. However, she was torn by the thought of composing the storyline first before selecting music.

> Most people think dancing is simply using your body to express your feelings and emotions, just like writing a poem. But I think dancing is always telling a story. Your feelings and emotions come out of that story. So it's like writing a narrative, just like the first assignment we wrote in your class.

Manna was referring to the writers' literacy autobiography, in which she recounted fascinating stories of how the "romantic relationship" between her and her writing in Chinese and English evolved. The reason she was hesitating between composing the story and selecting the music was that she believed that if she was too preoccupied with the music and emotionally invested, the music would end up devouring, as opposed to lending, her inspirations about the story. "Now I realized the wisdom of the Confucian philosophy that values '中庸 [*zhōngyōng*: the Golden mean].' Not too much, not too little. I need to balance everything out just right." Manna invoked the Doctrine of the Mean from Confucianism to rationalize her decision making. She eventually decided to choose the music first, because she was working with a dancing partner this time, which meant they needed to prioritize the concrete manifestation or product that they could work on. "You don't literally 'write' a story with pen and paper or on a computer, you know. The story is all in your head and you have to use your body to tell it."

As the event was approaching, Manna increased her practice load, occasionally at the expense of her schoolwork. "I knew I would always catch up. I

FIGURE 2.1. Manna meeting with her dance club members.

would never completely abandon my academic work just to be a good dancer. I love dancing, but I know I need to latch it onto something real." Her co-dancer Daniel was supportive of her. He looked slightly older and more mature than Manna. They met in a dance club on campus and soon developed friendship as well as mentorship. Manna learned new moves from him, practiced with him, and invited him to critique her moves. This healthy friendship/mentorship cheered Manna up and carried her through the miserable days when she had to constantly juggle upcoming exams and dance practice. They graciously allowed me to observe several of their practice sessions, which granted me access to the moments when they began negotiating the storyline verbally, modified and justified their moves using their bodies, gestures, and eye contacts, and eventually synchronized their moves and completed co-writing the story of the dance.

The story, as Manna recounted, dealt with the shifting power dynamics between a puppet and a puppeteer. Manna played the puppet who was relentlessly manipulated by the puppeteer, played by Daniel, and eventually rose up, cast off the mental shackles, and transformed into a puppeteer who took control. Translated into dance moves, the story was dramatized with patterned and synchronized moves that Manna and Daniel performed together and that represented the domination/submission dynamic. In addition to their patterned and synchronized moves, Manna and Daniel also composed their own idiosyncratic moves. For example, Manna's moves were characterized by her reaching to the ceiling or abruptly opening her arms and sprinting forward, which embodied her desperation for freedom; whereas Daniel's signature moves were pulling backward, locking his arms, and chasing Manna, which embodied his intensified craving for control. Manna said,

> If picking the music to dance to is like gathering academic sources to back up my argument, choreographing the dance with Daniel is like collaboratively writing up the argumentative paper, except, it's more fun, to be honest, and I have to sweat more.

The use of writing as a simile emerged yet again in Manna's reflection on the experience of choreographing a dance. I prompted her to say a bit more about this analogy. She paused and thought for several seconds and continued,

> As we learned in our writing class, you always need to analyze your rhetorical situation, think about who you are writing for, and how to appeal to them. To create a dance out of nowhere, I need to picture my audience sitting or standing in front of me cheering for me. Who would they be? Where would they come from? What would excite them or make them sad, angry, or even tear up? Also, what would the stage be like? Would it be a huge stage and far away from the audience? Or would it be a small and intimate one surrounded by the audience? How would the speakers be set up? Where would the music come from? As for the story itself, we wanted to create a story that's understandable and relatable, but not too understandable and too easily relatable. Here's where choreographing a dance is different from writing an essay in school. Dancing is a type of art, and like other types of art—poetry and impressionist artwork—we want to keep our audience guessing and encourage them to interpret it in their own ways. But when writing an essay, we always need to be as clear and straightforward as possible.

Manna and her partner's performance at the competition was a success. Although they didn't win the grand prize, their innovative choreography and well-executed moves were recognized by the referee committee and earned them an honorable mention. "I could have done better!" Manna seemed utterly disappointed.

> I was so nervous for some reason, which was unusual, so for a minute my mind went totally blank right before we were about to go on the stage.

Daniel helped to calm me down and boost my confidence. But I still felt that my body was someone else's and I had to tell my muscles to contract the way I wanted them to.

Despite the frustration, Manna approached the principal judge after the competition and requested feedback. "It's a learning experience after all. Now I have a better understanding of the taste of this particular audience."

As Manna recounted, after the competition, she rushed straight back to the dance room in the recreation center the next week, as she was eager to revisit her moves after taking into consideration the judge's suggestions. "I had to do it, you know, it was stuck in my head and stopped me from sleeping tight," she explained. A week later, I invited her to sit down with me and reflect on her experience of this competition and her dance career up until now.

> People like dancing for a lot of different reasons. Some dance because they like performing in front of an audience. Some dance because they want to make friends. I like dancing because there's no better way to fully express myself, my feelings, emotions, and even stupid ideas. I think writing is definitely irreplaceable when it comes to delivering thoughts with accuracy, because unless it's poetry, we tend to want our readers to interpret our writing in a certain way. But dancing is different. It could be richer in terms of expressing emotions. And as a dancer, I want my audience to interpret my moves based on their own experiences and find 情感共鸣 [emotional resonance] in my moves. What's even better about dancing is that it doesn't have to be representational, and that it doesn't need to embody or be attached to any real-world experience. It could simply be an expression of an intense but abstract emotion, just like you would jump up high the second you know you won a million-dollar lottery.

Manna's dance world is rich in networked ecological affordances that together enabled her to practice her rhetorical difference via a three-dimensional and nonverbal modality. First, the campus dance clubs of which Manna was a member, street dance styles familiar to Manna, basic choreographic principles, dance competition, music that Manna selected, and competition referees' evaluation rubric, among myriad others, formed a nexus of structural affordances within the rhetorical ecology. These structural affordances are invisible and need to be latched onto material entities to be manifest, such as textual documents and bounded space. Yet these indivisible structures nonetheless enabled Manna to be highly visible on campus, especially among the Chinese undergraduate student community and the dance community at Wabash, by repositioning Manna within the institutional discourse irrespective of her national, cultural, and linguistic identity. It provided Manna with a new identity: a talented and accomplished dancer.

Second, the most salient affordance is Manna's body and its kinesphere. Years of experiences practicing different dance styles maximized the expressive potential of her body and substantially extended her kinesphere. Manna was critically reflective of the expressive capacity of her body and was thus able to transform her bodily affordances into rhetorical affordances that empowered her to create affective bonds with her audience through nontextual and nonrepresentational means.

Third, Manna's experiences of taking the introductory writing course, minoring in dance, and reading the fundamental doctrine of Confucianism afforded her semiotic resources in the form of tropes to reflect on her choreography. For example, the writing course she took added to her repertoire terms such as audience awareness, and the structural and creative nature of writing turned the process and rhetorical features of writing into optimal tropes to discuss dancing. Courses Manna took in the school of performance also afforded terminologies and concepts that enabled her to develop a meta-awareness of her kinesthetic expression.

In addition, Manna's social affordances also constituted an integral part of her ecology. Her memberships of two independent dancing clubs, mentor-friendship with Daniel, and the connection built with the dance competition judge formed a convoluted relationship web that constantly provided social resources. These social resources then transformed into different ecological affordances when needs arose: moral support, professional guidance, co-dancership (partnership), and feedback. These social affordances directly contributed to Manna's perceptions of her differences and construction of her dancer's persona to defy and redefine her perceived differences. As her story on the dance floor shows, Manna's structural, semiotic, experiential, social, and bodily affordances are emergent, dynamic, transformative, and constitutive. They are in a constant state of becoming, from one type of affordance to another. Inhabiting this ecology of affordances, Manna was rhetorically empowered to complicate and problematize her oversimplified institutional label of Chinese international student and carve out her own space of difference on the dance floor.

An Adventure in the Unknown: Unlocking the Writing Center with Differences

As if the dance floor wasn't big enough for her to extend her kinesphere, Manna sent in her application for a writing consultant position at the writing center during the summer semester she was taking my writing course. It took me by surprise when she invited me to write a recommendation for her for the position because back then she had just completed the first assignment—writer's literacy autobiography—in my writing course, and I was aware that she was an engineering major. In other words, I was concerned about her eligibility to be a strong candidate, given her still-developing English proficiency and writing competence and her rather "irrelevant" disciplinary background. Now looking back, I feel mortified by my concerns, which were at best unfounded and outright insensitive and naïve as they were based on my institutionalized false assumptions about Manna's linguistic and literacy competence as well as her disciplinary preparation. Fortunately, Manna was offered the opportunity to enroll in a writing center practicum in the fall semester and be in full consideration for the position once she completed the training. During the course of data collection for this book, Manna's experience in the writing center emerged as a salient theme of her literate activities. From making the decision to apply for the position and practicing tutoring writing center clients, to composing weekly reflections and presenting the final project infographic report, Manna drew on various ecological affordances that enabled her to achieve her literacy goals.

When Manna reached out to me and requested a recommendation, she did not at all sound hesitant, as if she had planned this a while ago. Manna was not ambivalent about her rational decision, either.

> As you know, I was still using the writing center's service back then for the papers that I wrote in your class. I was and still am struggling with verb tense and prepositions most of the time. I still don't feel perfectly confident about my English writing in general. But I just wanted to do it. I didn't think of these issues as some kind of stigma that held me back. As a matter of fact, the real reason why I wanted to do it is because I would like to take advantage of this opportunity to practice my interpersonal skills. I know writing is the subject matter here, but tutoring in the writing center is more about communicating effectively with people. Being engineering majors, we often forget how important it is to hone our communication skills. In

the writing center, I get to learn how to communicate with clients and at the same time improve my writing—两全其美 [the best of both worlds]!

Manna's rationale for applying for the writing consultant position was primarily instrumental. Yet meanwhile she was not blindly optimistic; on the contrary, she was cognizant of and open about her weaknesses that may potentially disqualify her and even turned them into reinforcements of her decision.

Regular class meetings of the practicum were held in the writing center with the assistant director of the writing center leading the discussions. Manna, as usual, would sit quietly in the corner of the room, listening to the discussions and observing her classmates' reactions. Although Manna's East Asian face stood her out in a class of five white domestic students and two Indian students, nobody seemed to notice her the majority of the time, unless they were going around the table taking turns responding to a prompt. Her responses were characteristically concise and to the point, as if she made a conscious effort to shorten the period of visibility in the classroom space. Noticeably, the Manna in the writing center was nearly completely different from the one on the dance floor; the former was reticent and introspective, while the latter was expressive and spontaneous.

> I know I signed up for it with all my enthusiasm as if I was about to do something too cool for my Chinese friends to even think about. But when I actually sit in the classroom with seven native English speakers who not only speak perfect English but also know the culture inside out, well, at least the five Americans among them, I feel nervous and self-conscious whenever I speak up. It's different from speaking up in a regular class, for example, a mechanical engineering class. In a regular class, I don't usually feel that nervous when I answer or ask questions, because subconsciously I know we are all students, and the only difference between me and my American classmates is that I sometimes make grammar mistakes. No big deal. But here in the writing center, I'm haunted by the thought that if I make mistakes, my classmates who are far more qualified to be writing consultants would secretly laugh at me and wonder how I could possibly tutor our clients who need professional help with writing in English.

When asked about her perception of herself when on the stage of the dance competition and in the writing center, Manna chuckled,

> Honestly, I feel more like myself when I'm performing in front of my audience. I know I'm different and we are all different in our own unique ways.

> But I'm more conscious about the fact that I'm different in the writing center than when I'm dancing, because my differences as an international student, a non-native speaker, and an ME [mechanical engineering] major seem to be magnified, or at least I feel that way. For example, no matter how hard I work, they [American domestic colleagues] would probably still be skeptical about my language ability just because I'm not a native speaker. But 身体语言 (the language of body) is borderless and worldly. People wouldn't so easily judge you just by how stunning or how terrible your dance moves are or judge you by the type of dance you perform. Of course, I know our body language is extremely limited, but it's more efficient and effective in terms of connecting people heart-to-heart. That's also why I think that sometimes I can express myself better through dancing, because there are feelings that cannot be expressed through words—not because there are no words to communicate the feeling but because people intentionally avoid communicating it even though they feel it.

Caught up in the unbalanced structural and social relations networked in two material spaces, Manna's bodily and semiotic affordances enabled her to construct two distinct literate identities, suggesting how difference can be perceived differently.

A month into the writing center practicum, Manna and her colleagues were assigned to conduct a hands-on tutorial session, which means they needed to, for the first time, experience what it would be like to be a writing consultant by tutoring a "client" in a mock tutorial session. Manna was paired up with one of her American female colleagues, Blair,[2] also a current undergraduate consultant. In a regular 30-minute tutorial session, Manna was assigned to work on "client" Blair's research proposal that she wrote earlier.

> I was under so much pressure when we were about to start. I didn't know what was coming. What if the instructor encouraged Blair to challenge me just because she wanted me to realize how intimidating an authentic session would be like? What if she asked Blair to go easy on me just because I'm a non-native English speaker, which would be really embarrassing?

Despite the insecurity and fidgeting, Manna's session proceeded smoothly. Blair presented her research proposal to Manna and requested that she offer her general feedback on the organization and coherence of the essay. Because of her sense of insecurity, Manna adopted a proactive rather than defensive strategy, which is commonly practiced in a tutorial setting, in response to Blair's request: she invited Blair to read the essay out loud.

As a first timer, I wasn't sure how to ask appropriate questions. And after I took a glance at her paper, I noticed a couple of unfamiliar words. I said to myself: 'Calm down. You can do it.' So, I asked Blair to read it out loud, hoping she could realize her incoherence while reading, so that I wouldn't destroy my credibility and authority.

To Manna's relief, Blair did indeed correct herself several times while reading. Manna, on the other hand, pinpointed a few citation errors, and suggested that Blair replace some outdated sources with newer ones. The session completed without unanticipated drama. Blair indicated to me afterward that she thought Manna would make a highly approachable and professional tutor.

During the same week, as requested by the instructor, Manna wrote a short reflection on her first tutoring experience.

Tutorial Session Reflection (October 2018)

In this week's in-lab activity I had done a practice with being a tutor. I worked with Blair, who is a tutor in the writing lab. But instead of she is a tutor and I worked as a client, this time we switched our job.

Blair brought a proposal of her research project for the tutorial session. After the small talk we had about her day and school, we started our session. The first thing I did is ask question about the assignment. Questions like "What this assignment is about," "When will the assignment due?," "Have you work with other client before?" After knowing those general questions about this proposal, we talked about what she want to work on for this session. Blair said she wanted to work on the structure and see how well the proposal delivered messages. Base on those information, I wrote on the to-do list for the day, and we double checked once to make sure that is what she wants. The whole setting agenda process only takes about 2 minutes.

I asked Blair whether she is willing to read the assignment, and we worked paragraph by paragraph. Other strategies I used in the session was giving the client to control the pen and computer, thus she can work on own. Also, after I gave advices about Blair's work, I would ask her whether my suggestion making sense. If she seems confused, I would explain to her one more time. Besides, when gave her reflection on each paragraph, I always start with compliment. I would say "I think you did a great job on . . ." or "I really like how you addressed . . ." This strategy could help clients feel motivated and relaxed.

I learnt a lot from this experience. Even though I had been to a writing tutorial session and I had shadowed few sessions before, I still felt it is very different than being an actual tutor and saw everything on the tutor's perspective. When I was tutoring, at the beginning I felt very nervous, but as things going on, I felt more relaxed. This is partially because Blair was acting as an active client, so that I will feel more comfortable to talk with her too. Also, since Blair read the paragraph and I was listening, I felt sometimes it is a little bit hard to catch up when she is reading fast. Thus, I was going through a mental process about what I can do about this. Overall, I felt this experience is very nice. I knew even I felt nervous, I just needed to control myself to be able to still give constructive suggestions.

I think the most comfortable things doing in this tutorial is the small talk. After this practice, I think the small talk before the start of session can not only help client relax, but also comforted tutor as well. The small talked help the session goes more naturally and bring the client and the tutor closer to each other.

The other thing I think I would do differently was I will sit facing the clock. I noticed this part is important because the practice tutorial session was 30 mins, and it is very hard to stay in this short amount of time. During this practice, I was sitting in the same direction as the clock facing, I found it is hard in this way was because I didn't bring my phone with me and I also didn't feel natural to look back and see how much time we have left. Thus, during the session, there was a struggling about how to check the time remaining.

Other strategies I think I need to work on was ask question. I think when the time I can barely catch up with my client's reading speed, I should tell them just slow down a little bit. Also, when there are some words I felt confused about, I should also ask for clarification. During the class we learnt a lot about asking question, and when shadowing other sessions, I noticed other tutor ask questions too. However, when it goes to me, I still have problem with asking question. I think next time I will try to do better.

Manna clearly laid out the tutorial strategies she learned and internalized and used during the session, such as initiating small talks, building rapport, taking a supportive stance, creating a to-do list, reading out loud, and offering compliments. She was also vocal about her shortcomings: timekeeping and question strategies. Yet Manna seemed reticent in her reflection about her emotional disturbance and mental pressure that she experienced as a multilingual speaker assuming the position of perceived authority. Admittedly, Manna had full right and autonomy to be selective about the focus on the reflection. However, her perceived difference emerged frequently during our conversations and active reconstructions of her experiences and had mediated her decision making with respect to her tutoring style and strategies.

Manna's major struggle, which remained hidden, is not ascribed to her bodily or semiotic difference per se; rather, it is with her perception of the potential barriers and challenges as a result of her difference in the contact zone of a writing center. Without her reflective account of this struggle, her practicum instructor (assistant director of the writing center) and her colleagues would have no way of truly understanding her, particularly given the institutional discourse of cultural diversity that stresses "celebrating," not "questioning," diversity. Manna's difference was flattened; her struggles remained unseen and unheard; and so did she.

However, Manna was not entirely pessimistic and cynical about her perceived difference. She was also consciously aware of the cultural capital of her linguistic resources. For example, Manna believed that her upbringing in a different cultural context and her experiences of learning and using her mother tongue embedded in her a cultural sensibility and enabled her to view and interact with the world from a unique perspective.

> Not to mention other cultural activities, just in terms of writing, for example, the Chinese wisdom that has been programmed into us allows us to do things that Americans who only speak English can't do. We get to use lots of rhetorical devices they don't, such as 比喻 [simile and metaphor], 拟人 [personification], and 对仗 [roughly translated to "antithesis"]. These are very fancy ones. Especially 对仗, it's just not possible to be done in English, because English words are not of the same length, unlike Chinese characters. Plus, I'm always under the impression that people who write in English just want to get done with business, because they are so straightforward.

I was on the verge of correcting her that writers do employ similes and metaphors fairly frequently in English, but probably not so much so in the academic discourse of engineering, which is what Manna was exposed to most of the time. Nevertheless, I kept my thoughts unexpressed, as I knew Manna was simply and possibly carelessly offering examples, and as I knew, sharing a similar cultural upbringing with Manna and struggling to make my voice heard in the dominant discourse, sometimes a tiny dose of false pride is all we have.

Although Manna had to constantly reposition herself in a contact zone in which a complex assemblage of asymmetrical relations is entangled with Manna's histories and desires—the supposed authority of a writing consultant, status of a practicum trainee, perceived privileges of white domestic colleagues, and dominant language and discourse—she was sometimes able to articulate her sense of self in the writing center when enabled by her semiotic affordances. Not too long after the mock tutorial activity, Manna and her colleagues were assigned a small research project, for which they needed to explore a topic of interest related to writing center practices and report the findings in the form of an infographic. Upon completing the infographic, they were prompted to reflect on the designing process and explain the rationale behind it in a short essay.

Having experimented with several topic candidates—APA citation, punctuation, thesis development—Manna eventually dwelled on the topic of plagiarism, and decided to create an infographic to help writers avoid plagiarism. Titled "How to Avoid Plagiarism?," the infographic depicted a cartoon character of a thief holding a stolen "idea" and fleeing from a police cruiser. It defined what plagiarism is and listed six sequential questions intended to help students self-evaluate and avoid plagiarism. As she explained in the reflection, her motivation to undertake such a topic partly originated from her personal experience as a discourse outsider:

> The target audience for this infographic poster is in a big range. I think all the student can use it. For students who just start writing, they will learn what is plagiarism in this poster, and they can also check whether they unconsciously plagiarize someone. For international students, just come to a different country is very hard, especially language-wise. It is very important for them to know there are certain line they should not touch. For me, when I was back in China, our teacher will tell us not to cheat, however, they won't spend time to tell us what will be considered as cheated. Thus, when I just came to America, I found surprising when I know you can self-plagiarism if you used your own past paper without properly cite it. Thus, I think for other international students should pay more attention when they write their papers. Also, the audience can also be native speakers who is in business, college, or even high school. I think no matter what kind of career you are thinking to pursue in the future, it is always necessary to keep in mind for not plagiarize.

Manna did not automatically assume an authoritative authorial position. On the contrary, she sought empathy from her audience by acknowledging that she herself belonged to the intended audience and a beneficiary of this infographic. In other words, she was advocating for a respect for intellectual property and a means of doing so among what she perceived to be the less informed group, namely, the international student community and Chinese student community in particular.

> When I was doing this project, I felt it was not me against the Americans anymore like when I was in the classroom; it was more me within my Chinese circle. I know I don't speak much in class. It's not because I don't have any ideas or I don't want to participate. I have lots of ideas, but I'm constantly stressed out about the possibility that my ideas may sound different once I translate them into English words. But in writing, I feel more comfortable, because I have more time to organize my language and some wiggle room to make myself understandable. So, in writing, I don't have to feel self-conscious about who I am, and I actually want to be who I am in my reflection. I knew what we Chinese students struggle with because I had been there, so I wanted to side with them and create something useful for them, well, us.

Following the rationale for selecting the topic of plagiarism, Manna also elaborated on her thought process behind the design of the poster; for example, adopting the analogy of theft, developing a storyline of the police chasing the "idea thief," and constructing affective connection with her audience by using comics and visual narrative, claiming that "the goal is to entertain but also educate [her] audience." Although the narrative didn't seem logically impeccable (e.g., affirmative answers to the bullet-point self-check questions should facilitate the capture of the thief instead of slowing it down with stop signs), Manna's argument for the need of informing students of the danger of plagiarism was effectively and affectively delivered.

Interestingly but not unexpectedly, during a stimulated recall interview with me, in which Manna contemplated her written reflection on the designing process, the motif of grammar emerged yet again. She was well aware of the grammatical errors that abound in the infographic and the reflective essay, yet she was not able to pinpoint the errors without active attention. As I noticed in the paragraph quoted above from her reflection, Manna seemed to struggle particularly with verb tense (e.g., "our teacher will tell us not to cheat"), gerund (e.g., "just come to a different country is very hard" and "without properly cite it"), and dangling modifiers (e.g., "for other international students should pay more attention when they write their papers").

> I told you before that I feel extremely nervous about making grammar mistakes when I have to speak up in a group or in front of people, but when I write, I'm not always self-conscious, probably because I don't see my audience picking on my grammar through the page?

Manna grinned. "As long as my readers understand my content, I think I've done my job." Since Manna began her studies at an international high school where the majority of classes were taught by instructors from the US or the UK, she has paid more attention to effective and efficient, rather than grammatically perfect, communication in writing, although she was aware that grammatical accuracy was also a key factor in effective communication.

> My English competence back then was barely enough to help me understand the content of the courses. And I had to spend most of the time struggling to get good grades in those courses, how could I possibly pay attention to grammar? My 外教 (foreign teachers) didn't seem to be bothered, not to mention my Chinese classmates. So I lowered my guard, and over time developed a habit of focusing on my argument and logic instead of grammar. That's why you probably found lots of grammar mistakes in my reflection.

Manna then shifted to recounting one of her recent anecdotes:

> But something happened lately somewhat changed my perspective. Two days ago, I did my very first writing center tutorial session with a real client. She was an undergraduate student from Nepal, and just like every other international student that comes to the writing center, she wanted me to focus on her grammar on top of the flow of sentences. I freaked out a little bit, but forced myself to stay calm and try my best to help her. I was able to pick out some obvious verb tense issues or third-person singular forms and corrected them, and that was about it. I was relieved when the session finished in half an hour, and needed to write a report. That was when I really felt the need of grammatical accuracy. My client would read my report, and how could she think of me if my report was full of grammar mistakes? If I were her, I would totally raise a question about my credibility as a writing consultant—even the so-called writing consultant writes in broken English! That moment, I realized that in some situations, my English IS my professional image. If I ever tutor an international student again, I would definitely make it clear from the beginning that English is not my first language, but I'm willing to work with you and learn with you.

Manna's adventures in the unknown space of the writing center were networked into an assemblage of intricate asymmetrical relations, tensions, resolutions, and growth. Caught up in this dynamic cultural, semiotic, and bodily contact zone, Manna needed to incessantly reevaluate her social and material surroundings as well as her affordances and realign herself to the shifting construct of rhetorical difference. For example, the decision to claim membership in a traditionally homogeneous social group that also requires a certain threshold of experience and expertise was solidified by both Manna's semiotic needs to accumulate linguistic capital and her social desire to be recognized by the dominant cultural group. Yet her needs and desires were put under scrutiny as soon as Manna began engaging with other actants: practicum colleagues and instructor, consultants, clients, assignment papers, clients' writings, seating in the practicum, and countless others that were in action yet did not emerge in Manna's account. Her original motivation to be assimilated into the dominant discourse in the US academic context was compromised by her habitual indifference toward the grammatical flawlessness of the dominant language and eventually put in doubt when she sought emotional sanctuary in the power of her Othered discourse—the Chinese language. It was not until Manna's perceived identity shifted from a marginalized linguistic minority situated in a practicum to a writing consultant representing the dominant discourse positioned in authority within a tutorial session that she began to grapple with the ramifications of her difference, and as a result realigned herself with the public expectation. Manna's desire to be recognized by the dominant cultural group, on the other hand, was intertwined with and neutralized by her fear and frustration of her lack of the cultural and linguistic capital. Again, her experiential affordances stemming from her internalized consultation strategies came to her rescue by enabling her to perform a professional persona during the mock tutorial session.

Feel Thyself: Performing the Introspective Self through Reading and Journaling

Apart from the dance floor and writing center, a third literate space that Manna occupies and dwells in is invisible, intangible, intimate, and personal; it is the space carved out between her sensitive inner world and the readings and writings she performs that connect to and reify that inner world. In other words, it is the space that enables Manna to verbalize and communicate her introspective ideas and emotions to herself and her imagined audience. It is also the space where she can perform herself *for* herself, as opposed to what she was used to—performing for her audience on the stage or in the writing center.

Manna maintains a rich extracurricular literate life. In addition to her time spent on the dance floor, she reads widely and reads curiously. Finding it tedious and thus difficult to settle on one area or topic, Manna indulged in her intuitive biblio-exploration and covered genres such as novels, short stories, and nonfiction essays, and topics such as Greek philosophy, detective stories, and wine appreciation.

I wouldn't say I'm a book maniac, but I think I read more than most of my friends in my Chinese social circle here. I'm not picky about the topics. I just grab whatever is available. I browse Weibo [a popular Chinese Twitter-like microblogging site] on a daily basis, and sometimes I would see book recommendations. I would just buy them without hesitation. Although most of the time I end up reading just a few of them. This is because I'm always curious about anything I don't know about, and I think every part of the world deserves attention from us. And books are like windows through which I get to see those parts of the world without actually reaching there.

However, after Manna realized that she had squandered money on too many books that she eventually stacked unopened in her big storage box in her tiny dorm room, she became more selective. "Now I only buy and read books whose titles attracted my attention. I don't know about others, but I'm the kind of person who's easily drawn to the cover artwork, especially those provocative ones." Manna pulled out a book from her backpack as she spoke. It was a novel written in Chinese, entitled 早上九点叫醒我 (*Wake Me Up at 9:00 AM*), by A Yi.

Quite a few famous literary critics on social media recommended this book. I didn't even see its title but immediately locked my eyes on the cover. At first sight, it's just a really dark and depressing image of a sad old man's face and a group of people circling around some blood-like redness. But if you take a closer look, the lines on the old man's face that represent his wrinkles are so rough, and his mouth is even blurred. And look at his eyes, they are so hollow and spiritless, as if he has been through a lot and completely lost his will to live. Oh, and that piece of redness there—so catchy and even disturbing and provocative on the gray background. But of course, at that time, I wasn't able to make sense of it before I read the book. But the cover stirred up strong mixed feelings in me, something like a combination of disgust, annoyance, and depression. And I became immediately interested to read what's going on.

Manna seemed to possess sophisticated vocabulary (in Chinese) to describe her emotional reactions to the artwork and demonstrate her conscious awareness of how her rhetorical decision of selecting a reading was mediated by the image.

Although Manna was lured to the book by its provocative cover artwork, she did capitalize on her experiences of reading and critically engaging with the storyline, the implicit argument, and the stylistic features of the book, as a brief reflection found its way into her writer's literacy autobiography and became a piece of supporting evidence.

> I like to read books since I was young, started with bed-time stories, novels, and professional publications and so on. When I was young, my favorite books were *Harry Potter*. I loved J.K Rowling's imagination of magic and her description of the fight between Harry Potter and Voldemort. After I started to be interested in philosophy, I began to wonder about lives. There was a book wrote by a Chinese author A Yi, *Wake Me Up at 9:00 AM*. This author had cancer when he wrote this book. One of the reasons that this book attracted me is that I believed when you were reflecting on your experience you will have some philosophy of life. This book talked about the humanity. The book shocked me by how it only used simple words but created a strong feeling that made you almost cry for the main character. By learning through reading, I realized fancy words and hard techniques was not enough for good writing. In my opinion, a good writer can always make the readers feel what the writer feels or picture the story in the readers' mind. A good story can also keep the readers reading. Also, writers also should use the most straightforward and precise languages to create the most durable feeling. Writing is like a non-verbal communication between the readers and the perception of the writer.

The short paragraph taken from Manna's literacy autobiography is quite dense. She packed her transformation of reading taste, evaluative reflection on A Yi's novel, thoughts on language style and writing's impact into this short excerpt. Although these ideas and reflections read quite scattered, disorganized, and sometimes crude and simplistic, suffice to say they betray Manna's literary predilection for microscopic and in-depth analysis of human nature that also arouses compassion or empathy in her readers. Having moved beyond her childhood obsession with imaginations and fantasies, Manna began tapping into the reality of the present-day human conditions. As an ideal illustration of the sensitivity to the mankind's well-being and sufferings, A Yi's novel successfully appealed to Manna's taste with its simple yet powerful language and its provocative cover artwork, evoking deep compassion from the equally sensitive Manna. In addition to the affective connection built between Manna and the novel, there also seemed to be an attempt at rationalizing the association between the author's stylistic maneuvers and the intended rhetorical consequences on readers. The association seemed unapologetically prescriptive, though:

> In my opinion, a good writer can always make the readers feel what the writer feels or picture the story in the readers' mind. A good story can also keep the readers reading. Also, writers also should use the most straightforward and precise languages to create the most durable feeling.

Just like a dancer who practices making use of her bodily and kinetic affordances to directly express complex feelings and emotions, Manna values the most straightforward, unaffected, and purest expression that is less mediated or, worse still, contaminated by words. And of course, the trope comparing dancing to writing emerged again, except this time it is used in reverse order: "Writing is like a non-verbal communication between the readers and the perception of the writer."

Consuming language-mediated "third-party" thoughts and feelings did not suffice to satisfy Manna's literary appetite; at best, it served as semiotic and structural affordance that enabled Manna to carve out a discursive space for catharsis. It was Manna's private and intensive introspective activities in response to or enabled by her literary consumptions that ultimately kept her intellectually and spiritually entertained.

> I think a lot when I'm alone. But I'm not like those serious philosophers who wrestle with big global issues such as global warming or immigration. Those political and historical subjects are too difficult for me to study. Plus, I'm just not interested in them, perhaps because I'm too naïve or selfish to see how they directly affect our ordinary people's lives.

Manna smiled and continued,

> Those subjects could be references whenever I need them to help answer my questions, but I don't need to master them. When I think in a quiet environment with nobody around, I usually think about the philosophy of life. You know, different 人生境遇 (situations, conditions, and contingencies of life) and who we are and who we become in those 人生境遇.

Manna had cultivated her sensibility to her own emotional homeostasis and her social and material surroundings long before reading and thinking about a "philosophy of life" and self-reflection. The meta-reflective ability she had developed alongside her sensibility allowed her to respond quickly to her emotional disturbance and readapt to the shifting dynamics around her. During one of the interview sessions in October, Manna seemed melancholic and somewhat quieter than before. She didn't withhold her anxiety and gloominess when I cautiously inquired. She recently withdrew from a major course in mechanical engineering, as she realized that with a 21-credit-hour course load this semester, it was plainly impossible to keep up with anything, and she had been sleep-deprived for two weeks due to the horrendous wave of midterm exams. Yet the direct cause of her dropping the course was not her physical or mental inability to carry on with the heavy course load.

> I know this may sound crazy, but I just can't accept even one B or C on my transcript. I've already gotten a few A minuses, which is not ideal, but I have to be able to live with that. But B or C? No way. It's totally non-negotiable. The course I dropped was very challenging. But if I work really hard and forget about sleeping, I'm sure I can do it well. But I just can't when I'm taking six other equally challenging courses. So I'd rather not do it if I can't guarantee an A in the end.

As serious as she was about maintaining her straight-A academic status, she did not develop this obsession with As "by default," that is, conforming to the cultural and racial stereotype that Asians, especially Chinese students, are naturally overachievers. Rather, she did so "by choice."

> I know Americans all seem to have this idea that we Chinese students are supposed to be the best students, especially in math. And they always expect us Chinese students to be the most hardworking ones on campus. Plus, they tend to think that the reason why we are hardworking is because our parents put a lot of pressure on us. So first of all, I want them to know that none of those are true. Of course, my parents expect me to have the best of everything, but they never give me any pressure. They encourage me to do what I want. And second, I want straight As not because I want to be just another hardworking Chinese, but because I'm determined to prove it to myself that I can do well on anything I want: dance, writing center, and my major courses.

Manna's obsession with excellence and perfection, however, turned out to be the ultimate cause of her anxiety and gloominess. Not long after the withdrawal, Manna's anxiety about her slim chance of getting an ideal grade in the course transformed into a different type of anxiety: peer pressure—a sense of insecurity that if she did not exhaust all her potentials, she would not be able to emulate her friends' achievements.

> It's not that I'm jealous of my friends' accomplishments. When they achieved something, I'm genuinely happy for them. It's my sense of insecurity that everybody else is so passionately fighting for the life they want, but I'm already burned out and even have to drop a course? I know it sounds funny, because I'm still taking six courses, which gives me more than enough work to do. But I'm used to pushing myself hard. I'm contradicting myself, aren't I?

Manna managed a smile.

> Have you heard of a trendy term in Chinese called '阳光型抑郁症 (sunshine depression)?' In front of people, you are like the sun: wherever you go, you

would bring sunshine—positive energy—into people's lives and make them happy. But at the end of the day, you may be alone at home, that's when you feel depressed and stressed out. So it's like you have to constantly put on a show in front of people because you don't want to negatively affect people you care about. But the more you hide and pretend, the more bitter you feel. I think this word I saw on social media characterizes the recent me well.

Manna needed a space for catharsis. She invested more time and energy in the dance practice room, as intense bodily movements helped her release some portion of her stress and temporarily escape from the noise in her mind. Yet Manna had never been an escapist in her life; instead, she always actively sought solutions. Indulging herself in reading novels or nonfiction that implicitly inculcated what she terms "life philosophies" became her new after-school therapy. During the time when mid-semester crisis struck her, Manna began reading a collection of short stories titled 从你的全世界路过 (*Passing by Your Entire World*), written by Zhang Jiajia. The collection can be aptly characterized as fictional bedtime stories, in which the author complied dozens of independent stories. These stories do not follow any systematic pattern in any sense—form, setting, characters, length, or language style. The morals of the stories vary as well. Yet it has gained tremendous popularity in China since its publication in 2013, as critics claimed that every reader could find themself in some of the stories. Manna opened the book that she carried in her backpack and presented the following quote to me:

世界上，总有一个人和你刚见面，两人就互相吸引，莫名觉得是一个整体。这就是你的反向人。为什么叫反向人呢？你们的运气是共同的整体。两人相加是一百，那么你占五十，那么他也占五十。如果你占九十，那么他就只剩下十。(Zhang Jiajia, 2013)

[In the world, there must be someone who, upon meeting you, will attract and be attracted to you, as if the two of you are a complete being. This person is your "reverse other." Why is the person your reverse other? It is because your and his/her fortune makes up the whole. If your fortune plus his/hers equals 100%, then yours accounts for 50%, and his accounts for the other 50%; if yours accounts for 90%, then he's left with only 10% (my translation).]

The first time I read this quote, frankly, I found it so pretentious. It doesn't make any mathematical sense. So according to this theory, the world population has to be a perfect even number? Otherwise, someone's going to be incomplete and thus can't access their fortune. Or, everybody may potentially have multiple different reverse others, because among seven billion people in the world, there must be more than one person whose fortune is negatively correlated with yours. Plus, how can we possibly quantify our luck in the first place? And who knows how much luck my reverse other and I can have in total? But yesterday, since I started going through some mood swings, I've revisited this quote a couple of times, and tried to temporarily block the "critical engagement" my college professors in America, including you, taught me to do. And then I started to taste the spices that Zhang Jiajia carefully and subtly put on this very light dish. I learned a new idiom the other day in my computer engineering class: benefit of the doubt. If we give Zhang Jiajia the benefit of the doubt, then perhaps we do have a reverse other waiting for us somewhere in the world, whose luck is always inversely proportional—when I gain, he or she loses. After all, there are seventy billion people on earth! So maybe the fact that I'm going through some hardships now—and I know my so-called hardships may sound like 无病呻吟 (moan and groan without being sick) to a lot of people—actually means that my reverse other is having a good time somewhere else. Thinking about that, I feel my heart has been lightened up, because by going through some down times, I'm actually allowing another person to go through some up times. The more I think about it, the more eager I want to meet him or her. I hope it will be a him, though.

Manna smiled again, and the smile this time seemed less forced than before.

Manna also revealed to me that some of what she said during our interviews was also documented in her sporadic journal entries and thus not completely impromptu. Yet due to privacy concerns, I respect Manna's request not to share her journal entries. Her books and journal entries and her sensibility toward her emotional and environmental equilibrium together constructed a sanctuary where she sought catharsis and regained energy. Manna referenced her diary book in her literacy autobiography: "I found myself a 'home,' where I could keep my little secrets and feelings. I felt a sense of belonging when I wrote." Although Manna's literate world has become more sophisticated and intertwined with her emerging identity as well as material conditions compared with the diary entries she wrote during teenage years, it still, and ever more greatly so, affords her the rhetorical power to reposition herself in the face of changing dynamics.

We could intervene in the construction of Manna's literate world by taking stock of the complexity of the affordance. First, bodily and material affordance. Manna's body played a crucial role in supporting her action of using dance moves to express her literate ingenuity. Here again, Manna's bodily affordance, along with her perception of her bodily capacity, enabled her to effectively and nimbly recreate her rhetorical self when sensing potential threats to her emotional homeostasis. As a long-time dancing practitioner, Manna had developed cognitive as well as conscious awareness of her bodily capacity. In other words, years of practice and attempt to maximize the physical possibility allowed Manna to develop an implicit theory of her body that helped her to operate the complicated organism. When external stimulants were at work, Manna would immediately respond by seeking emotional outlets. The books she carried around in her backpack functioned as a synthetic semio-material affordance that grounded her catharsis in reflective terms. The semio-material affordance of books distributed her agency by providing a heuristic to rationalize her emotional disturbance. The physicality of the books themselves that otherwise only served to add weight to Manna's backpack turned out to also intervene in her emotional homeostasis, as they were handy and accessible whenever Manna needed to consult them about "life philosophy." That material being of books provided a sense of security. In other words, the books were an extension of Manna's bodily and emotional being. Second, social and structural affordance. It seemed as though Manna was constructing her own psyche-literate silo where she had conversations with the authors and her own situated thoughts. Yet, as a matter of fact, this activity is itself highly structural and social. On the one hand, reading and journaling are inherently social activities, as Manna needed to engage herself in a series of communicative activities: negotiating the title to read, negotiating the text content, negotiating the text style, negotiating the interpretations, and, finally, negotiating the responses and implications. On the other hand, the outcome of the afforded activities is Manna's created emotional response mechanism in dealing with social and structural challenges: course credit hours, graduation, peer pressure, and fragmented and oftentimes trivial others. Eventually, after ecologically afforded therapeutic engagement with reading, thinking, and writing in her introspective world, Manna repositioned herself in the external social world, regained emotional homeostasis, and found reconciliation with her own shifting literate identities.

Conclusion: Manna's Literacy Affordances

Manna's bodily affordances that enabled her to craft her rhetorically different persona of a competent dancer were entangled with her structural and semiotic affordances that shaped her literate identity as a critical and reflective reader and writer. The entanglement found its manifestation in the writing tropes she used to discuss dancing and dancing tropes used to discuss writing. Manna's participation and immersion in both literate activities (and seeing both *as* literate activities) afforded her a new perspective to view the relationality of the two ecologies and afforded her a new discourse to articulate her own position within that relationship.

Caught up in the liminal space of the writing center where her competing identities were fronted, Manna needed to constantly make decisions to highlight or suppress her cultural and linguistic differences. Fortunately, the audience awareness she developed through years of stage performance and her introspective ability strengthened through reading and journaling intervened in her struggles. Manna was quick enough to identify these experiential affordances and capitalize on them by, for example, incorporating tutorial strategies practiced in the practicum, drawing on her cultural sensibility and difference, and building rapport by acknowledging her difference. These affordances enabled Manna to reevaluate her expectations and her rhetorical situations and modify her rhetorical choices accordingly.

An observant and sensitive individual, Manna was accustomed to building affective ties to her social and material surroundings, and when the affective ties broke down, Manna needed to seek help from her affordance-scape to rebuild the ties. Her habitual literate activities of extensively (then selectively) reading, journaling, and reflecting served to restore her emotional homeostasis. Dancing, unsurprisingly, afforded Manna another emotional outlet to fully express herself. But the difference was that Manna translated her emotions into bodily movements that may not be representational at all times, as opposed to embodying her emotions in semiotic resources.

3
Wentao

A Structuralist Poet in Disguise

Wentao began his undergraduate studies at Wabash in its internationally renowned program of aviation management, and during the course of my research, decided to pursue a double major in both aviation management and data science. When asked why he chose his majors, he responded with uncharacteristic excitement: "I've loved to know anything about aviation management and airlines since I was little. And I'm aware that data analytical skills are important for working in the aviation industry." As a junior student, Wentao enrolled in several upper-level major courses during the time of my research, including airline management, aviation finance, and aviation safety problems. At the same time, he was also taking an entry-level computer science course, an intermediate Japanese course, as well as a physics course. Out of his 23 hours of coursework every week, Wentao managed to meet with me every other week for a 1-hour-long interview session, and he willingly did so, as he took it as an interesting and rewarding opportunity to learn from me and know himself better.

Outside of the classes, Wentao maintained a no less hectic schedule by participating in a student club called Performing Arts[1] that provided a platform for students of any major to be involved in performing arts, as he wanted to enrich his extracurricular life by participating in different social groups and experiencing cultural activities. Although he was not particularly interested in acting on stage per se, he was nonetheless eager to learn the management side of a performance, and thus ended up filling a secretary position and assisted the president of the club in team communications and public relations. In addition to his conscious sociocultural integration, Wentao also actively attempted to understand personal finance by investing a small amount of money in the US stock market. As he noted, he based his investment decisions on "extensive research of individual stocks and the economic and political context." As a hobby, Wentao watched trendy and classic movies on a weekly basis, occasionally writing movie reviews on a popular online Chinese movie forum.

In general, my meaningful interactions with Wentao over the period of 9 months have yielded ample evidence for me to characterize him as a sensitive, meticulous, gentle, composed, expressive, observant, and sometimes cynical individual. These characteristics as reflected in his literate activities labeled him a structuralist poet under the guise of a Chinese international student.

Craftsmanship and Teamwork Meet in the Game of Words: Writing for Aviation Management Courses

Wentao is a self-proclaimed perfectionist, so much so that he once spent 2 hours searching all over the Internet to find *the* right image for a PowerPoint slide. This pursuit of excellence in academic work is fueled by his passion for his major studies and in turn drives his craftsmanship in completing course-related reading and writing assignments. As Wentao composes for his course assignments, either independently or collaboratively with group members, he demonstrates an extraordinary level of linguistic ingenuity that immediately sets him apart from his peers, international and domestic alike. Yet overall he plays the game of words by the rules, which, rather than constrain him, afford him the maximum level of flexibility in executing his linguistic ingenuity.

Wentao was taking three aviation management major courses while I was collecting research data: Airline Management, Aviation Finance, and Aviation Safety Problems. The three courses all involved some reading and writing components, and reading and writing skills were integrated into the course objectives. For example, to complete the coursework for Airline Management, students needed to, as stated on the course syllabus, "demonstrate oral and written communication skills on topics related to the airline industry." For the upper-level course Aviation Safety Problems, students were also required to read, comprehend, and critically engage with literature in the disciplinary field, which clearly served as a stepping-stone to more intensive reading and writing tasks in their graduate program. Although Wentao used to regularly write for recreational and reflective purposes outside of school before he came to the US, such as keeping a journal and reviewing movies, he had stopped doing so altogether since the course load increased dramatically, and he focused almost exclusively on reading and writing tasks assigned in these major courses. These reading and writing tasks assigned by Wentao's course instructors and professors are structural affordance that provided him with an outlet to express his evolving expertise in the field while at the same time suppressed his extracurricular literate activities.

Course syllabi usually afforded the first overarching structure that segmented Wentao's course of the semester into meaningful pieces (topics, quizzes, exams, writing assignments, presentations, etc.), stipulated the requirements and expectations, described the material and social aspects of the course (textbooks, class meeting locations, group assignments, etc.), and explained the consequences (grading, certification, etc.). Wentao indeed took these syllabi seriously, as he frequently referred to the requirements and guidelines presented on them. With the help of the latest iPad and a compatible stylus, handy and expensive material affordances, Wentao took differently colored notes right on the PDF files of these syllabi, which he could easily retrieve within seconds whenever he needed them (see Figure 3.1). These notes were combinations of English and Chinese words as well as mathematical signs for simplicity and clarity. For example, in the margin next to the assignment "Article Review," which accounted for 300 points, Wentao noted the length requirement ("3 pages + single space") and emphasized in red ink a tip that the instructor provided ("可以先把 draft 给老师 comment, 然后再修改": "I can send the draft to the instructor to get some comments before revising it"). Wentao's material and semiotic affordances intertwined with structural affordances, empowering him to maintain his membership in his classes and to practice differences.

Wentao seemed consciously aware of and confident in leveraging these structural, social, and semiotic affordances during a collaborative research-based review essay assignment. The project was assigned in his Aviation Safety Problems course and asked student groups to first, self-select a topic concerning aviation safety, such as hazardous behaviors, decision making, human factors for pilots, controllers, wildlife hazards, and weather and turbulence, among others, then, discuss the importance of the issue and finally,

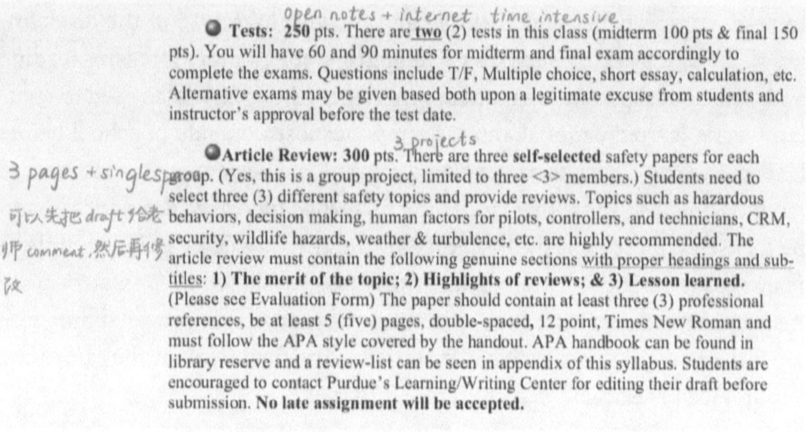

> **Tests: 250** pts. There are **two** (2) tests in this class (midterm 100 pts & final 150 pts). You will have 60 and 90 minutes for midterm and final exam accordingly to complete the exams. Questions include T/F, Multiple choice, short essay, calculation, etc. Alternative exams may be given based both upon a legitimate excuse from students and instructor's approval before the test date.
>
> **●Article Review: 300** pts. There are three **self-selected** safety papers for each group. (Yes, this is a group project, limited to three <3> members.) Students need to select three (3) different safety topics and provide reviews. Topics such as hazardous behaviors, decision making, human factors for pilots, controllers, and technicians, CRM, security, wildlife hazards, weather & turbulence, etc. are highly recommended. The article review must contain the following genuine sections with proper headings and subtitles: **1) The merit of the topic; 2) Highlights of reviews; & 3) Lesson learned.** (Please see Evaluation Form) The paper should contain at least three (3) professional references, be at least 5 (five) pages, double-spaced, 12 point, Times New Roman and must follow the APA style covered by the handout. APA handbook can be found in library reserve and a review-list can be seen in appendix of this syllabus. Students are encouraged to contact Purdue's Learning/Writing Center for editing their draft before submission. **No late assignment will be accepted.**

Handwritten annotations: "open notes + internet   time intensive"; "3 projects"; "3 pages + single space group"; "可以先把 draft 给老师 comment, 然后再修改"

FIGURE 3.1. Course syllabus annotated by Wentao.

provide solutions. Fairly confident in his disciplinary knowledge and writing skills, Wentao volunteered to work with three other students who also came from China. When asked why he decided to group with three other Chinese students, Wentao didn't seem ambivalent about his choice at all:

> It's way easier and more comfortable to work with Chinese classmates. We can use WeChat [the most widely used and popular instant messaging/social media smartphone application among Chinese students] to text each other whenever we want, and we can get instant responses. Can you imagine how easy it is to be able to speak Chinese while working together? Plus, my previous experiences working with American students left me the impression that they are 不靠谱 [unreliable]. So I guess it's not all about language barriers.

Then he told me stories of domestic teammates finding excuses to skip group meetings and staying inactive until the very last minute before deadlines. "I wouldn't have rushed into my judgment if they [referring to the domestic classmates he worked with] had stopped being unreliable. But the truth is, besides being unreliable, some of them didn't seem to respect my ideas." To illustrate his claim, Wentao recounted another experience of being dismissed by his domestic teammates. During the previous semester, Wentao and his teammates were working on a report, for which they needed to analyze a pilot's data set consisting of flying time and other information and make predictions about the pilot's probability of completing their 45-hour requirement. One of Wentao's domestic teammates dominated the discussion when proposing analytical models. Wentao was quick enough to notice the limitations of that model and attempted to voice his disagreement. However, before he could finish his thought, his teammate interrupted him and argued back. Wanting to continue his claim, Wentao suddenly found himself at a loss for words, and ended up saying "never mind." Feeling embarrassed and frustrated, Wentao wrote a long message to articulate his thought, and eventually prompted the team to make changes. "That's when I decided that I prefer working with Chinese classmates, not only because it's easier to communicate my ideas with them, but also because I get more recognition from them."

Leveraging his social resources, or *guanxi* (network), as well as semiotic access, as affordance, Wentao assembled his team of Chinese classmates/friends to work on the project together. With this affordance mediating the rhetorical action of selecting group project teammates, Wentao's previous unpleasant experiences of being dismissed and silenced by those he took to belong to the generalized group of "American students" as well as working with this group that he characterized as "unreliable" offered him the simple remedy—to work with classmates that share similar cultural and linguistic backgrounds. Luckily, his social and semiotic capital easily afforded him the collaborative relationship he desired, and was, meanwhile, transformed into an experiential affordance that enabled him to make agentive decisions in similar future situations. Wentao's perception of the notion of difference had also become rhetorically powerful, as he articulated and defended his position in relation to his perceived difference (work ethic, language barrier, respect for divergent perspectives) during the decision-making process.

Among the four teammates, Wentao was typically regarded, if not respected, as the "写手" ("language guy") and usually assumed the responsibility of composing the more time-consuming and challenging sections, as he made his name early on in the first-year writing course I taught. He successfully demonstrated his linguistic ingenuity and creativity in the very first paper he wrote in the class, which was a writer's literacy autobiography. The assignment prompted students to share experiences of and reflections on their development as writers in both their native and second or foreign languages. Wentao's draft stunned me with its vivid and detailed descriptions, meticulous and intimate reflections, and melodramatic metaphors and similes:

Farewell to Shadow and Embrace of Dawn (September 2016)

"No way!"
   Upon turning to the final question page, I screamed within heart.
   Several seconds ago, I thought my 90-minute self-starring movie *Strug-*

gling in English Exam would culminate in a smooth and perfect end. Much to my surprise, nonetheless, the last question turned out to be a lovely picture, where a girl danced happily in a farm with cute animals. "Describe the scene with the title *Mary's Happy Farm* in no less than 30 words." Never had I tried a Chinese composition portraying a picture before, let alone an English one. My mind went totally blank . . .

That was the very beginning. The winter exam in Grade 3 introduced me to the world of English writing, and I apparently stumbled and fell at the gate—the gate of hell.

When it comes to writing, the first word appearing in my mind is *shadow*, partly because of my limitation in language proficiency as a starter.

During that exam, for instance, I merely listed some sentences—words, I mean—which barely made any sense. I even got stuck in spelling "rabbit." Unlike my sister, who enjoys novels and fictions, I prefer comics. Words can be abstract and sometimes complex to digest. Cartoons, in comparison, are more accessible with concrete pictures. Besides, some of those manga features variegation and thus seems far more attractive. My resistance to literature masterpieces, to some degree, blocked me from honing writing skills and nurturing creative ideas. Consequently, whether in Chinese or in English, words often failed me in properly demonstrating emotions or developing opinions. Particularly when composing in English, I felt like staggering blindly in the dusk, struggling in pain for every step. Writing, therefore, became my shadow, which I used to be extremely reluctant to face bravely. Usually for a writing assignment, I would not start until the last few hours. However, the less I practiced, the less progress I would achieve.

Such a downward spiral gradually ceased and turned upward as I entered junior high school and began accumulating writing techniques through varieties of reading. Then came the constraint from exams, which became my another shadow.

Instead of a platform encouraging diversity and styles, the entrance exams are more of a boundary or even a designated path for writing. At the mercy of academic success, which is generally considered equal to high scores in China, I was supposed to follow the so-called "success patterns" in my essay so as to achieve satisfying results. I did enjoy the pattern at first. The structure made it pretty clear where I should write what, so all I had to do was to fill the blank with gorgeous sentences. What teachers said then became my bible. Rather than using "Looking forward to your reply" at the end of an e-mail — the most common type of compositions — I wrote down "I would appreciate it a lot if you could reply to me at your earliest convenience," simply to please teachers. And it did work. Handsome grades soon kindled a sense of achievement in my heart, particularly when my essay in an English exam was printed to be read by all the classes.

However, when I opened my diary and decided to continue logging my daily life after the college entrance exam, what I noted down was just like zombies dressed perfectly. They gathered and danced with such stiff bodies.

"Breeze rustling leaves in a kind of dry and diaphanous distance, clusters of lilacs in full blossom incessantly sent out charming fragrance. Everything appeared the same as the day I first stepped into senior high. Dressed in various styles, everyone gathered early in the morning, chatting and waiting for the photo taking. With flashlight on, grins spread on our faces amid the subdued sunshine . . . I seethed with great ambitions and the approaching freedom, while driven into tears when watching classmates swallowed by the pedestrians. Gazing upon the school, which witnessed my prime time adorned with highlights and dearest companionship, I felt a sense of belonging and obsession although I used to count time to escape away . . . Still the memory we shared would serve as a firm belief, glittering and bestowing me with a warm embrace during sticky patches."

I got too accustomed to the patterns. I laid so much emphasis on the superficial facet of writing as to spare no effort to insert as many "high-level" expressions as possible, thereby forming a hardly approachable diary featuring lengthy sentences. Grandiloquent and complicated combinations of words, indeed, made my "masterpieces" seemingly fabulous yet actually short of insights and emotions. Boasting florid language, the old Wentao succeeded in throwing the new Wentao at a loss, with adjectives coming like "diaphanous" and overwhelming non-predicate verbs. What a disaster!

The outpouring of feelings and opinions ought to have been blessed with enough freedom and not strictly adhering to rigid rules. College, by contrast, applauds to distinctiveness, therefore allowing me to completely develop ideas within my own styles. It serves as a fertile field, which grows various real flowers. What a relief!

Writing appears to me as a prime way to voice out what is truly in our heart. Once we go beyond restriction of articulation, what we are supposed to do is to follow our inner thoughts. That is the real "success pattern."

Unlike the writer's literacy autobiographies that his peers wrote, which were mostly saturated with birds-eye views of their entire literacy developmental trajectories, Wentao's narrative zoomed in on several critical moments of his English writing and provided such rich details and honest critical reflections that instantly elevated his writing from a stack of rather mundane papers. Not only did Wentao highlight the critical incidents of his literacy history to reflect on his change and growth, he also showcased his confident manipulation of semiotic affordances—a wide range of lexical and metaphorical resources. For example, to dramatize the rough beginning of his journey of writing in English, he wrote: "The winter exam in Grade 3 introduced me to the world of English writing, and I apparently stumbled and fell at the gate—the gate of hell," and "I felt like staggering blindly in the dusk, struggling in pain for every step." Later on, when reflecting on his diary writing, he helped the readers visualize the dreariness by comparing his diary entries to zombies: "What I noted down was just like zombies dressed perfectly. They gathered and danced with such stiff bodies"; he even presented an example from his "zombie-like" diary to illustrate his claim. Interestingly, Wentao was consciously aware of his language style, which, as he himself characterized in this very paper, rests on "grandiloquent and complicated combinations of words," as if he was composing this paper purposefully in this style to pay tribute to the "old Wentao."

Wentao's flamboyant display of rich lexical resources in a narrative essay also earned him the reputation as "人民的诗人" ("people's poet") within his Chinese social circle, remediating the communist notion of collective ownership in a witty way, as he was generous enough to frequently help his friends polish their writings. The article review assigned in the Aviation Safety Problems course required three sections: (a) merit of the topic, (b) highlights of reviews, and (c) lesson learned. Striving to maintain his reputation and title, Wentao volunteered to take over the first section (merit of the topic) and third section (lesson learned)—the two sections that required substantial engagement with relevant literature in the field and the ability to synthesize the literature and construct a model based on it. "I like the fact that people trust me. It gives me a sense of belonging and achievement. And I love the title they gave me. I would do anything I can to live up to it. I don't think I feel this way when I work with American classmates." Wentao said to me with a confident wink.

Again, within the ecology of a collaborative writing project, his multiple experiential, social, and semiotic affordances were operating together and giving rise to his actions and reactions. Wentao's recent literacy history of being recognized as an outstanding poetic writer who contributed his expertise to his immediate social community afforded him the motivation to position himself in a leadership role in writing-intensive assignments. Wentao was self-assured and fulfilled that his linguistic ingenuity and creativity demonstrated in writing a narrative essay was regarded as an essential skill that not only distinguished him from people in his social group but also earned

FIGURE 3.2. Wentao's writing's room.

him respect that he didn't believe he could receive among his "American classmates." Interestingly, Wentao's semiotic resources marked him *different* in both of his imagined binary communities—those of Chinese students and US domestic students who are perceived as native speakers of English. Wentao was labeled as different in the Chinese community because of his skillful use of his lexical and rhetorical resources in English, yet he was labeled as different in the US domestic community due to his evolving communicative competence. These *different differences* on the one hand suggest that affordance is in constant flux and that affordance in one context could transform into constraints in another; on the other hand, the different differences intervene in other affordances and ultimately reposition the agent in their decision-making and meaning-making activities.

The actual writing process kicked off on a weekday night around 1:00 a.m. in Wentao's bedroom/study in his apartment. He had already met with his teammates informally and discussed and settled on their topics, approaches, and specific claims and evidence. Before sinking himself into the writing mode, Wentao set up the camera that I loaned him, facing his laptop and its immediate environment, to film his composing process (see Figure 3.2). The video presents a tidy workstation of Wentao's writing's room (Rule, 2018). The laptop was placed against the backdrop of complete wee-hour darkness. Next to it, there was a bottle of water that kept Wentao hydrated throughout the session. His iPad was also placed within easy reach.

> I like doing homework after midnight. It's quiet. And there's no distractions of emails and WeChat messages . . . I get easily distracted by anything, messages, objects around me, light, and sound. That's why I cleaned up my desk and just left the stuff I needed.

Wentao explained to me. He continued to reflect on the rationale behind his decision making in terms of the spatiotemporal specifics:

> I used to, for the most part, do my homework or write papers in the undergraduate library. It's of course not as quiet or private, but I guess sometimes being too quiet and private is not a blessing, because you might feel too relaxed to concentrate on your work. Also, and I think this is more important, in the library, you get to share a space with so many other Chinese students, which provides me with a sense of security and motivate me to work harder. But since I moved to my new apartment two months ago, I felt the room was refreshing enough for me to stay focused, which is why I have been writing papers at home. Once I become too familiar with this space, I will move my mobile workstation again, because I know I would retreat to being comfortable and watching movies and doing other distracting things.

As he was explaining his rationale, he replayed the videotaping from the beginning. "See? As I was about to dig into the paper, I closed the window of a video player. I had been watching that show for a while." I followed up, "I'm curious about the sense of security that you feel when working alone but together with other Chinese students. What about that ecology in particular that makes you feel secure?" Wentao smiled yet remained collected:

> The fact that I *know* them. I 朝夕相处 [live day and night with them] during my two years in Beijing. I know their aspirations, their frustrations, and shared understandings of the American culture. That familiarity makes me feel secure.

He continued, "But then again, sometimes I just need to find a really quiet and private space to work, especially when I need to think hard and create something." Wentao did not appear ambivalent about his ecological affordance. He deliberately chose his working environment and time in accordance with his perceptions of the ambient sound, privacy, security, material surroundings, social dynamics, as well as his own bodily conditions and his emotional connection to the ecology. After shutting down the irrelevant computer programs running in the background, Wentao opened the file that he and his team had been working on, reread the existing finished sections and paragraphs, and began refining the model in the lesson learned section (See

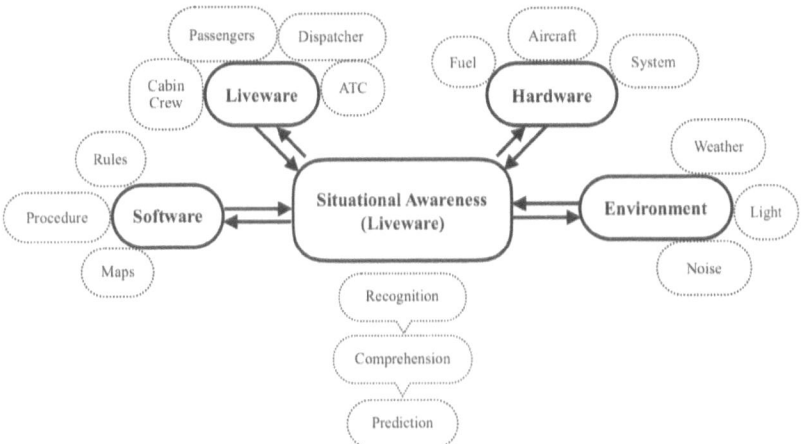

FIGURE 3.3. Visual representation of "situational awareness" created by Wentao and his team.

Figure 3.3). The model representing the components of a pilot's situational awareness was already half constructed when Wentao began reworking it. He began moving around the bubbles corresponding with each situational factor—hardware, software, liveware, and environment—and drawing and deleting arrows between the bubbles in an attempt to connect or disconnect them. He also attached more bubbles to each situational factor: fuel, aircraft, and system were attached to hardware while cabin crew, passengers, and dispatcher to liveware. Occasionally, his flow of actions was interrupted by his need to use references, such as searching for synonyms in the online thesaurus or looking up an English word in an online English/Chinese dictionary, retrieving a journal article he documented using source documentation software, and pulling over his iPad to skim through the notes he took in class or to directly doodle the bubble chart with the stylus and play with it with his fingers. With the involvement of multimodal and multilingual resources as semiotic and material affordances, after 30 minutes, Wentao declared the completion of the "situational awareness model" by reopening the video player window and continuing the show from where he left off.

The interplay and interaction between and among networked affordance—structural, semiotic, experiential, social, bodily, and material—became rhetorically powerful as they enabled Wentao to constantly position and reposition himself in relation to other actants—human agents and ecological conditions—in the making of rhetorical decisions. The act of positioning and repositioning is essentially marking differences as they emerge. From the moment Wentao entered the agreement to co-/re-construct his ecology of writing for aviation management courses and the Aviation Safety Problems in particular, his positionality had been in a constant flux; at one point, he positioned himself in opposition to who he conceived to be "American classmates"—the oversimplified aggregate of everybody non-Chinese, despite the fact that the "othered" group may also include students from other nationalities and ethnicities. Then he strategically capitalized on his social resources to build an academic legion of several other students from China that he trusted and that trusted him and recognized his expertise. The difference that mediated Wentao's act was his emergent understanding of collaborating with classmates from other linguistic and cultural backgrounds, and it was centered on not only the discrepancy between communicative competences in a certain dominant language but also divergent conceptions of work ethic. However, immediate repositioning was called upon once the dynamic of the affordance transformed. Wentao's linguistic difference that initially constrained him in effective and efficient communication when working with domestic classmates was suddenly remediated to function as his affordance when working with his team of fellow Chinese classmates. His attention and sensitivity to the details of English writing conventions and relatively elevated linguistic ingenuity that were overshadowed, unrecognized, or suppressed in a different socioacademic group—that is, the domestic team—were also repositioned as dominant affordances that enabled Wentao to assume a leadership role in the writing and editing of the review essay and maximize his value and contribution. Later on, Wentao's individual composing process was afforded and mediated by material and environmental affordance, including the physical space of a private and quiet room, time of the day, technological tools, texts, online resources, and, inevitably, the camera with which he filmed the writing's room. As the analysis demonstrates, Wentao was always caught up in the network of relationalities between and among humans and things that enabled him to make rhetorical decisions.

Student Club as a Gateway to "American" College Life: Working for the Performing Arts Club

As a large land grant university with over 30,000 undergraduate enrollments, Wabash takes pride in providing a culturally rich and diverse student experience. There are nearly 1,000 registered student organizations on campus ranging from the cutting-edge ones such as 3D Printing Club to the more classic and academic-oriented ones such as the RoboMasters Club. Most students would be able to find their niche if they so choose. It's no exaggeration to say that the involvement in student organizations is an integral part of students' college life. Wentao is no exception. Soon after he transferred to Wabash in the fall of 2016, Wentao secured his membership in an emerging student organization named Wabash Performance Collaborative (WPC), which sought to "provide a platform for students of any major to be involved in the performing arts without the immense pressure and commitment of participating in a Wabash Department of Theatre production" (Wabash Performance Collaborative, 2016). Wentao's reason for joining the WPC is rather simple and uncharacteristic of his otherwise meticulous and cautious decisions:

> I've always seen the crazy part of student club life in American movies and TV shows, and I just wanted to experience what it's really like to be a part of a typical American college club. As to why I chose this particular club, I saw the name, a 'drama club?' Sounds cool. I always like watching performance anyway. So why don't I take this opportunity to know more about how a theater works.

Upon settling down in the club, Wentao chose to serve as the spotlight person. Surprised, I asked him why he did so, as I assumed he would be eager to express himself on the stage, given my impression of the performative rhetorical style exhibited in his narrative writings.

> I didn't join a theater club because I wanted to shine on the stage. I'm more interested in the structure and the system. I wanted to figure out how everything is coordinated and operates together to provide visual entertainment for the audience, just like I wanted to figure out how an airport operates in such an organized way so that planes don't crash, though flights are always delayed, to be fair.

Wentao smiled. At the beginning of the second year, however, Wentao took on the duties of the organization secretary, which, according to him, was a "promotion." As he reflected,

> I used to be in charge of things, but now I'm focusing more on relationships between people, because a big part of my job is to keep email exchanges with lots of people—the president, performers, logistics, and prospective members . . . and I also need to reach out to sponsors and other student organizations. So it's a great opportunity for me to learn how people work in the organization after I learned how things work.

The first job Wentao needed to take the lead on as the organization secretary was the yearly recruitment event. The organization had already documented contact information of students who revealed their interest in becoming a member, and Wentao was appointed as the primary contact who was in charge of maintaining communication with these prospective members. "I felt powerful yet nervous at the same time, because my email will reach around 80 people. I thought to myself, this email would definite make or break the deal, but how should I compose it?" Wentao shared with me his initial thrills and jitters. During the first week of the new semester, when most undergraduate students were still hectically orienting themselves, Wentao sent out the first callout reminder. The email was addressed to 85 interested students:

> Hey y'all,
> Our callout will be at **WALC 1055 starting from 7:30p on August 22 (wed)**. Feel free to come and chill:)
>
> Also, for those of you who are interested in acting in our shows of this semester. **WPC auditions** will be at **KRAN G04 from 6 to 9pm on Aug 28 and 29 (Tue & Wed)**.
>
> Hope to see y'all.
>
> Wentao

The email was apparently composed in an informal and even playful tone, as evidenced by the abundant use of colloquial expressions ("y'all," "come and chill"), contractions and abbreviations ("wed," "Tue & Wed"), and emoticon (":)"). It also appeared plain and straightforward, completely stylistically and rhetorically foreign to me, whose understanding of his writing was dominated by his carefully crafted narratives and arguments. Yet this simple five-line email was by no means casually composed. Wentao was well aware of the consequence of it once it reached 85 people and invested no less time and energy crafting it than writing a homework essay. Without knowing that "y'all" is typically associated with Southern American English or vernacular English, Wentao adopted it from a movie to more effectively connect to his audience—prospective members—and to establish his ethos as a friendly, approachable, and down-to-earth person. The smile emoticon was used to create the same rhetorical effect, according to him. With the bolded phrases that Wentao used, the emphasized key information (time and location) nearly accounts for the entire email, which further suggests its directness.

Four days later, immediately after the first callout meeting, Wentao sent a follow-up email to prospective members with a list of upcoming events. This

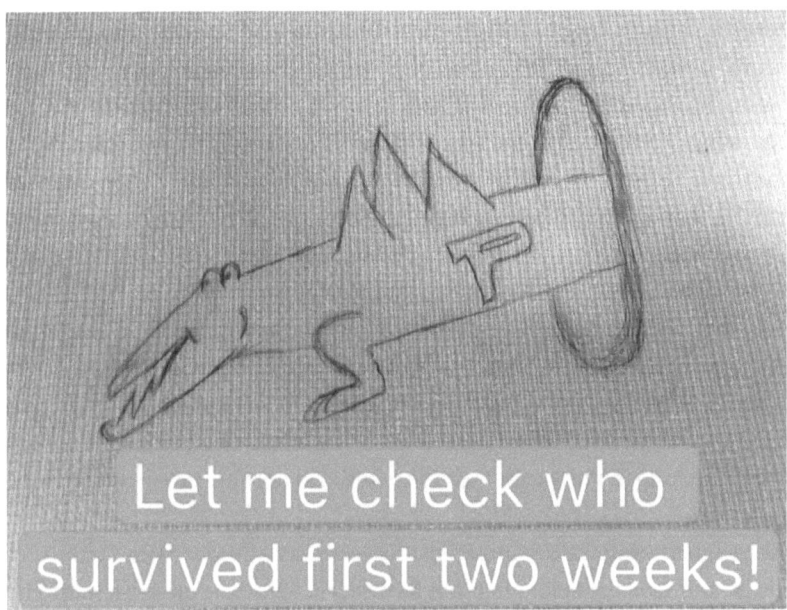

FIGURE 3.4. Promotional image created by Wentao.

time, however, the recipient list became substantially longer; there were 121 names in the "To" box, many of whom were not included in the initial callout list but attended the meeting spontaneously.

> Hi WPCers,
> Thank you all talented boilers for making our WPC family bigger and stronger. Here is a list of upcoming events.
> . . .
> The Callout slides has been attached and feel free to ask questions via emails or social media. Plus, there will be more information about watching shows and ushering in GBMs (general body meetings). See y'all then:)
> Boiler Up!
Wentao

I immediately noticed that instead of using "y'all" to address the receipts, this time Wentao opted for "WPCers," a more intimate address that signifies the membership and exclusivity. Wentao confirmed that it was precisely his intention to more effectively build rapport with his audience/prospective members while presenting himself as a personable individual. Yet, interestingly, Wentao himself seemed to be invisible in this email, as marked by his consistent deployment of a passive voice that concealed his identity ("has been attached" and "there will be"). "I was sending this email on behalf of the organization, so I thought maybe I shouldn't use 'I.'" Wentao explained. "What about using 'we' to refer to the organization as a whole?" I asked. "Hmmm I didn't think of that. I vaguely remember that our high school English teacher taught us that when we want to hide ourselves, we would use passive voice. They would know who I am anyway, because my name is spelled out at the bottom." Wentao winked. The image attached at the end of the email was a doodle that Wentao drew with a pencil, which shows a dragon-like creature with the Wabash imprint sneaking out of a space hole. The caption states, "Let me check who survived first two weeks!" He seemed to blush when I asked him about it. "It's something silly. I'm far from being an artist. But I just wanted to throw something in there to lighten the mood. I'm not sure how helpful it was, but anyways."

Although serving the organization as a secretary afforded Wentao the recognition and sense of belonging that he desired, being the only international student in the organization, he still felt somewhat marginalized, if not invisible, when engaged in other activities within the community, such as auditions, rehearsals, or even sometimes the general body meetings.

> I know it sounds self-contradictory, that sometimes I feel that I belong whereas other times I don't. For example, when I'm responsible for contacting a large group of people, I feel that I'm irreplaceable and I'm needed. But when the major activities of the club are going on, such as auditions, I'm only minimally helpful. I thought about it, I guess it's mainly because of my English. When writing an email, I can take the time to 把玩和斟酌 [play with and ponder] the language till it's perfect, at least to me; but when I need to work with people offline, I become reserved, because I'm afraid that I can't keep up with their conversation, and I don't know how to crack a joke like they do all the time.

To compensate for his lack of verbal contribution in club activities, Wentao worked harder on the tasks assigned to him and always made sure that they were completed in a timely manner. "I have to make myself useful in some ways. If I don't speak, I do."

Regardless of the organizational structure and value system that seemed to spotlight extraordinary individuals who made exceptional contributions while leaving the others in the shade, Wentao displayed strong favor toward the structure of the WPC compared with that of college student organizations in China. The entire organization workflow at WPC was, according to Wentao, "very mature and organized." He continued to say,

> Things were crazy and messy in the organization that I was part of at the university in China. Bureaucracy and hierarchy were everywhere. You have to learn how to 巴结 [fawn on] people who are in even the lowest powerful position and use your 关系 [pull some strings] from the day you decide to join any student club, as if they regarded these organizations as some kind of exclusive clubs that would guarantee your bright career future. Organizing events would be an even bigger hassle. One time I was trying to get some signatures, approvals, and paperworks done for an "English corner" event where we invited an American teacher who taught English at my university to have conversations with students who were interested in improving English communication skills, I had to literally run all over campus and ask different people. Some of them even felt annoyed and seemed dismissive. Yet getting things done here is much smoother. People seem genuinely willing to help you out. And every procedure has already been well-thought-out and carefully instructed. You just need to simply follow the procedures.

I saw a different Wentao as a rhetorical agent in the student organization. He is still expressive, meticulous, and cautious, but he is also more sensitive and self-conscious compared with the Wentao I observed in collaborative writing activities. Here in the organization, Wentao was wired up with and networked into a complex assemblage of relations that connects people, things, and structures, some of which are asymmetrical and constantly mediate Wentao's perception of difference. His desire to join a student organization grew out of his cultural experiences as an outside observer: he learned about the student club culture in US colleges through a highly dramatized and stereotyped artistic form—films, as well as his enthusiasm in deconstructing organizational structures. He was cognizant of the affordances the student organization membership would bring him—social community, recognition and visibility, and the opportunity to not only learn but also shape the organizational structure. He was also aware of his own experiential, semiotic, and bodily affordance and how these would enable or constrain him. For example, his craftsmanship that was manifested in his academic writings was also exhibited in composing emails in an attempt to make connections with intended audience. In addition to his genre awareness that was reflected in the clarity and simplicity of the emails, Wentao also incorporated multimodal forms of expression, such as emoticons and a self-drawn doodle to connect with the audience on an affective level. Yet despite the recognition he received from the broader student community, serving in assisting roles in a performing arts organization as the only international student, Wentao was still on the structural, semiotic, and bodily periphery. He did not participate in any acting roles, was not involved in any major organizational decision making, felt linguistically disadvantaged when communicating with other members, and undeniably looked different from other members. His semiotic, experiential, social, and bodily affordances that were otherwise enabling were now turned into constraints, mediating his practices of perceived differences—community role and language—as he tried to downplay or silence them.

Japanese Learning as a Gateway to a Transcultural and Cosmopolitan Self

Learning Japanese has played and continues to play a pivotal role in Wentao's literate life in college. At the beginning of his second year at Wabash, Wentao had to select courses to meet the outcome of the general education elective requirement of gaining insights in the humanities and social sciences. After tapping into his social resources by consulting friends who had chosen different courses, Wentao eventually decided on Japanese.

> It seemed super popular among my Chinese friends. Some of them said, "learning a language is easier to get an A, and it's more fun, and also, you start running at the same starting line with Americans. You would certainly be disadvantaged if you take political science or history." What they said made sense to me, so I hopped on the train named Japanese.

By the time I became more involved in Wentao's literate world, Wentao had already moved up the ladder and enrolled in an intermediate-level Japanese course.

Without a well-articulated intrinsic motivation to study Japanese when entering the foreign and mysterious language-learning world, Wentao gradually found his refreshed passion in the new East Asian language and in language learning itself. I characterize his passion as "refreshed," as Wentao mentioned that he used to invest a substantial amount of time and financial resources in learning English when he just began doing so; not out of an instrumental and opportunistic ideal of using English effectively in a predominantly English-only monolingual context, unlike some other international peers, but out of his pure enthusiasm toward mastering a new language. Not unlike most of his peers, however, Wentao lost his enthusiasm after several months; what was left was his duty of maintaining his title of a "good student" granted by his course teachers and parents. His first Japanese 101 instructor at Wabash helped to rekindle his passion in learning Japanese and the culture associated with it, and the process of language learning, too.

The intermediate-level Japanese course that Wentao enrolled in highlighted the development of students' communicative competence in various social settings, basic understanding of Japanese cultures and customs, ability to read and comprehend simple essays and stories, and ability to compose simple essays in Japanese. The first essay assigned was poetically titled: "夢の旅" ("Dream Trip"). The stated purpose of the assignment was for students to practice using the syntactic structures that they learned in previous class sessions. Yet Wentao claimed that the stated purpose was far too limiting and that, despite his still evolving Japanese literacy, he would strive for what he conceived to be the elevated artistic expression—carefully crafted and poetically decorated language.

> When I learn a new language, I become more adventurous. I like to test the boundaries in terms of grammar and vocabulary and try out new ways to express my thoughts and ideas. Of course, I make mistakes all the time, sometimes really laughable mistakes. But what do I have to lose anyway?

The resulting short essay Wentao wrote in Japanese in October 2018 was well recognized in Wentao's class by the instructor and his classmates.

理想の旅行 (October 2018)

今日は。私は Wentao です。今日は私の理想の旅行をしょうかいします。

　私は、漫画がとても好きです。漫画で、スタンドアップというのが一番好きです。スタンドアップは、絵が綺麗で、成都の高校生の生活のことを話します。そして、成都は、私の理想の旅行のところになります。

　成都は中国の西南だから、冬に、雪があまりふりません。天気は、よく曇りだけと、夏の気温は高いです。でも、春と秋はいいですよ。

　成都で、パンダを見たり、美味しい料理を食べたり、多い景勝を行ったりできます。

　成都に、パンダがたくさんすんでいます。パンダは、顔がまるくて、背がまるくて、とても可愛いですね。

　成都の食べ物は、四川料理なのて、とても有名です。私は、胃が

元気じゃないけど、いつもホットポットを食べたいですよ。多くの人は、よく、四川料理が辛いと おもっていますが、成都のデザートも 美味しいですよ。

　成都の景勝の中で、古いのも新しいのがいます。例えば、杜甫草堂は、1260年の前に、一番有名な詩人杜甫のうちでした。今、博物館です。太古里は、古そうだけど、新しい建物で、人気なショッピングセンターです。

　みなさんも 成都に 行きましょうか。ごせい ちょう ありがとうございます。

Dream Trip (Wentao's translation, October 2018)

Hello, I'm Wentao. Today I am going to introduce the trip of my dream.

　I like cartoons very much. Among them, my favorite one is titled "Looking ahead while Standing on Tiptoes." The pictures are beautiful, and the narrative is about high school life in Chengdu. Therefore, Chengdu became the destination of my dream.

　Chengdu is located in Southwest China, so it does not snow a lot. Although it is cloudy quite often, the temperature is high in the summer. However, the weather in the spring and fall is good.

　In Chengdu, you can go see pandas, taste delicious dishes, and visit a lot of scenic spots.

　There are a lot of pandas in Chengdu. Pandas' faces are round, and bodies are round. They are very cute.

　Food in Chengdu is famous because it is Sichuan cuisine. My stomach is not good, but I always want to eat hot pot. Many people think Sichuan food is always spicy, but desserts in Chengdu are delicious.

　Among the scenic spots of Chengdu, there are new and old ones. For example, Du Fu Thatched Cottage used to be the residence of Du Fu, who lived 1260 years ago. But now it is a museum. Although Taiko Ri looks old from the outside, it is a set of new buildings, and a popular shopping center.

　Let us go to Chengdu, too. Thank you very much.

Apparently, Wentao's lexical and syntactic resources in Japanese were still relatively limited. The essay may, at first sight, seem like a collage composed of pieces of common objects, as the different topics that typically emerge in discussions of a particular location—climate, food, points of interest—are scattered. There are no clear transitional phrases that serve to connect different topics except for a few conjunctions indicating causal relationships. Yet despite the seeming incoherence and simplicity, Wentao did consciously and courageously venture into the unknown through his deployment of short narrative components at the beginning of the essay and the historical account at the end. He did not open the essay with superficial descriptive coverage of the different topics; rather, he attempted to draw his readers' attention by rationalizing his choice of dream trip through a personal anecdote. In the second to last paragraph, to further justify his attachment to the city of Chengdu, he located a historical account of a popular tourist attraction on the Internet and incorporated it into his description in simplified Japanese.

> I know the paper looks like a piece of 流水账 [running account, used metaphorically to refer to a tedious bare-bones account of day-to-day events that lacks meaningful details] that just covers the basic aspects of a trip. But I did try to use all the resources at my disposal: dictionaries, my instructor, classmates, Google, and some words from Japanese anime that I've watched. I wanted to introduce a city that I thought was very representative of China, which may be unique in my class. And although my paper is simple and basic, I think the writing style somehow resembles that of Chinese prose. We tend to focus on describing the 意境 [ambient mood] rather than organizing logically sound expository prose.

Taking Japanese courses and exposing himself to Japanese cultures, Wentao gradually aligned himself with a set of strategies for language learning and constructed his own theories of practice regarding language learning. For example, the habit of listening to Japanese pop songs (known as J-pop) that Wentao developed long before systematically learning Japanese has been consistently feeding him with literary inspirations and lyric rhythm. He particularly liked several classic and timeless J-pop singers and musicians such as Ayumi Hamasaki and Namie Amuro. He would copy the lyrics, look up each word he didn't know in a Japanese-Chinese dictionary, figure out the meaning and 意境 (ambient mood) of the lyrics, and tried to memorize them.

> It [listening to J-pop songs] not only helps me to add new words to my vocabulary, but also, not to sound too pretentious, deepens my understanding of Japanese people's general 情绪 [mood and sensibility] and 意识流 [stream of consciousness]. They are totally different from the American pop culture. Here in America, pop songs that are played over and over again on the radio sound so "greasy" . . . I mean they are full of superficial and straightforward expressions of their greed, lust, pursuit of immediate gratification. But Japanese songs, just like their cuisine, are much subtler and refreshing, and sometimes philosophical.

In addition to listening to J-pop songs, Wentao has also been engaged in experiencing Japanese cultures through a Japanese student association. The association was run by Japanese international students at Wabash to provide service for the community, such as organizing cultural events geared toward the Japanese student community and the campus at large. To Wentao, a language learner, the involvement in a student organization established upon the target language transcended the limitations of the structural affordances he received in the Japanese class, as it afforded him social, bodily, as well as material resources that he would not otherwise have easy access to. During the cultural events organized by the Japanese student association such as bento box tutorials and Japanese movie nights, Wentao actively sought opportunities to meet Japanese students, engage himself in small talks or topic-oriented discussions in Japanese, and inquire about Japanese cultural norms. Understandably, he frequently struggled with comprehensibly expressing himself in Japanese due to his developing proficiency and currently restricted linguistic resources, let alone skillfully incorporating into his repertoire rhetorical devices he typically deployed when he spoke Chinese. To compensate for his lack of comprehensibility and sophistication, Wentao chose to opt for English verbal annotations when their discussions exceeded his capability. The discussions, as a result, usually transformed into translingual and multimodal interactions. The Japanese students he connected to and the friendships he built have had a positive impact on his development of language proficiency.

When prompted to reflect on his experiences learning a third language, Wentao exuded controlled exhilaration.

> Learning Japanese definitely opened a door to a new world for me, and a really interesting world. I was exposed to so many cultural experiences in a more informed way. Although I was exposed to Japanese cultures when I was little through cartoons and anime, but I was ignorant about why the world looked so different from their perspective. For example, the wonder worlds in Miyazaki's *Spirited Away* and *Castle in the Sky*. They were just so fascinating to me back then. But now I sort of understand the structural and historical conditions that brought them the inspirations. I came to this realization because I got to read, although not fluently, simple books in Japanese, and more importantly, talk with my Japanese friends. Their perspectives really matter.

Despite the benefits of learning Japanese, Wentao was also critically aware of his constraints. According to him, Japanese is 中西合璧 (a fusion of Chinese and Western linguistic features), since the characters (kanji) resemble those in Chinese whereas the structures are similar to those of English. At the current level, Wentao was not able to employ a variety of linguistic resources at his disposal, particularly resources and structures associated with and affording higher-level abstract thinking.

> I want to initiate some deeper discussion of a certain topic, for example, the notion of loyalty in Japan. But my vocabulary and grammar just don't allow me to do that. So I began to wonder if our language really shapes our thought. I didn't used to believe that, but now I think there's some truth to it.

On the one hand, Wentao harnessed the language resources to develop his linguistic and cultural sensibility; yet on the other hand, he laments the constraints of not only his but linguistic resources in general in terms of making sense of the world.

More deeply, Wentao connected his language-learning experiences to his identity formation. He believed that the process of mastering a certain language is ultimately gaining and possessing membership of a discourse community.

> Only when we speak the same language can we really claim that we belong. And it's not simply about the language itself, it also has to do with the style, the accuracy of your vocabulary, and the emotions your language evokes. One of my high school classmates in China was a language artist. I still remember him and admire him for his ability to 遣词造句妙语连珠 [manipulate words, create sentences, and consistently quip] when he spoke as well as wrote papers. By talking with him, I was able to not only learn new stuff, but also feel entertained. That single trait of his made him popular among us and made him a good leader in organizing activities. So his language made him who he was.

Wentao shifted the attention back to himself.

> My Japanese proficiency is definitely not worth mentioning now. My English, though, helped me to get some recognition from my peer Chinese friends and earn the title of "people's poet." But it's far from getting me a membership card to enter the "real" American community. I mean I can communicate basically without much trouble, but there's always an invisible wall between me and Americans. I thought about it, it may be because my English is "empty," like a 枯井 [dry well], meaning I don't have enough content to talk about. I haven't read enough literature in English, nor have I watched enough TV shows, movies, news reports. So I don't know their 梗 [Chinese Internet slang, literally meaning "stem," remediated to mean the punchline of a joke], and so naturally I can't make any 梗 to connect with them, either. So I feel I'm kind of stuck in-between.

Wentao's Japanese-learning experience—classroom interaction, essay composing, strategies, socialization with native speakers, and theorization of language learning—is a miniature of the actor's complex and even convoluted affordances within which he leveraged various resources to achieve his rhetorical and material goals: becoming a cosmopolitan citizen (Appiah, 2006; You, 2016) and honing the ability to fluently communicate in three languages. The very decision to learn Japanese was reached as a result of Wentao's desire to transcend his bodily and linguistic difference perceived by the university and proactively mark his alternative difference by gaining new linguistic and cultural capital. To do so, Wentao carefully, though subconsciously, evaluated his affordances, identified affordances that empowered him, such as experiences writing essays in English, structures of English and Chinese, social groups embodying the target language and culture, and pop songs and films representing material and semiotic resources. Once identified, these affordances were assembled and networked as Wentao engaged himself in different literate activities, enabling him to make decisions while imbuing the decisions and actions with rhetorical meaning. For example, as Wentao reflected, his language-learning endeavors built into his entire schooling so far were closely tied to and may well track and characterize his emerging, shifting, and dynamic identity construction. Who he is as conceived by himself and perceived by his surroundings, how he desires to be recognized, where he belongs, and to what extent he wants to belong are but a few rhetorical considerations Wentao constantly wrestled with during the ongoing journey. At least for now, Wentao confidently claimed his evolving cosmopolitan sensibility and transcultural competence to make sense of and cope with the world of institutionalized power asymmetry.

Making Translingual and Transmodal Affective Connections: Constructing Social Media Persona

In a posthuman condition (Hayles, 1999; Pennycook, 2018) where technologically extended biological and cognitive beings are perpetually wired into a gigantic, invisible, and powerful online network, it's nearly impossible for us to lead a life offline without leaving any traces of online presence. The constant surveillance makes some people panic, confuses others whose online identities are not articulated, yet offers a few the most convenient and accessible means of crafting from scratch their new identities. Like most of his friends, classmates, club members, and his family members in China, Wentao maintained an active online presence on popular social media platforms such as Facebook and WeChat. WeChat is a mobile platform that provides users with ways to instantly connect with each other (instant messaging) and publicize their life moments through verbal and visual means (social media). It is the most widely used social media platform in China and some of its neighboring countries with monthly active users exceeding 1.2 billion in 2022. Wentao explained,

> I have both accounts [Facebook and WeChat], and I used to think of them as my two different selves: Facebook is more popular in America but banned in China while WeChat is what everybody uses in China, so I post different contents to be shown to different audiences. Facebook is my American identity and WeChat is my Chinese identity.

To Wentao, every social media post is a legitimate rhetorical project that requires careful deliberation and measured execution, as he regards it as the most effective and impactful way of constructing his persona and connecting to a world bigger than his immediate material surroundings.

> When social media just became a thing, people were genuinely enthusiastic, and they would just post whatever happened to them in all honesty without any filtering. At least I was like that. The first social media account I registered for was Renren, which back then was the most popular one that all of my high school classmates were using. We shared even the tiniest and most stupid moments in our mundane high school lives on Renren. Ah . . . those fond memories! We were honest on social media because we were using our real names and everybody knew everybody. The time has changed, though. Today, people in general became less honest: some of them always peek at others' posts but never share their lives, and those who *do* post regularly, they spend a lot of time wording and rewording the post and retouching the pictures till they look like a perfection. It's understandable, though, because you never know who might see your post—your parents, your boss and colleagues, your elementary school friend that you haven't seen in person for 10 years. . . . That's why people would usually block certain people when posting. Although I don't like it, but I don't want to be a clown that everybody watches and laughs at, so I had to go with the current.

Cynical as he is about his social circle's obsession with public images, Wentao is no less careful and deliberate when constructing his own. Over time, Wentao developed his own social media posting protocol that he followed strictly and consistently. First is timing and frequency. Wentao didn't follow a particular schedule. Sometimes he would post about a recent event

3 days in a row, while sometimes he would be silent for a week. "I always make sure to update my friends about my life once in a while just so they know I'm still alive." Wentao grinned while joking.

Second is content. The sources of Wentao's social media posts were embedded in yet transcended his ordinary life as a college student, as he drew on moments of particular importance to *him* and remediated the narrative in a way that, on the one hand, conveyed his poetic expression, and on the other, dis-limited the linguistic and genre norms of daily life. For example, on his 22nd birthday, Wentao shared on WeChat six pictures taken in drastically different geographic and temporal contexts: the first three were taken years and months before; the latter, three weeks before, leading up to the current moment. As usual, he composed a caption to accompany the pictures, which reads: "二十二 · 头发(fà)越来越长，希望见识不要越来越短" ("Twenty-Two: Hair is getting longer, I wish my sight is not getting shorter"). As the first half of the caption explains, the six pictures present the trajectory of Wentao's hair getting longer over time. The caption came from an idiom in Chinese that originally reads "头发长见识短" ("The longer the hair, the shorter the sight"), which originated around the Ming Dynasty and had been used in the patriarchal ancient China to demean or even insult women for their lack of skills, expertise, and social experience. Wentao remediated this outdated, outrageous, and caustically criticized idiom into a mildly self-mocking birthday wish that blurred the gender boundary and entangled the change to his physical features over time and his desire to be a farsighted and learned individual. The parenthesized pinyin in the caption (fà) was also carefully deployed to remediate the sound of the character "发," whose normal sound is "fà," to pay tribute to Beijing—the place that Wentao had studied and lived for 2 years, as the sound "fà" is how the character "发" is typically pronounced in Beijing dialect.

Third: structure and language. What distinguishes Wentao's literate activities that took place in the online virtual space is his insistence on a rigid structure across all posts that maintains uniformity yet allows poetic creativity. The structure consists of a brief title of one or a few words and explanations/descriptions of a few phrases or sentences, segmented by an interpunct. This structure that Wentao adopted resembles that of "词" (cí), which is a type of classical Chinese lyric poetry particularly prevalent in the Song Dynasty, and the short title segmented by the interpunct resembles a "词牌" (cípái)—the title of a 词 that regulates its rhythm, rhyme, and tempo. For example, the title of one post reads "霞空多彩" ("colorful sunset glow"), and the body of the caption states: "沿着这条路走下去吧，/ 登上金色的山峦，/ 俯瞰这宁静

·霞空多彩·
沿着这条路走下去吧，
登上金色的山峦，
俯瞰这宁静的村庄。

FIGURE 3.5. Wentao's WeChat status.

的村庄。" ("Walk down the road, / climb up the golden hilltop, / and overlook the tranquil and serene village"). Although the title, unlike a real 词牌, does not operatively structure the body text, it does evoke a nostalgic sensual experience through the use of visually stimulating words and set the rhythm for the body text to follow. The uniform structure of three interconnected yet independent imperative sentences demonstrates Wentao's careful contemplation and execution of his linguistic structural knowledge borrowed from Chinese. The two pictures of sunset on campus he added reinforces the visual stimulation.

> The other day I was walking to the bus station after my classes, and all of a sudden, I noticed the beautiful sunset, so immediately snapped the pictures. That very moment reminded me of some Chinese classical poems I read in high school, as well as some contemporary ones I read outside of school. So I decided to merge two types of poems together to express my feelings at that moment.

Wentao described the ecological affordances available to him when constructing the post.

In yet another post, Wentao incorporated an English abbreviation into the creation of the title: "ThxGvng," which stands for "Thanksgiving." The title here, as usual, indicates the temporal setting. What follows is the narrative: "通宵收拾五天行李" ("Stay up all night for five days straight to pack my luggage"). Interestingly, Wentao began the brief narrative with an emoji that symbolized unlocking, and he completed it with another emoji showing a shrugging man. Put together, the narrative reads: "Thanksgiving is around the corner. I'm unlocking the holiday mode: staying up all night for five days to pack my luggage. Well, there's nothing I can do about that." Two Internet memes illustrate the narrative: the left one shows a door sign that says "push" in Chinese and English, and the right one shows an anime character with a petrified look.

> I was incredibly busy during Thanksgiving break, as I had to prepare for final exams, write up term projects, and at the same time pack my luggage for my trip back to China during the winter break. I thought maybe some of my friends were going through the same challenges? The memes I posted to go with the caption were just something funny to attract my friends' attention. But on second thought, they implied my status back then: I was pushing myself to the limit but still shocked at how much left to do.

When asked to reflect on his rhetorical choice of dwelling on the structure of remediated lyric poetry while drawing broadly on resources from multiple languages, cultures, and modalities to territorialize the virtual social space, Wentao said,

> I like to play with words, as you know now [he smiles]. Even when I write papers for my courses, I would be very careful with what words to use, how and where to put them. So I think there's no better place than social media to experiment with some creative wording, because people are not usually rational when they are on social media and they don't come to social media to find ration. I chose to use this format just to establish my own signature style and connect with my friends who see my posts on an emotional level.

Wentao seemed to have seriously grappled with the meaning and purpose of social media and applied his theorization to the composing of every post.

Wentao's literate activities in the virtual space, as they were in the physical and material world, were bound up with, given rise to, constrained, and mediated by various structural, semiotic, experiential, social, bodily, and material affordances, and in turn shaped Wentao's positionality and subjective experiences in the physical and material world as well as virtual space. First, the material reality—smartphones, power plants, base station, social media application—afforded the manifestation of an intangible yet real social space through digitized multimodal texts projected onto a tiny OLED screen. That digitally materialized social space served to connect Wentao to not only the world he was familiar with but also the world he was entering, that is, a digital rendering of the US college life. In the physical world infiltrated by the institutionalized discourse of cultural diversity, Wentao was marked as different by his physicality and his linguistic and cultural behaviors. Yet in the virtual space of social media, Wentao was only visible through literate performances such as creating original posts or sharing other posts. His differences were marked from bottom up by friends, family, and acquaintances sharing the same social space.

Second, in addition to the material ecology Wentao inhabited and reacted to, structural and semiotic affordance—the invisible forces that created nexus among the material affordance as well as human agents—also enabled Wentao to perform his literate ingenuity and linguistic creativity through the integration of multimodal and translingual resources into poetically framed texts. These structurally and semiotically afforded and remediated textual performances singled him out from his social circle—virtual and physical—as a cosmopolitan and rhetorically sensible individual.

Third, the temporal dimension of the affordance manifests itself in Wentao's literacy histories. For example, his habit of reading extensively, especially Chinese science fiction (e.g., Liu Cixin) and essays (e.g., Wang Xiaobo), tremendously enriched his rhetorical sensibility and literary repertoire, which were reflected in his short yet thoughtfully crafted WeChat posts. The affordance, material and structural, semiotic and experiential, was inextricably entangled and networked and enabled Wentao to position himself and mark his emerging differences in his virtual social sphere through literate inventions. Just as Wentao inhabited the liminal world that blended the structural, semiotic, and cultural synergies from his home and college life in the US, he dwelled in the hybrid literate world that textually materialized his fluid identity and practice of "togetherness-in-difference" (Ang, 2001).

Conclusion: Wentao's Literacy Affordances

The permeability of Wentao's affordances allowed him the flexibility and mobility to cross material and social spaces, adapt to new rhetorical ecologies, and claim his "literate being" (existence as represented in symbols and signs) with ease. Cognizant of his bodily and linguistic differences institutionalized within the university context, Wentao strategically carved out his niche in the liminal space between the structural constraints and affordances ascribed to the university discourse. On the one hand, Wentao's bodily experiences of being positioned unfairly in the power dynamics of a group meeting with domestic students—because of his institutionalized status as a Chinese international student with developing English proficiency—prompted him to suppress his perceived differences by repositioning himself in other groups.

On the other hand, his once-suppressed differences—bodily features, linguistic and cultural upbringing—were rhetorically transformed into affordances in the other group, enabling him to take the leadership role and shine. Similarly, as a peripheral organization member, Wentao did not possess the institutional, social, or linguistic capital his fellow members did in the WPC when he initially joined it. Yet his linguistic creativity and rhetorical sensibility afforded him the semiotic resources and affective support necessary to venture into a broader social space and connect with prospective members. Admittedly, what is presented here is a tiny fraction of Wentao's complex, multifaceted, and continually emerging and unfolding literate world. Nevertheless, the fragmented yet tightly networked accounts offered a meaningful glimpse into the myriad ways in which an institutionally labeled international student's perceptions and practices of difference are shaped and mediated by his literate activities.

4
Yang

A Translingual Gothic Musician in the Making

After completing her entire pre-college schooling in Shijiazhuang, China, the capital city of Hebei Province, Yang enrolled in undergraduate courses in biology at Wabash in 2016. After a year, due to personal reasons, Yang transferred to a college in the Boston area, subsequently moved back to Wabash in 2018, and signed up for the first-year writing course I taught that summer. During our initial interview sessions, Yang appeared ambivalent about her choice of major studies. Raised in a family rooted in art, Yang was exposed to art, music, and design at a young age, thanks to her father and stepmother who are both art designers, and learned how to artistically express her thoughts and emotions. She always thought she was preparing herself to follow her parents' lead and work in the arts/culture industry. Yet when her journey to the art world suddenly encountered a disruption—her family's decision to send her to study in the US, following the fad of studying abroad that swept across China—Yang became disoriented and overwhelmed by the gigantic pool of options. Feeling insecure about the career prospect of studying arts-related majors in a foreign country, Yang consulted her father's friend, a college professor, who advised her to explore majors in the natural sciences. Eventually settled in biology, Yang struggled to discover her passion. During the fall of 2018, after painstaking soul-searching and negotiation with her parents,

https://doi.org/10.7330/9781646426447.c004

Yang finally decided to change her major to electrical engineering technology. She explained,

> I'm happy to have finally decided to make the big change. Now I have the luxury to focus on audio engineering, although I'm not entirely sure what it is yet. But if things go as I planned, I will eventually be able to do both engineering and music. Now I have a better chance of reliving my childhood dream and making my hobby my career.

Yang confidently claims her trilingual status. A native speaker and writer of Mandarin Chinese and proficient speaker and writer of English, she has also done substantial independent study of Japanese language, literature, and culture to the extent that she can artistically manipulate the Japanese language to compose song lyrics in response to her mood and the melodic prompt. After taking the graduation qualification exam in high school in her hometown, Yang invested all her time and energy in aggressively learning Japanese. She took courses from private language-training schools in Shanghai, gradually moved up the comprehension difficulty ladder in Japanese literature, and spent hours a day watching anime and listening to Japanese pop music. As soon as she mastered the basic sentence structures and accumulated a reasonably large vocabulary, Yang boldly attempted writing simple poems and lyrics. Not until years later, when the lyrics she composed gradually added sophistication and subtlety and even took on a Gothic style, did she realize that lyric writing had become her expertise, her love, and her life.

Contentedly residing in her music-creation world, Yang cautiously avoided being involved in a complex social network. She didn't make much effort to mingle with her classmates in the writing course beyond in-class group discussions, nor did she actively seek social connections outside the classrooms. She did, nevertheless, maintain productive relationships with a few friends who were also creating music as a hobby or as a potential profession.

> I don't socialize much for two reasons. First, making new friends and maintaining friendships cost a lot of energy. I like hanging out with just a few friends who know me well enough to make both or all of us comfortable. You can also say I'm a bit lazy, but I'm happy with just a couple of quality friendships. The second reason is that I don't usually feel insecure when I'm alone, and honestly sometimes I prefer spending time alone doing something productive, like, recording new demos or painting. And I guess having a boyfriend helps, too, because I need to visit him in Boston every month, and sometimes he comes to town to visit me.

Yang seemed quite rational about her disposition. Because of her disposition toward maintaining a distance from people in the social communities she involuntarily participated in, Yang was viewed by some of her classmates as someone who stands aloof, despite that in a seamlessly networked contemporary world where engagement has become a bandwagon, it's rather difficult to be disengaged. Consciously disengaged, Yang had been adequately open to me and vocal about her introspective observations during the research process.

A Translingual Muse at Work: Lyrics Writing across Borders

For international students studying in the US, learning a third language in college has become so popular that it has defined their polyglot competence. Yet students' translingual creativity manifesting in artistic expression in more than two named languages is still a rarity. Yang's literate world constructed upon lyrics writing in Japanese that is then translated to English and Chinese embodies this translingual creativity in its highlighted form. I first learned about Yang's experiences with and reflections on composing song lyrics in Japanese in her literacy autobiography written in my class in 2018. In the paragraph where she fondly "lamented" the lousy classroom environment stifling students' literary creativity during her high school years, Yang contrasted the discouraging context with her "spiritual world" created upon her artistic expression.

> Another form of art, music combined with painting have totally taken over my spiritual world. By the time I graduate, I consider myself already fairly knowledgeable in the music genre of Jazz and Japanese contemporary (Then it proves to be a dumb ignorance). Though I haven't been so obsessed in writing in high school, the experience I learned from other composing method still make school writing a rather simple task for me.

As evidenced in this excerpt, a major motif of Yang's high school literacy experience is the constant tension between "school writing" and extracurricular writing/painting/composing. Yet she artfully resolved the tension through the transfer of techniques, which, however, she did not specify here. Her first attempt at composing short lyrical sentences and stanzas could be traced back to the second year during her systematic Japanese learning. By the time Yang was about to embark on her undergraduate journey, she had accumulated a fairly large vocabulary. She also went beyond the basic "survival" Japanese vocabulary that focused on observable entities and common verbs and grasped the meaning and use of abstract concepts such as eternity and reality. Yang, too, was able to skillfully use a variety of syntactic structures.

> Although I still made a ton of grammar mistakes at that time, like verb conjugations or polite versus plain forms, I felt the urge to create something with the language, because I had all kinds of weird thoughts left unexpressed in my head. Some of them came from the Japanese songs I listened to, some from the Japanese PS4 [Play Station 4th generation] games I played. For example, lately I have been playing the game called "Horizon Zero Dawn." I liked the electronic music in the background, so I found it online and downloaded it. Then I tried to write lyrics to go with it.

When I expressed my skepticism as to why she did not attempt to write lyrics in English or Chinese, Yang somewhat proudly responded:

> I think writing English lyrics is too easy, so I've never actually even tried. I like doing things that are challenging, and set me apart among other people in my circle. A Chinese native-speaker writing Japanese lyrics in an English-speaking country is one of those things. Maybe one day I'll study in Japan, then I would try writing lyrics in English.

Yang grinned and continued,

> Another reason is, I have been immersed in the Japanese culture since I started learning the language. And I have been so fascinated by their cultural stuff: the Shinto religion, Ikebana, sushi, ramen, anime, video games, Haruki Murakami, Keigo Higashino. The more I know, the more I want to know. So writing lyrics is also a way for me to learn and participate in their culture.

Not only does Yang write lyrics to the songs her boyfriend—who studies music and composition at a renowned performing arts conservatory on the East Coast—writes, she also records herself singing the songs they write every now and then and publishes them on a music-streaming service based in China. The most popular single amassed more than 30,000 hits. After 2 years of active engagement in extensive and intensive lyric experimentations as well as cultural exposure, Yang began to identify and develop her own lyrical style without formal training. The lyrical style that Yang has grown accustomed to composing in may be best characterized as a synergy among postmodern surrealism, stream of consciousness, and Gothic, as represented in the use of metaphors, non sequiturs, unexpected juxtapositions of things, subjective experiences, emotions, and imaginations, and a touch of gothic myth and darkness. To Yang's anticipated audience, average members of Generation Z or millennials who grew up in China listening to Mandarin pop songs that revolve around the eternal theme of love, her lyrics may sound simply eerie and pretentious. Yet Yang claimed that it was her intention to create discomfort and disjunctions, and it was not at all by accident that she gradually adopted and adapted to this signature literary style. Rather, a variety of literate and ecological affordances have shaped Yang's lyrical styles and empowered her to challenge and redefine the boundary of her literacy creativity, including her extracurricular reading, the musicians she had been following, and the lyrical attunement to her boyfriend's (songwriter) melodic style.

Yang's most recent lyrical adventure began as her boyfriend sent a recorded music demo to her. Once in a while, her recent emotional ups and downs that are entangled with her sensual experiences in daily lives need a verbal vent to be released and communicated. Yet Yang would usually wait for a music muse to inspire her so that she can translate her entangled emotions and experiences into words. The music demos her boyfriend sends her almost always serve as her muse, as Yang noted:

> Maybe this is the reason that I write lyrics rather than poems. Poets write poems because they are inspired by visual stimulants. I write lyrics because I tend to get high when I hear things. My ears turn me on more effectively than other organs.

Yang listened to the demo for an hour with her headphones on in her apartment bedroom before lying down in her bed, launching the note application on her smartphone, and beginning to type up random words in Chinese: "依存" (interdependence), "许可" (permission), "囚禁" (incarceration), "羔羊" (lamb), and "陷阱" (trap). Upon stimulated recall, Yang explained the rationale behind her initial lyrical invention:

> My boyfriend sent me a prompt along with the demo. He only gave me one word, "love," in the prompt, and asked me to be creative, and assured me that he would be openminded about anything I'd come up with. I listened to the music over and over again, and tried to find a point of entry as well as a particular angle.

Yang further reflected,

> The music is a mixture of digital piano, cello, violin, drum, and sound produced with other electronic instruments. The use of electronic musical instruments determined that it was a love fantasy, and the irregular beats during the first half created a lot of tension, as if the music was questioning

FIGURE 4.1. 絵馬/えま/Ema, courtesy of DLKR (unsplash.com).

the eternal hardships in love. But there was also this not-so-easily-captured undertone of care and hope. It reminded me of the love stories in Murakami's novels, and also some fragmented scenes in the Japanese game I was playing. So I just typed up the words that hit my mind in the moment. They don't seem to make much sense as a whole, though.

As wild a ride as Yang's imagination was taking her on, she was cognizant of the need to tame it and make connections between the images; as she noted, "after all the lyrics must make sense, even though they don't necessarily tell a complete story." Upon more contemplation, Yang decided to begin the first chorus with the symbolic imagery of a lamb, as in the biblical account, the lamb is considered a representation of innocence and sacrifice.

I want the "punch" of my song to be the contrast between the darkness and the brightness of love, you know, the selfish, greedy, manipulative, and deceiving part of love and the altruistic, kind, humble, and innocent part of love. So I thought of another cultural symbol in Japan that I often see in movies and anime, which is called 绘马 [Ema]. It's basically a small wooden plaque where people draw a horse and write wishes and then hang up at the shrine. It sounds like a good thing, but I see it as a lure, or something seductive that gives you false hope. So I'm comparing Ema to the innocent lamb here.

The completed chorus reads as follows.

> ひつじになる事 *(To be a lamb)*
> えまになる事 (To be an Ema)
> 引っ掻き回した標べは (The mark that I scratched)
> 明確な場所で餌を釣る (Hangs the bait at a clear place)
>
> 網膜で狙う *(Aiming at the retina)*
> 千本鍼で貫く (And perforating it with a thousand sticks)
> 痛感もないの罠で (With no pain in the trap)
> 割り込む圧縮して餌となる (Broken and compressed into the bait)

The chorus is saturated with Gothic romance and presents a surrealist collage of fragmented representational images. Some images, for example, lamb and Ema, represent certain religious symbols and rituals (Christianity, Shinto, and Buddhism). Others, such as retina and pain, are directly associated with bodily experiences. The images are sensual and provocative to a grotesque level and create strong visceral reactions. Yet the emotional disturbance is precisely what Yang was aiming for. To her, writing song lyrics is in stark contrast to writing professionally or academically; the primary criterion to judge the quality of lyrics is whether or not they emotionally move or engage the audience, whereas to judge the quality of professional or academic writing, whether or not it engages people in rational thinking and decision making. In terms of the form, Yang didn't particularly strive for rhyming verses, which she believes is constraining and dogmatic. The lines are just as broken and fragmented as the scattered images, further intensifying the audience's emotional responses.

> I was trapped in my own complicated thoughts while I was "squeezing" the lines out of my head. I tried to close my eyes and create the 意境 [ambient moods, meanings, ecologies] in my head and then translate that into Japanese words as if I was taking a photo. That's probably why it looks messy. But I would say it's my style, which is to defy any particular existing style.

Yang reflected on her composing processes.

Although through oxymoron, Yang claimed that her lyrical style is idiosyncratic, it's not difficult to trace the sources that have had an impact on her style. As a matter of fact, she left clues and evidence in the writer's literacy autobiography she wrote in my first-year writing course. Learning Japanese has been an essential part of her entire literacy developmental trajectory, which is rightfully highlighted in her autobiography. In the paper, Yang unfolded her experience of coming to terms with the cultural importance embedded in song lyrics and illustrated her understanding by analyzing the lyrics of a Japanese musician's work, which had meaningfully shaped her lyrical style. Here is an excerpt from her autobiography.

During the self-learning process of the third language, Japanese, I gradually learned that though vocabulary and grammar could be easy to handle in a brief period, the cultural knowledge and the communication skill would take me much longer to master, while learning to read and write in Japanese become a challenging but fascinating goal for me to reach. If you don't get to know haiku, then you may never to know the meaning of "いろはにほへと　ちりぬるを," which is a simple song for the kids to learn romaji or understand its other format as "色はにほへど　散りぬるを," which means "Flowers will fade away no matter how" or even its Buddhist version "以呂波耳本へ止　千利奴流乎和加," which represent "void" as the core of everything in the world. What's more, I encountered several artists who gave me surprises all the time not only with their music but also the lyrics. To my understanding, Music itself is purely art that is emotional and rational. With the meaning given by the composer, it gives life to the lyrics that gives purpose back to music. I want to give an example of one of Treow's song. He used to be my favorite Japanese composer. In <triplantena>, the first chorus goes like:

溢れた風に乗る/乘上流溢而出的风
Afureta kaze ni noru/乘上流溢而出的风
Take the flooded wind

雨色の降灰/雨色的落灰
Amairo no koukai/雨色的後悔
The fallen ashes of a muddy rain

笑顔が飽きるほど砕いた/笑容碎去得几近令人生厌
Egao ga akiruhodo kudaita/笑容碎去得几近令人生厌
Laughters shatter away as if they are too much

小さな夢撥ね返る/将细小的梦境 拨转覆始
Chiisana Yume hanekaeru/於微弱的梦境 辗转反复
Spring back in the tiny land of dream

(Lyricist: NaturaLe; Interpretation: foolen, Liwei, Fe; Translation: foolen, Yang)

This poetry-like piece has used a lot of Japanese writing skills like 当て字, which means to "borrow" meanings from other words. It also includes words which have same pronounce but different meaning. E.g. "雨色の降灰(後悔)," "降灰" and "後悔" are of same sound but different meaning. Though they are different, either one can fit perfectly into the lyrics. Its beauty and romance were a total shock to me during high school. The dedicated phrases and connections between them was more than just fascinating to me. Though I was never trained to understand what the definition of beauty in Japanese culture is, it is true to me that I feel the resonance coming from this masterpiece. I have made up my mind to write lyrics that's as good as these ones but failing to do so which contributed to my unyielding lyrics writing practice to go on and on until today.

In the excerpt, Yang *demonstrated* by invoking linguistic and religious legacies, as opposed to merely *claiming*, that learning Japanese had opened the door to a new cultural experience. Then she zoomed in on a Japanese musician named Treow, whose works had inspired her to adopt lyric writing as a means of articulating her affective self. She quoted the chorus of the lyrics of Treow's song, which were written by NaturaLe, and retranslated the lyrics to English based on foolen's original translation based on her own interpretation of the lyricist's rhetorical purpose. Through the analysis of the lyricist's rhetorical strategy of "当て字" (to borrow meanings) and the use of homophones ("降灰" and "後悔"), Yang also showcased her rhetorical sensibility that later afforded her own lyric composing in her third language. As she noted beautifully, the affective power transcended the linguistic and cultural representation and entangled her subjectivities in the world of lyrical creation. After I initiated a stimulated recall of her experience of writing the autobiography in relation to her emerging lyrics, Yang realized and acknowledged that her lyrical style was indeed shaped by lyrics whose style resembles that of NaturaLe's lyrics.

There's a 淡淡的忧伤 [mild sense of melancholy] flowing in the lyrics. The 意象 [topoi] in the lyrics, as you see—风 [wind], 落灰 [fallen ashes], 破碎的笑容 [shattered laughers], and 梦境 [dream]—are all conveying that melancholic message. Everybody feels blue or down or even depressed every now and then. And when I feel down, I would look for some sort of comfort from others' expression of similar feelings. And the lyrics as well as the melody of this song sets me up well for emotional 宣泄 [catharsis]. And because I feel blue more often than I feel happy, so I appreciate this type of songs and listen to lots of them. Plus, there's something particularly about Japanese songs that attract me. For example, lyrics like those for this song are very poetic and implicit, unlike American pop songs that explicitly sing about strong emotions. I can better relate to it, because the poetic style is similar to that of our Chinese poetry that we grew up learning, which is very subtle, indirect, and yet provocative. So thinking about this, I think my style has indeed been affected by these lyrics. But I guess my style has also been influenced by Western pop songs, because I tend to use topoi that would evoke stronger emotions. So my style is kind of a combination or a hybrid of both worlds.

Generally contented with the chorus, Yang continued to compose the verses, which were aimed at contextualizing the chorus. She employed the same strategy used to write the chorus, that is, typing up keywords in Chinese in the note-taking application on her phone, and rearranging them while making connections. The initial keywords entered into her phone were "杂讯" (noise), "淡绿色" (celadon), and "记忆" (memories). "As you can feel, these 意象 (topoi) are not as provocative and disturbing as those I wrote in the chorus, because I want to take it easy at the beginning and ease my audience into the more intense part." Yang explained her rationale. Extending—or, rather, foreshadowing—the tension between positive and negative forces often experienced in love, Yang decided to contrast desire with reality, and interdependence with free will.

> 雑音で 依存を 捜す *(Searching for dependency in the noise)*
> 青磁色のパーミッションで *(With the permission of celadon green)*
> 現実を はらう *(Escaping reality)*
> だけど いつか 見つけられだろ *(But I will find it someday)*
> ならば ちゃんと その記憶を隠す *(And then hide the memories properly)*

> さあ どうか自分を守る *(Please protect yourself)*
> 囚われた僕にも *(Even to me who was caged)*
> 飛んでいる機身(きみ)にも *(Even to you who are flying)*

The salient disjuncture here is between the "self" who is held captive and the "you" who is entitled to complete freedom. The "self," desperately suffocating, seeks ways to escape reality while holding onto the fading connection.

I struggled a lot when trying to write the verse, because different ideas and images were messed up in my mind, and I had a hard time sorting them out or expressing what I wanted to say properly in Japanese. So I followed the chorus backward and introduce the background and previous actions that eventually led to the falling apart of the hopes. The music that my boyfriend wrote and that I was supposed to write the lyrics to reminded me of some unpleasant memories of the conflicts we had in our relationship. Most of them were caused by our desire to be free but also be connected, and our desire to control each other and to break out of each other's control. Sometimes we seemed to have lost hope, but other times we regained hope. Having recalled all that, I found it easier to put things together and translate my messy thoughts into words and lines.

Interestingly, and as Yang admitted, she would always construct 意境 (ambient moods, meanings, and ecologies) by leveraging linguistic resources rooted in Chinese. Yet as she transitioned to the phase of reconstructing 意境 in words on her smartphone screen, Yang opted for Japanese.

> Honestly, I still compose most of the lyric lines in my head in Chinese. There are usually quite a few words that I haven't learned in Japanese, so I need to look them up on Google. Although I organize my words in Chinese, the images that pop up in my head are all associated with Japanese culture, for example, Ema, celadon, retina and so on, because I learned about them in Japanese literature or music or anime. That's why I said my ideas are messy. When I write down the lines, though, I would always use Japanese, as I want to make sure what I write looks authentic to my future audience who wants to experience Japanese culture. Have you seen the movie *Lost in Translation*? Although the screenplay is not directly about translation, but I learned that a lot can be compromised during translation, even your identity.

As the above thick description of Yang's lyric-writing ecology illustrates, her literate activity of composing translingual lyrics were assembled into complexly networked affordance: her literacy experiences of learning Japanese, emotional and sensual experiences of managing a romantic relationship, semiotic resources hoarded through years of linguistic and cultural immersion, structural guidance for composing lyrics, technological tools used to perform writing, the material environment of the writing ecology, as well as her bodily reactions to the imagery created through the lyric lines. An independent thinker, writer, and a somewhat self-proclaimed proud loner, Yang invests substantially more time and energy into orchestrating her own performative identity by engaging in lyric creation in multiple languages. First of all, Yang's rhetorical disposition toward embedding her affective experiences in a popular literacy genre—pop song lyrics—and circulate the lyrically mediated affective experiences in the pop music community marks her unique performative identity in the mainstream university environment. Also, Yang's rhetorical choice of drawing on her Japanese linguistic and cultural resources in lyric writing defies the assumed national sentiment that ties a writer's language practices to their nationality. Further, the literature, artwork, entertainment and popular culture, and other forms of cultural flows that Yang has been immersed in have been instrumental to her growth as a rhetorically versatile and sensitive writer in that they afforded rich cultural tropes and symbols that enabled Yang to attribute her emotions more aptly. Deeply entangled in the affordance that assembled different materials, representations, and forces, Yang's lyric writing is constituted and also constitutive as it circulates in the wider pop music community she's trying to enter.

An Onlooker/Player's Insights into the Game of Pop Music Industry

An idiom of conventional wisdom in Chinese says: "当局者迷，旁观者清" ("The onlooker sees more of the game"). Being deeply involved in a certain activity or culture blinds one from seeing the big picture and misleads one to pay excessive attention to trivial matters. Yet Yang seems to demonstrate otherwise: only by being an engaged game player does one *care* to see the game critically and make it a fairer one. Yang has been actively interacting with the online pop music community in a multitude of ways since she began to create music. She learned the basics of writing lyrics by following online tutorials and consulting experienced writers using online forums. She downloaded unpublished raw music samples to practice writing lyrics to. She shared her experiences and ideas in social media groups of amateur musicians. She also promotes her song demos through massive music resource hubs and streaming services such as NetEase Music. Being involved in the pop music community in her various capacities has bestowed on Yang the confidence to claim her authority as a seasoned "player" in the game of the pop music industry and a "peripheral insider"—who knows a lot yet lacks the power to meaningfully impact the game.

"The market is never predictable. We wouldn't have seen so many struggling artists or musicians if anybody can beat the market," Yang claimed, with her usual composure, when I asked her about her intrinsic motivation that drove her to create and share music and about her general impression of the broader context of the music industry. Soon after she wrote and recorded herself singing her own song, Yang registered for an account on NetEase Music, a music-streaming service and one of the biggest and most popular music-sharing communities based in China, to publish her recordings.

> I was extremely nervous the first time I shared my demo with the world out there. When I say 'the world,' I literally try to include everybody: my family and friends, classmates, strangers that include lay people, average music consumers, and maybe professional critics or even record company agents. On the one hand, as you can imagine, I longed for people's feedback, otherwise I wouldn't even share it in the first place. On the other hand, I was so anxious about how people might react to it. Would they like it or hate it?

Yang compared her experiences of sharing a recording to sharing a piece of writing.

> It's sort of like spending days or months writing an essay or a short story and you need some audience and some recognition. But there are differences, too. For example, the type of pop songs that I make require little from the audience, as long as they have a speaker or a pair of earphones, they can listen to them and judge them. As for a piece of writing, though, the audience definitely needs literacy, and some background knowledge about the writing. In this sense, my songs can reach a broader and more diverse audience. So it's more difficult to ask for everybody's positive feedback.

Quickly enough, Yang had overcome the initial jitters triggered by uncertainty and successfully gathered an encouraging number of loyal fans over the past several years: her subscriber base grew to approximately 3,000 and the most played single among those published acquired 30,000 hits. Contented with the steadily increasing popularity in the community, Yang was, however, still bewildered by the unpredictability of her audience's tastes.

> I'm doing something that fewer people are doing, which is writing original lyrics in Japanese and share them, because I don't want to follow the trend by doing something silly or easy. From what I know the community that likes or creates original Japanese music in China is very small, well, in a relative sense, largely because fewer people are passionate about or know enough about J-pop, not to mention to write original songs in Japanese. So I often wonder who my subscribers are and what they really think about my music. For one, I want to continue to find my own style by trial and error; for another, I want to tailor my songs to attract more listeners or at a least produce something new and interesting for the current subscribers.

Indeed, Yang characterized her own lyrical style as "lacking 大众适口性 (appeals to the general public)," not because she's blissfully unaware of what lyrical genres sell or incompetent at composing one but because she does not prioritize the circulation over expression. In other (her own) words, she "writes lyrics for (her)self first then waits for the public to find meanings in them." As a matter of fact, she even dismisses, if not despises, the way in which distasteful music has saturated the market and to a greater extent shaped the public's collective predilections.

Yang presented to me several widely recognized and trusted Billboard-like lists of recent top-ranking pop songs in China; for example, the ones compiled and published by Tecent Music and NetEase Music, and singled out a few of the titles from the list. "Just by looking at the titles, you can imagine how 三俗 [triply vulgar] they are." With a contemptuous smile, Yang explained to me what she meant by 三俗:

> It's a term that got its notoriety in the Internet social community, which basically refers to something that's 庸俗 [philistine], 低俗 [vulgar], and 媚俗 [mercenary]. How can a song be sān sú? Well, first, the melody can sound super corny or cheesy, and too simplistic or repetitive just so people can remember it. Sometimes I hear the melody playing in a shopping mall, for example, even if the melody is forced into my ears without me paying attention for a few seconds, I can remember it, and it will resound in my mind over and over again for the rest of the day, which is really disturbing. Also, the lyrics may be even worse than the melody. I understand that most pop song lyrics in China are about the universal human emotion of love, because it simply sells. But sān sú songs take it to the extreme. The lyrics are about the stupidity in love. For example, some lyrics are written from a guy's perspective about how much he misses his girl. The lyrics sound as if he's desperate and cares about nothing but being with the girl, not even self-esteem or responsibility. Some lyrics could even be childish or explicitly sexual. I feel not just annoyed, but embarrassed and angry every time I hear them on the street. I can't imagine what kind of impression the songs would leave on foreign visitors or simply any educated people in China.

Yang clearly believes that pop culture, including pop music culture, is an essential part of a teenager's or young adult's literacy life.

> In China, well I think anywhere in the world, teenagers grow up listening to pop music, and some of them not only listen, but also create, like me. It's just an indispensable part of our life and also an indispensable source of information. We learn about the world through pop music as much as we do so through textbooks.

Yang's observation here resonates with my personal experiences of gaining literacy. When I was a middle schooler back in the early 2000s, the Internet was just beginning to gain momentum as one of the sources of information, far from being the dominant one as it is today. Schooling, including textbooks and teachers, were our primary, or rather, orthodox, gateway to the unknown world. Yet when we needed an escape to explore the differences in the world hidden from the textbooks, we would either open the pages of Jin Yong's "wuxia [martial arts and chivalry]" novels or Chiung Yao's romance novels, or put on a pair of headphones, turn on the portable cassette player, and tune in to Jay Chou's R&B songs. The pop music industry in mainland China was young and booming, and it was shaped largely by a few influential musicians and singers based in Hong Kong, Taiwan, England, and North America. Also, lacking the speed and reach of the Internet as a medium of circulation, the creation and production of a new record takes much longer. As a result, we used to listen to the same record for a year while anticipating the new one to be delivered on a cassette tape or a CD. And due to the limited channels that connected us to the "outside world," we would ruminate on the lyrics, copy them in a notebook, and sometimes memorize them verbatim and sing along as we listened to the trendy pop songs. Looking back, if not for Jay Chou's culturally rich lyrics, I wouldn't have been fascinated by the ancient Babylonian culture or Japanese bushido; if not for Westlife's poetic lyrical style, I wouldn't have fallen in love with the art of the English language. In short, the collective memories of my generation vouch for Yang's claim that the pop music culture affords her literate growth.

> If such vulgar lyrics and tacky music overflow the pop music market and continue to rape our ears, how long will we be able to confidently say that China has a great culture and expect the next generation of Chinese kids to embrace it and love it?

Yang lamented the detrimental impact of the still maturing yet mercenary pop music industry in China on students' development of literacy and cultural sensibility.

> Of course I'm not trying to be a police here, and it's way beyond my ability to police the sort of free market of over a billion consumers. People listen to what they find appealing anyways. Because I participate in the market a bit differently than most of the people: I'm simultaneously a creator while being a consumer, and I have first-hand experiences interacting with musicians and producers from other cultures, so I sort of know what's going on in the Chinese market, and I'm concerned about its future.

Cynical and concerning as Yang may appear to be, she is not entirely pessimistic. As Yang particularly clarified, although she doesn't find 三俗 (triply vulgar) music appealing, she does not deny the colors it brings to the world and people's lives. Her marketing acumen helped her to make sense of the complexity and diversity of individuals' tastes and dispositions.

> Despite the fact that these 三俗 songs sound so tacky and vulgar to most modern educated people, and I bet the creators themselves know this, they still attracted hundreds of millions of consumers. What does it mean? It means these songs still deserve a spot in the market. You don't have to like them, but they will always be there, because others do like them and they provide some kind of entertainment to others. I don't want to be like "oh I'm writing and singing exotic Japanese songs so I'm superior to you guys who enjoy 三俗 songs." No. My argument is, we need a little bit of everything in the world, and everything is equally valuable.

Ang's (2001) notion of togetherness-in-difference is well represented in Yang's outlook toward the good and bad in the pop music industry in China. In other words, from Yang's perspective, diversity does not differentiate values but preferences. Diversity is objective reality, and at the same time, subjective (and oftentimes collective) perceptions and constructs of the differing relations. What Yang embraces, then, is not the dominance of any particular strand of form, but coexistence of and synergy between different strands of forms.

Yang had demonstrated her cosmopolitan insights into not just the pop music industry but also music education before we began to schedule interview sessions regularly. In the research-based argumentative essay she wrote in my first-year writing course, Yang compared the differences of music education in higher-ed institutions in China and the US, demanding more diversity and flexibility in music education in Chinese institutions. Her motivation to undertake such an ambitious project during a short summer section is based upon her observation and assumption that music education in China has witnessed a more problematic developmental trajectory in comparison to other countries where music education is more mature, such as the US. As Yang pointed out in her research proposal written in my class:

> The booming industry of entertainment in China have brought flourishment to the music education system as a result. However, not every time could education system catch up with economic growth, especially when it comes to music education. There are myriad of issues we face on copyright infringement, tolerance of plagiarize, low-quality works that's

uncompetitive in the global market, etc. These issues have raised lots of concerns from music enthusiastic across China. It's not fair to deny the improvement we have made over the years; however, it is even more than necessary to continue to find out problems and make adjustment in the system to keep up with the pace international wide.

In a series of well-balanced acknowledgments, concessions, and criticisms, Yang showcased her knowledge of and expressed her concern with the status quo of music education in China. The concern, however, is not justified through an introspective observation of the system itself; rather, it is done through a comparison with the system in the "global market." Here, Yang's togetherness-in-difference takes on a subtle layer of nationalist ideals, despite that she seems to hold an egalitarian belief when it comes to music creation. To understand her grand research questions regarding the differences between music education in China and the US, Yang collected both firsthand and secondary data from various sources; for example, the publicly available recruitment policies and course curricula of five major music schools (or conservatories of music) in mainland China and the US and academic journal articles that covered different aspects of the topic. She also interviewed several professors and students from two music schools whom she was introduced to through her social networks. The completed project ended up being a 3,000-word report fully detailing differences in terms of student recruitment, course curriculum, and student experiences in and beyond college. The comparison itself is not what Yang ultimately aimed to achieve; rather, as Yang herself noted during student conferences with me, she always had a rough sense of the current status of music education in China, being someone who nearly applied to one and who had well-maintained social connections with students enrolled in those schools. What she needed was some evidence to confirm (or, less fortunately, disprove) her hypothesis. Although to definitively and authoritatively answer her research questions and conform her hypothesis she may need a substantially longer research period and more data, Yang was confident enough to articulate the argument she had been wanting to make for a long time:

> My central argument is that Chinese music conservatives, while having gained impressive improvements in its quality of education, retained reputation through its orchestra band and traditional music, could still make further improvement and replenishment in some brand-new subject in music, such as music production and music business, which needs

attention, and thus should take the responsibility of diversifying the employment opportunity, work with the government and education bureau to create a more flexible and welcoming academic environment for students, and keep the ongoing educational reformation in enrollment which create a fair competition environment for students.

In her statement of argument, Yang made three mega-sociopolitical points addressed to the government educational policymakers and higher-ed institutional administrators: first, diversify the job market in the music industry; second, create a "flexible and welcoming" academic environment; and third, continue educational reform to stimulate fair competition. Apparently, the evidence based on four sample schools may hardly substantiate such an ambitious argument, despite the fact that it indeed seems cogent and attested. Yang explained:

> I know my argument is huge. And you can say that to some extent I made it based on confirmation bias, which means I had had some hypotheses or beliefs before and only found evidence to confirm that I was right. I remember reading news articles and op-ed pieces about politicians constantly talking about reforming music education in China and strengthening our cultural soft power, but after so many years, nothing visible has changed, or at least not to my knowledge. And I have friends who study at music institutions in both China and America. They share similar concerns. I'm not a musician. And I didn't receive any official and professional training in one of those music schools. But I do make original music and I do participate in the development of the music industry, however minimal my contribution is. So I wish those who are lucky enough to go to a music school and pursue their dreams to create the future of the Chinese music industry.

Although the research Yang conducted may not have yielded adequate results to buttress her claims, which may themselves originate from established scholars, the bold argument does indeed demonstrate her peripheral insider's status and her genuine care. Her insights into the music industry transcend linguistic and cultural boundaries yet do not fully translate to borderless and uncritical optimism. The imaginary border that resurfaced in this instance is Yang's perception of the national border: national borders rarely interfere with the circulation and access of music yet they delimit the origins, histories, and cultural implications of the music. Regardless of the language in which she writes song lyrics or for whom she does so, Yang's literacy that enabled her to write in the first place is always rooted within the sociopolitical construct of nation, as the literacy education she received in China is fundamentally afforded or constrained by the sociopolitical and educational system.

Yang's peripheral insider's status in the pop music community afforded not only firsthand experiences interacting with different stakeholders in the industry and gaining insights from within but also a distant bird's-eye view of the social context within which the industry struggles or thrives. Her semiotic resources enabled her to freely and skillfully communicate with professionals and semiprofessionals who have built or are building a career in the industry, through multiple semiotic channels—music and words alike. Her social networks established within and around the community in both China and the US broadened her horizons and lent her a new lens through which she views the "deviant" or the "vulgar" and encouraged her to embrace togetherness-in-difference in the industry. Yang was also able to take advantage of the research methodologies briefly introduced in a writing course to analyze the structural differences between the music education systems across the Pacific Ocean and properly express her patriotic sentiment regarding the future of the industry in China in tune with her cosmopolitan philosophy.

Navigating the Rhetorics

Yang's rhetorical versatility found its manifestation in her translingual lyrical composition and marketing her creation to different audiences across the world. Yet somehow her rhetorical versatility failed to agree with institutionalized rhetorical education in the US Not so long after finishing her first-year writing course in summer 2018, Yang signed up to take the test-out exams for COM 114: Fundamentals of Speech Communication the following fall. Note here that due to Yang's transfer back and forth between Wabash and the college in Boston, she needed to take quite a few entry-level courses in her third year. COM 114 is a required public speaking course that involves introducing communication theories and training students to perform informative and persuasive speaking in a standard speaker-audience situation as well as interpersonal and small-group communication. Although the course credits are required, students may, alternatively, obtain the credits by successfully passing the test-out exams, which include a written exam and an oral presentation. The written exam, which Yang felt especially apprehensive about, consists of fifty multiple-choice questions checking test-takers' comprehensive understanding of key communication and rhetorical theories. These questions include, for example, identifying rhetorical strategies such as ethos and pathos, effectively visualizing information when delivering a message, identifying logical fallacies and facts, value, policy, and intent, among a number of others.

Unfortunately, Yang failed the test, as she regretfully indicated during an interview session in the fall. Although she acknowledged that she did not devote adequate time and energy to studying the recommended textbook and preparing for the test, Yang attributed her failure primarily to her lack of sufficient rhetorical preparation and repertoire overall.

> The education I had so far in China owed me for this. During my entire schooling in China, I had never been taught how to effectively make a public speech in practice, not to mention any relevant theories that help you do that. What's worse, nobody had ever told us that communication is such a big deal and a scientific study in itself. We always believed that communication is some kind of "street art" that one can only pick up by either being born into a business family or mimicking businessmen or politicians. Rhetoric? I had never even come across the term before I set foot in America. I thought the test out would just be asking you very simple questions about how to do presentations, which I have some experiences with after studying in an American college for two years. I didn't expect and was surprised that they would ask about lots of theoretical stuff that I was too confident to have paid attention!

She continued to describe how she "freaked out" immediately upon seeing questions about unfamiliar concepts in communication theories.

> If I had learned about it or even just heard about these concepts in high school, I could at least make some educated guesses. It was in your [first-year writing] class that I first learned the concept of rhetoric, thankfully, but then again there were lots of other concepts particularly related to verbal communication that I didn't know.

I decided that this topic merited further discussion and coconstruction, thus I began to assume a more active participatory role in the interview and explore with her what communication and rhetoric meant. "What does rhetoric mean to you?" I asked Yang. She hesitated and tried to retrieve relevant information from her repertoire.

> I remember we spent quite a bit of time talking about rhetoric in your writing class. Rhetoric to me means, like we discussed in class, being aware of the context when you are speaking or writing so that you can more effectively convey your message and persuade people to take certain action. It's interesting, though, that we don't seem to have a perfect translation in

Chinese. I looked it up in an online English-Chinese dictionary after you introduced it in class. And it said something in Chinese like empty, exaggerated, or even false remarks. Totally negative. The study of rhetoric in Chinese is 修辞学 [xīu cí xúe], which as far as I know is the study of how to use strategies like simile or parallelism to make your sentences and passages more beautiful. In that case, we did study "rhetoric" in China, even in elementary school, because our Chinese teachers would always ask us to analyze an essay in terms of what strategies the authors used to make their texts more appealing.

"Let's say we [Chinese students] did study 'rhetoric' as you just defined it in China. What are the differences then?" I asked a follow-up question.

I've never seriously considered the differences. But my impression is, our *xīu cí xúe* in China is intended to express our thoughts and emotions in a more artsy way, to create some kind of aesthetic pleasure for the readers. Western rhetoric, however, focuses more on effectively using words to get people to do something and take action.

"What do you think contribute to these differences?" I continue to ask Yang. She answered,

I would say historical and political reasons, maybe. Scholars living in ancient Chinese dynasties did debate regularly on different matters, if we consider "rhetoric" as also implying debating. For example, the essay we read in our Chinese textbook talked about the debate between Zhuangzi and his friend about whether or not they know what fish enjoy. I remember it clearly because I thought it was so clever and fun. And also, other philosophers like Zhuangzi, such as Confucius, travelled to different kingdoms to lobby or advise the lords. I guess these all have to do with rhetoric. But not a lot of scholars back then, as far as I know, were interested in studying it as if it's something important. In terms of political reasons, I think the primary reason rhetoric is a big thing in the West but not so much in China is because the public seems really interested in participating in politics. And what's more, they are able and allowed to participate in politics. For example, here in America, people vote for their presidents. When I first came in 2016, I watched students lining up in the Union and casting their vote. Back then, I didn't understand why they would feel proud to vote and why would that one vote even count. Of course that's the perspective of someone who had never voted or were allowed to do so. Now I realized it's the power of rhetoric: it moves people to do things and lots of consequences will follow. You watch, read, and hear the debates of those presidential candidates, and you are convinced by someone and agree with him or her, so you want to be part of the politics that changes people's lives. But in China, since we don't get to vote, people developed this idea that what we say doesn't matter or can't be heard, and politicians developed the idea that what they say can be heard but doesn't affect their career anyway, so rhetoric doesn't mean anything in politics. It's only useful in terms of making what you say sound prettier.

Although Yang's emerging understanding of "rhetoric" is derivative of brief class discussions and rough empirical observations, her slightly overgeneralized description of her rhetorical understanding does reflect her sensibility to how communication is conceptualized and executed differently across different cultures. She is also apparently cognizant of the social and political consequences of rhetoric as well as its nature in different contexts. Yet she lacks the canonical terminologies and phrases typically seen or heard in conversations situated in the Western rhetorical tradition due to her limited exposure to formal and systematic rhetorical training. This may also be the major contributor to her unsuccessful attempt at the written examination. It did not bother Yang to a great extent, however she later indicated that she learned from her friend, who had taken COM 114, that the course was worth the time and money. More importantly, Yang was aware of the necessity to continue to hone her communication skills and develop her rhetorical awareness and sensibility, especially in cross-cultural contexts, because it became clearer to her that, in her words, communication skills are "what get things done here in America" and rhetorical awareness and sensibility are "what get things done effectively and morally."

Yang's emerging rhetorical sensibility also extended to the realm of nonverbal communication during the course of research data collection. In this case nonverbal communication refers to any type of information exchange through nonlinguistic means, such as visual presentation. In a cross-cultural context, appearing to belong to a certain identity group tacitly delivers substantially more information than verbally communicating information in a certain manner, as Yang's experiences seem to suggest. During our conversations, the notion of "face" surfaced as a dominant theme. It does carry the connotation of the stereotypical notion of "face"—public self-image—that is entrenched in the Chinese value and circulating in North American public discourse (Mao, 2005). Rather, the "face" that Yang kept referring to should be understood at its face value, that is, the literal face that bears and delivers a vast amount of identity information in nonverbal communication: race, ethnicity, gender, age, and even class and education. These identity messages exchanged involuntarily in communicative situations are always intertwined with power dynamics and cultural nuances.

Her initial realization of the communicative information embedded in people's face was prompted by her interactions with course instructors and teaching assistants coming from, in her term, "non-mainstream ethnic backgrounds," particularly those of Chinese origin.

> I went to an international high school in Shijiazhuang so I was accustomed to being taught by "foreign teachers." But not until I came to America did I realize that I would be taught by "foreign teachers" too in a foreign country. Of course, foreign teachers from Americans' point of view.

Yang used the term "foreign teacher" to address those non-US-born or non-native-English-speaking instructors and professors in general. Over the course of 2 years, Yang had taken multiple beginner-level or intermediate-level courses from "foreign teachers"; for example, introduction to statistics and applied calculus. Some of her other courses were staffed by international teaching assistants in addition to the course instructor. Yang continued to share her perceptions of attending classes taught by "foreign teachers."

> It would be a lie if I say I wasn't surprised at first and I don't have reservations about their credibility. Like other international Chinese students, I came to study in America to experience a different type of education system—different and, well, I try not to compare, but—better education system. But it never occurred to me that I would end up coming all the way to America from China to take a course from a Chinese professor. During my first semester, I signed up for a calculus class. It turned out that on the first day, the professor that showed up was a Chinese who looked just like a random teacher I had in China and who spoke heavily accented and soft English. I felt disappointed. I didn't know I would have to pay thousands of dollars for a class taught by my own people. After the first class, though, my impression changed a little bit. Although her appearance and teaching style reminded me of my middle school math teacher and the terrible experiences that came with her, she turned out to be pretty effective. She made the otherwise chewy stuff easy to understand, and she was super nice and always smiling at us. And she even threw a joke or two during that class. And my American classmates seemed to enjoy her class as well. I almost forgot the fact that she had the look and accent of a Chinese just like me.

The nonverbal communicative information presented by the mere appearance, or face, of the Chinese professor was associated with the value of the course in Yang's discourse. Her earlier discursive construction of the notion of "American education" is shaped by her previous schooling experiences and media portrayal in China that presented US higher-ed institutions as staffed entirely and uniformly by white native-English-speaking American citizens. Yet this discursive construction soon collapsed as Yang continued to negotiate the meaning of "face" with her emerging cosmopolitan mentality in an institutional environment characterized by difference as opposed to uniformity. By the time Yang enrolled in the ENGL 106 Introductory Writing for International Students course I taught in summer 2018, she had already taken at least four courses from non-US-citizen or non-native-English-speaking instructors at both Wabash and the transfer institution in Boston. She had internalized the idea that American institutions openly embrace faculty members from diverse racial, ethnic, linguistic, cultural, and disciplinary backgrounds or are usually required to do so in their hiring practices. However, it still took her by surprise that the very class offered by the English Department would be taught by a non-native-English-speaking instructor.

> Now, of course, I know you are an excellent teacher. But back on the first day, I had mixed feelings when you walked into the classroom. My first reaction was curiosity. By seeing your face, I immediately labeled you "Chinese" in my mind. But then your hairstyle and outfit and more importantly, the fact that this is an English writing class made me less sure. Maybe you are an ABC [American-born Chinese]? But what if you are a "real" Chinese, how is it possible that you are teaching an English class in an English-speaking country? It's like an American come all the way to China to learn Chinese from an American. You must be really, really good at English then. All those questions popped up in my mind within the first three seconds I saw you and got me interested and curious. I was at the same time a bit relieved and worried. Relieved because I knew I would be able to better connect with you if you are a Chinese, you know, because of our similar cultural background. Worried because I was still not convinced that a foreign teacher would teach English writing well. Then your slight accent confirmed my hypothesis that you are a "real" Chinese. No offense, but although you spoke fluent English and made the class fun and enjoyable, it still took a little longer for me to be convinced and trust your competence than it would have if you are an American.

Having been immersed in the institutional culture of celebratory diversity for 2 years, Yang still needed to battle against the powerful nonverbal argument one's "face" made. Yet thanks to her ever-sharpening rhetorical sensibility and critical reflective ability, Yang was capable of responsively making a counterargument against the "rhetoric of face" and resisting the discourse around the tie between face and ethos. The counterargument Yang was making was dynamic and constantly strengthening as she collected more evidence through observation and interaction. For example, she soon noticed that the assumed cultural, linguistic, and experiential proximity between herself and me as indicated by the face may not always prove true, as she commented on my grading priority:

> I thought you would value long, complex, and beautiful sentences just as the other English teachers I had did back in China. But it turned out you seemed to value clarity in my writing, because you would always ask me to break up the long sentences.

In addition, Yang also tried to complicate the rhetoric of face by turning attention to the "sameness" as opposed to the mere focus on "difference."

> After I attended your class for a couple of days, I started to become blind to the fact that you are different from an American teacher and instead began to see the similarities between us. You shared in class how you learned English as a second language and the difficulties you had while writing academic papers in an American college. I could definitely relate to those experiences and your sharing them helped me gain confidence. Also, I think having been through those hurdles yourself means you understood what we needed, which I'm not sure a traditional American teacher who only speak English would be able to do.

Yang seems to navigate the cross-cultural and institutional rhetorics cautiously yet strategically. When she needs help with, advice about, or just an escape from the discursive formation under the umbrella title "US college life," Yang would approach the Chinese student organization named WUCSSA (Wabash University Chinese Students and Scholars Association). Unlike Bohan (the protagonist of the next chapter) who expressed concerns over the corporatization of the organization, Yang reflected more positively on her experiences and interactions. During her first year, Yang served as a committee member, working closely with several other members in the public relations division. Their responsibility is to manage the organization's relationships with the university and the external sponsors represented by small businesses or corporations. As a junior member, Yang did not directly participate in correspondence with other stakeholders; rather, she did some of the legwork such as preparing documents.

Although I left the organization before climbing up the ladder because I needed to transfer to Boston, I learned a great deal and received lots of help from the organization. Our public relations team leader would sometimes copy me on her email exchanges with representatives from other organizations or businesses, because I needed to do some follow-up work. And I couldn't help but notice how flexible her communication style—or is it "rhetoric?"—could be when dealing with different people. For example, I remember one time we needed to submit a report to the student organizations office at Wabash, she used very formal and straightforward language in the emails as well as the report itself. But later on when we were communicating with the owner of a local Chinese restaurant, who is also a Chinese, about the upcoming spring festival events, she completely changed the style: writing in Chinese and picking up a respectful and friendly tone. That experience made me realize that although we are in America, we communicate with so many different people for so many different purposes. We can't always use the style we learned in an English academic writing class to deal with different situations. Sometimes we need to use our native language to better connect with people, sometimes we need to use formal English to show seriousness and respect. It all depends on the situation and the people you are communicating with.

Apart from the routine service she was obligated to do as a member of the organization, Yang would also seek out rhetorical escapes away from the "institutionalized lifestyle" designed for college students, usually particularly for domestic students. As Yang recounted, one of the blessings of having a huge community of Chinese students is that she rarely feels isolated or disoriented in a foreign place. In a cross-cultural context, a "rhetorical escape" is an agential decision to temporarily abandon the rhetorical conventions and expectations of the hosting culture. When Yang occasionally feels frustrated about the still unfamiliar unwritten rules of interpersonal or professional communications here in a US college, instead of trying to decode the rules and adapt to them, she would choose to retreat to familiar rhetorical situations where she would more effortlessly speak and be heard with "more attention," in her words. Although Yang seems competent to navigate basic rhetorics assumed in the US college discourses, she admits benefiting from the freedom to fall back on the "sameness" and familiarity away from the "difference" once in a while when needed.

A number of ecological affordances enabled Yang's evolving rhetorical sensibility and cross-cultural rhetorical awareness: her failure in the communication course test-out as well as the reflections prompted by it, her experiences of attending courses taught by instructors representing various linguistic, cultural, ethnic, and racial backgrounds, her own "face" as well as her observations of others' "faces," and her social communities and memberships. Despite that Yang has not yet received formal training in public speaking or systematic rhetorical education by the time the data collection was completed, these ecological affordances that she was inevitably entangled with and actively coconstructing helped her form insights about and eventually navigate the emerging differences given rise to by the institutional structure, linguistic and cultural conventions, expectations, and histories.

Conclusion: Yang's Literacy Affordances

Yang's ecological affordances provide her with cognitive, conceptual, creative, and social resources to shuttle between or merge her literate worlds that are once demarcated by different languages, cultures, artistic and creative histories, rhetorical traditions, and identities. These networked affordances are structural, semiotic, experiential, social, bodily, and material. The structural ones include Yang's independent language study, different institutional configurations in China and the US, and genre conventions for lyric writing. The semiotic ones include Yang's communicative and creative competence in multiple languages (Chinese, English, and Japanese) and her emerging rhetorical sensibility. The experiential ones include writing lyrics, creating music and sharing online, failing the communication course test-out, and attending courses taught by non-native-English-speaking instructors. The social ones include her boyfriend, her involvement in the music-creation community in China and the US and in the Chinese community on campus. The bodily ones include her "face" as well as her understanding of its rhetorical implications. And the material ones include the online music-sharing platform as well as the lyrics she has written. Entangled in these affordances, Yang finds herself constantly in need of negotiating differences in the liminal spaces (Wargo & De Costa, 2017).

In some cases, Yang embraces her perceived differences, for example by writing lyrics in Japanese and sharing her creation in the Chinese community. Sometimes she recognizes differences that constrain as opposed to enable her, for example, her understanding of the term "rhetoric" that failed to help her pass the test-out; other times, she may not see the difference at all or tries to unsee it, for example, the instances of distastefulness and disorderliness in the community of music creation that challenges the structure yet also brings diversity. Regardless, Yang's perceptions, desires, decisions, and deeds are mediated by the communities she—sometimes involuntarily—claims membership of and the social, the institutional structures and systems that she needs to navigate, the material conditions, and also the literate activities she engaged herself in and the products produced as outcomes of the activities. Eventually, despite the sometimes unfavorable social and institutional conditions that deny Chinese international students like Yang full access to educational resources and privileges, she was able to make meaning of the "mess of multilingual experience" (Lorimer Leonard, 2014) and make her differences matter.

5
Bohan

A Cosmopolitan "Robot Master"

A graduate from a rare all-male high school in China, which is also the first all-male school in China, Bohan initially planned to go to a local college in Shanghai to pursue undergraduate studies. Yet, unfortunately, due to the excruciating competitiveness of Gaokao—the college entrance examination in China—Bohan failed to get into the top-notch universities in Shanghai. It's worth noting here that "to fail" may carry a slightly different undertone in the Chinese educational context. The notion of failing in the Chinese educational context, as Bohan explained, may fall anywhere between being second-to-best and being the worst. In his case, his failure was close to the left end of the continuum, meaning that, although not ideal, his examination scores would still qualify him for some of the prestigious universities in Shanghai. Yet he eventually decided that exploring the world and broadening his horizons would be substantially more beneficial to his personal growth than attending a less than ideal college in his hometown.

> I didn't hesitate when I chose to apply for colleges in the States. It's not because it's a trend in China now and a lot of my peers from well-off families study abroad and I have to be one of them; it's not because America provides better education and more resources like the media say. The main

reason that I wanted to come to the States to study is because I wanted to see with my own eyes what the other side of the world is like and equip myself with new ways of thinking. Shanghai is a very modern, international, and diverse city. I met countless foreigners growing up and got to listen to their fascinating stories. But looking at the outside world from within the "wall" [referring to the Great Firewall of China: legislation and technologies enforced by the Chinese government to regulate the domestic Internet activities, including restrictions on foreign sites such as Google and Facebook and heavy censorship on Chinese netizens' online activities], I oftentimes feel suffocated, and lost my ability to detect truth and rumors. So my "failed" attempt to get into a college in China actually helped to reinforce my determination to study abroad.

Upon arriving at Wabash, Bohan chose to dabble in the field of biology and consider the possibility of majoring in it. Two semesters later, after he took only the introductory course in biology, Bohan changed his mind and subsequently changed his major to mechanical engineering. As a self-proclaimed pragmatist, Bohan realized that a major in biology may not immediately and effortlessly guarantee him a well-paying and secure job upon graduating from a master's program, particularly given his immigration status as a noncitizen.

I've consulted my academic advisers, my biology professors, and my Chinese friends in biology who were about to graduate. The impression I got from them is that I should be prepared for 毕业即失业 [starvation upon graduation]. I know this is kind of an exaggeration, but still, I don't want to chance it. I need a job that provides secure funding so that I can explore other parts of the world. Mechanical engineering looks like a safe bet, especially at Wabash. So I did a lot of research on that and finally decided to take on the challenge. Luckily, I'm doing all right now and haven't been kicked out of school yet.

I first met Bohan in the introductory writing course I taught in fall 2016, when he had just set foot in the US and was still settling down in the college town. Unlike Wentao, who was sitting in the same classroom and later became his best friend at Wabash and who was quite active in classroom activities and discussions, Bohan fulfilled the role of a devoted listener and thinker. Occasionally, I would call on him to check his understanding of certain writing concepts or strategies discussed in class. He would almost always utter an insightful response in the most succinct manner. As a writer in my class, Bohan 惜字如金 (treasured every single word/Chinese character as gold), consistent with his public persona as "a man with few words but determination and actions." His philosophy of writing seemed highly aligned with his pragmatism, too, as he insisted that every single word should serve a purpose and make a difference in concrete terms, instead of "wasting" words just to appeal to readers' emotions. He ascribed this philosophy of "expressive austerity" to the generalized "concise English writing style" as he perceived it in comparison to Chinese style in a class paper:

> The main purpose of English writing is expressing your ideas as clearly and concisely as possible, which directly contradicts the Chinese standard of good writing. As a result, I developed a favorable impression for English writing when I was first exposed to it.

With 21 credit hours filling up every corner of his calendar that semester, Bohan learned how to entertain himself outside the classroom by organizing or participating in various activities hosted by a student club called RoboMasters, which gathered students interested in designing robots and developing human-robot interactions. Bohan's active involvement in RoboMasters club was, according to him, a worthwhile investment, as it granted him an opportunity to travel to Shenzhen, China, to compete with his team in a robotics competition, and it allowed him to add yet another important line on his résumé.

Redrawing Cultural Boundaries: Reflecting on Cross-Cultural Experiences

Although Bohan rarely exuded an air of superiority that usually comes with the Generation Z students born in the most open and advanced economic hubs in China—Beijing, Shanghai, Shenzhen, Guangzhou—he did reveal a sense of pride in the easy access he had been enjoying to diverse cultural experiences right outside his home. Shanghai is a particularly representative cultural contact zone in China, as the central and local government has invested myriad financial and political resources to, on the one hand, preserve the cultural legacies of the colonial era and, on the other, promote a neoliberal economic model to attract international trade and investment. Shanghai's colonial history as manifested in the various Western architectural styles on the Bund (Waitan, literally "outer beach") is subtly woven into its contemporary neoliberal culture reflected in the modern and postmodern skyscrapers clustered in the Lujiazui financial and business district. As you take a stroll down the sleepless Nanjing Road in the evening, while being amazed by the well-preserved neon lights, you might all of a sudden find yourself disoriented in an urban concrete jungle where numerous employees at local and international start-up companies are working overtime.

Growing up in such an assemblage of cultural and historical artifacts embodying the conflicts between the West and East and between the old and new, Bohan had the luxury to begin cultivating his rhetorical sensibility to cultural differences at a young age. For example, since he was 7 years old, Bohan has visited different museums on a regular basis, sometimes with the company of his parents, sometimes on his own. In addition to his favorite destination—Shanghai Natural History Museum—Bohan was also a frequent visitor at humanities-oriented ones such as Shanghai Art Museum and Shanghai History Museum.

> I started to go to museums not because of some sort of instrumental reasons, for example, I have to learn something and brag about it to other people. I went there simply because I was always a curious kid. And looking back, I think those experiences really offered me lots of new perspectives and made me more sensitive to different cultures.

Bohan also found his greatest extracurricular cultural classes outside the physical boundaries of concrete walls and in historical sites or sometimes touristic spots. However, his mentors and tutors were not historical artifacts anymore in these open-house classes; rather, they were visitors and tourists from all over the world that were caught up in the spatiotemporal ecology with Bohan. As reserved as he was, Bohan would approach them and initiate a casual conversation with basic English words and phrases he learned in middle school, and he would always be ready to provide guidance whenever visitors and tourists sought assistance.

> Friends who know me well wouldn't believe that I used to do that. Sometimes I can't even believe that I used to be so brave. But that was me indeed! Back then, the only way for me to learn about the 'outside world' was through reading other Chinese tourists' blog posts about their experiences abroad. Although there were quite a few excellent writers who told their stories in such vivid ways, I still felt like I was 抽二手烟 [inhaling second-hand cigarette smoke]. I always felt even more tempted to actually experience their experiences to find out if it's true or not. But of course, I was in school and didn't get to travel abroad a lot. So I made up my mind to seize the opportunity to learn from people who were from the 'outside world.' It was not easy, obviously, because I struggled with English back then. But most of the people I talked to were friendly and patient. So we tried different strategies to make meaning and it all worked out.

This "proxy cultural experience" certainly did not suffice to instill a full understanding of the notion of culture in the then teenage student, let alone initiate a lifelong research project on culture, yet it planted a seed in Bohan's mind that would later grow into a rhetorical sensibility to cultural differences or a heuristic to approach differences at large.

The rhetorical sensibility to cultural differences that Bohan had been, purposefully or unconsciously, cultivating came to be textually articulated during the fall 2018 semester, when he enrolled in a one-credit course titled Mentored Intercultural Communication Experience, which was jointly offered by the Department of Communication and Wabash's Center for Intercultural Learning (CIL).[1] Affiliated with the Office of International Programs, CIL was established in response to the increasing cultural diversity on Wabash's campus, and set out to promote and facilitate intercultural learning; foster inclusion and community; and cultivate knowledge, skills, and attitude of intercultural competence. The course that CIL offered through the Department of Communication was designed to fulfill the mission of cultivating intercultural competence. Yet despite its well-intentioned course goals, CIL's interpretation of "intercultural competence" is nonetheless aligned with the university's institutional discourse of cultural diversity that views diversity as simultaneously capital and issue. This is because although the course was aimed at developing intercultural competence, its "inter-" is unidirectional and implies an assimilationist undertone, as the course was only open to international students as opposed to welcoming the entire student body, domestic and international alike. Students enrolled in this course would complete a series of readings and reflective responses while working with a learning mentor to receive personalized feedback.

Although Bohan seemed generally content with the way the course was set up, he was somewhat skeptical about the purported course objectives.

> At first, I was happy that Wabash offered such as course that perfectly clicked with my ambition: to be a global citizen. I always have observations and ideas, and I want to systematically learn how to express my thoughts. Also, if I get an internship or job here in the U.S., I'm definitely going to work with people from different cultures. I need to learn some skills to get ready for that. And it's only one credit hour, so it wouldn't take up a lot of my time that I should spend studying my major. But as soon as I started taking the course, I realized that all of my classmates were international students, just like me, and none of us were American except the teacher and mentor. Isn't it a bit weird that they claim to teach "intercultural skills"

yet they don't expect American students to learn what it means to communicate and work with people from other cultures? Instead, they only teach us international students how to do that, as if we know less and we are less tolerant of other cultures.

Despite his skepticism, Bohan didn't intend to question further, and he quickly settled down, since his pragmatic orientation soon helped him turn this course into a useful professional-development course.

Just as Bohan began showing skepticism toward the purpose of the course, his then pragmatic and reductive understanding of cultural differences intervened. This pragmatic and reductive understanding of cultural differences were manifested in his first paper assignment written in August 2018, in which Bohan set a few concrete objectives and composed an "intercultural autobiography." For example, the objectives that Bohan laid out were based on a generalization of what he took to be representations of cultural differences.

1. To learn more about another culture and language other than English
   -I am taking Japanese level 3 and I hope I can get a better understanding of the culture and language.
   -Attend the scheduled Japanese movie nights and participate in the discussion with instructors.
2. To build a deeper relationship with people who are from another culture
   -Wabash has a really diversified student body and I have meet great friends. I hope I can foster a closer bond with at least one of them.
   -Try to start conversations with various kinds of people and be more proactive.
3. To be involved with activities in this course
   -Go to culture centers and attend events held there.
   -Participate in all of the events and take advantage of the resources offered in the class.
4. To read more
   -I have not finished a whole book for a while and I hope I can read more books in English this semester.
   -Spear [sic] time everyday from my commute and lunch break into reading.

In addition to these short-term objectives, Bohan also stated his ambitious long-term plan:

As people from different backgrounds are brought more and more together than ever, I see that in the future workforce, people with multi-culture experiences will be in a big demand. In this class, I hope to learn more about culture adaptation and awareness, as well as push myself to be more active in interacting with people from other cultures.

As his initial attempt at translating his perceptions of culture into words shows, Bohan viewed the notion of culture as reified in substances, if not products, associated with particular nation-states, such as language, movies, relationships with people representing a certain culture, events, and books written in a certain language. In other words, Bohan still needed to discuss the notion of culture in concrete terms and conceive, validate, and value it as structural, semiotic, social, and material forms.

Just as I was about to rush into the conclusion that Bohan's cultural awareness was still evolving and was yet to move beyond the representational dimension, Bohan sent the assignment prompt to me. As the first assignment of the course, the prompt was written in quite an inviting tone. Yet it was also fairly vague and lacked an articulated scaffolding in terms of the types of objectives expected.

> I didn't know what "culture" meant in the context of this course yet, and had to make up some objectives. So I had to think hard and pull everything that I thought was related to culture together, you know, language, movies, getting to know foreign people, and participating in their events. These are the things I used to do when I was in middle school and high school,

Bohan explained during a later interview session. The reductive view of culture at this point, then, cannot be solely ascribed to Bohan's lack of critical understanding of the situatedness, complexity, and contingency of culture, but was also partly attributed to the lack of meaningful structural affordances supposedly embedded in the pedagogical materials.

A month later, the weekly topic of the course turned to stereotypes and openness. Bohan and his classmates were assigned to read a chapter on stereotypes in the textbook *Maximizing Study Abroad: A Students' Guide to Strategies for Language and Culture Learning and Use* by Paige et al. (2002) and also some related articles, respond to the readings in writing, and interview a friend from a different culture than his about the topic of stereotyping. The reading responses Bohan presented to me contained two short paragraphs:

> It is interesting to read how people perform different when they are told about a cultural stereotype. From my experience with exams, I definitely think that thinking you can nail an exam helps improving the performance.

> People get anxious and therefore think more when they are told that they are naturally inferior.
>
> The second article talked about an American who was assumed to be better off. It also talked about the concept of forming a generalization and hypothesis. I sometimes get that too. People I know from China or here thinks that I come from a rich family. In fact, my family is not wealthy and I have the opportunity to live and study here because my parents value education.

Apparently, Bohan was barely scratching the surface of the notion of cultural stereotyping in this brief response. The readings prompted him to reflect upon his own experience of falling victim to the stereotypes about his family's wealth. Yet Bohan did not fully unpack this personal account to reach a more profound understanding of the causes and ramifications of cultural stereotyping.

> I had a lot to say about cultural stereotypes, actually. But I ended up only writing about the superficial stuff because I did not believe writing about it will really change how people think about stereotypes. I've read a lot of news about hateful people doing harmful things to others just because they happened to come from the same culture as those who did bad things before or simply didn't share the same value. For example, there was news about Americans discriminating against Muslims, and news about Americans calling Chinese people names and yelling at them "Go back to China!" What can we *really* do about it? Writing papers about it? I don't think it's enough.

In some sense, Bohan was protesting a stereotyped interpretation of stereotyping and demonstrating his cynicism through rhetorical "absence"—making a strong case by dodging the main argument and allowing it to emerge through the rhetorical exigency within which an audience is involved.

As Bohan continued in the reading responses, he maintained his minimalist rhetorical style and briefly touched upon the informal interview he conducted on this topic. The friend he interviewed was a second-generation Indian American.

> I asked how he thinks about Chinese international students on campus. He did find that Chinese students always stick together as a group. However, he also pointed out that you can also see groups of Americans anywhere but no one is saying anything about that.

Bohan's friend highlighted the stereotype associated with Chinese international students' social grouping, claiming that they tended to form close-knit small groups of the same members when participating in different social activities. Instantly, his friend attempted to defend the legitimacy of this social grouping by putting the dominant community under scrutiny and expressed his skepticism. What may potentially complicate the case is the fact that Bohan and I could not readily assume that the friend invoked the contrast of an American as someone from the dominant community or from a peripheral community, given his immigration status and ethnicity.

> I've known him for a while as we have been taking a few classes together in ME [mechanical engineering]. But still, we are not like really close friends. He hangs out with his American friends and I, like he described, hang out with my Chinese friends for the most part. I invited him to our Chinese social before, and he did join us. But it was sort of awkward, because all he could do was observing us talking in Chinese and occasionally jumping in and asking us about superficial cultural differences, like "do you guys like rice better or noodles better?" Maybe this is why he thought we were always stuck together? But he has a point though. We do tend to stay in our comfortable zones and speak the language that doesn't cost us a lot of energy. We do it, and Americans do it as well. But we are more noticeable just because we are the minority here? Or is it because *we* are *supposed* to mingle with the dominant group but not the other way around? We did open ourselves and let him join us, but for some reason we weren't able to move beyond the basic cultural differences topics.

Here again, Bohan deployed strategic rhetorical absence to tacitly critique the reductive view of the notion of cultural stereotyping, particularly as interpreted by his friend who was viewed to be from the dominant culture in this context. Had we not created the space for negotiation and expansion beyond the text, or had the exigency not allowed the fuller account to emerge, Bohan would not have had the opportunity and motive to share his unaffected and rational stance on this issue and offer his careful observation. Bohan's critical approach to the essentialized collective understanding of cultural stereotyping was supported by and entangled with his past experiences of interacting with people from a variety of cultural backgrounds. Granted, his conversations with them may not have gone beyond basic discussions of cultural norms, if not giving simple directions. Yet the consistent exposure over years and his active reflection on those interactions had turned those experiences into rhetorically meaningful affordance.

Outside of the intercultural communication course, Bohan is a self-proclaimed global citizen. Without the geographical limitation of his hometown, he is now able to travel around the world and experience diverse cultural conventions with the generous financial support from his family. During summer 2018, Bohan participated in a study abroad program in Tokyo, Japan. He took Japanese classes as well as mechanical engineering classes with local professors, attended project-oriented workshops, observed a tea ceremony, attempted meditation at a shrine, and interacted on a daily basis with local Japanese students. Bohan also tries to maximize the value of every holiday break during the semesters by traveling to new places and experiencing different local cultures. It has been his signature means of publicly reflecting on his trips within his social circle by, at the end of the trips, posting a Twitter-length message along with several pictures taken during the trips on his WeChat wall. For example, he traveled to New York City and Miami, respectively, in September and during the Thanksgiving break and posted the following social media statuses. The caption of the first status reads "坐在球场的边上看的美网。迷失在法拉盛的中餐馆之中。" ("Watching the US Open [tennis] from afar in the back row, and losing myself in Chinese restaurants in Flushing"). The caption of the second status reads "大西洋的日出 和墨西哥湾的日落。还有两周四个考试的恐惧。" ("Sunrise over the Atlantic Ocean and sunset over the Gulf of Mexico. Plus the fear of four exams in two weeks").

His social media posts about traveling experiences are characteristically succinct, yet uncharacteristically poetic in the sense that they weave his affect into them and juxtapose activities or feelings that emerged in different geographical spaces.

> One WeChat post per trip is my only way of announcing to my friends that I had some new experiences, because I travel to experience different cultures and gain new perspectives, unlike a lot of Chinese students who travel just to take pictures and show them off on social media. I admit that I'm not like an anthropologist who stays in one foreign place for years and years and studies how local people live and think and what they believe and value. But I like observing people wherever I visit, and I like participating in their local events to physically experience what they experience as a group. Well, I guess the US Open is not just a local event. But you get the sense. I think that's the ultimate way of learning a culture. You just can't confidently claim that you developed your intercultural competence by reading a couple of book chapters or interviewing a couple of people. And I don't think reading about kimchi and Korea helps me to move beyond stereotypes.

Bohan, in a caustic and sarcastic tone, vented his discontent with the way in which the course curriculum seemed to perpetuate stereotypes as opposed to offering students a heuristic to critically and strategically resist it. Yet Bohan performed rhetorical absence through his literate activities such as responding to the course readings and posting social media statuses, as if he was attempting to muffle the noise with silence. Bohan's pragmatic approach to written communication, if not communication in general, also played a role here, as his rhetorical absence might be partly attributed to his indifference. The belief that his class response paper may never reach an audience beyond his instructor discouraged him from engaging with the public discourse and voicing his concerns regarding how cultures were represented and interpreted.

Bohan's willingness to learn from, make meaning of, and make peace with divergent cultural norms in different geographical spaces helped to cultivate in him a cosmopolitan sensibility to how cultural terms are defined and interpreted from different belief and value systems. The cosmopolitan sensibility that Bohan developed within his transnational affordance enabled him to critically examine the rhetorical exigency in which culture is defined in stultifying categorical terms and allowed him to engage in culturally conditioned literate activities with his own idiosyncratic rhetorical style. Although Bohan recognized differences exhibited in the ways people see, hear, think, write, live, and ultimately believe and value, he did not dwell on the perceived differences; rather, he viewed them as dynamic and always in flux. Admittedly, Bohan is yet to enrich his repertoire to contribute his latent cosmopolitan ideas more effectively to the public discourse; he has already carved out the space for negotiation through social media presence. The structural (routine of visiting cultural sites, study abroad program, course syllabus, assignment prompts, etc.), semiotic (multilingual competence, rhetorical absence, multimodal composing on social media, etc.), experiential (interactions with people from diverse cultures), social (bonds with the Chinese community on campus and relationships with diverse groups), bodily (his appearance of a somewhat nerdy Asian student), and material (financial support from his family for him to travel) affordance is networked and entangled to shape his understanding of his own differences and differences in general and mediate his rhetorical practices in relation to the notion of difference.

Redefining Disciplinary Identity through Writing to Learn

Despite the fact that Bohan seems to tacitly wave his anti-essentialist sword at the university's pragmatic curriculum on intercultural communication, deep down, he is aware of his hardcore pragmatist's philosophy. His pragmatism is situated and easily finds manifestation in his work and literate activities in his major studies—mechanical engineering. His disciplinary community, as materialized in course lectures, collaborative lab experiments, and collaborative lab report writing, among others, happens to be the discursive space that he spends the majority of his time in. It's tempting and somewhat safe to speculate that Bohan's disciplinary identity is deeply caught up and entrenched in the assemblage of people, structures, relationships, and materials in the mechanical engineering community at Wabash University.

As a mechanical engineering student newly transferred from the natural science field of biology, Bohan seemed to have found his niche and appeared to be much more motivated. "I enjoy making things rather than remembering texts. And I enjoy the feeling of creating something new rather than knowing something other people have found." However, what Bohan was not able to foresee when he was peeking through the door of mechanical engineering was the countless hours he had to spend in the lab conducting experiments and writing up lab reports. For example, in fall 2018 when I began systematically tracing Bohan's literate activities, he enrolled in three required courses in mechanical engineering: an upper-level ME course titled Designing Prototyping, Basic Mechanics, and Electronic Measurement Techniques. Among the three registered courses, Electronic Measurement Techniques explicitly required that students develop their measurement and modeling skills through a variety of laboratory experiments. As the fall 2018 syllabus pointed out, the course may be conceived as the laboratory of the co-requisite lecture course, and students were expected to design, build, and test various circuits and "maintain a laboratory notes and create professional experiment reporting." "It's a ton of work. We basically need to submit a lab report every week from now on. And it seems there's no way around writing after all." Bohan couldn't conceal his frustration.

> Of course, it wasn't the main reason that I choose mechanical engineering, but I thought I could finally get away from writing papers. But now I started to understand why ENGL 106 is a required undergrad course—you never escape writing, even in engineering.

As a matter of fact, Bohan made a confession in 2016 in the literacy autobiography he wrote in my ENGL 106 Introductory Writing for International Students, which he interestingly titled "12 Years a Writer," echoing Steve McQueen's 2013 Oscar-winning film *12 Years a Slave*.

> I used to procrastinate when faced with an essay. Honestly, I do like writing. I enjoy expressing my feelings or describing to my friends the amazing taste of the dinner I had with 140 or fewer characters. I would describe myself as a bit introverted and consequently prefer to share my opinion in text rather than verbally. However, if it was an academic paper that I was about to write, I would not do it until the last few hours. The instant gratification monkey, who resides in a procrastinator's mind and tells him/her to "seize the day," would take control and make me do anything else other than what I was supposed to do. Of course I felt guilty, dreadful and anxious, I just did not feel motivated. I have heard fun facts about Balzac that allegedly he drank 50 cups of coffee a day when writing. I, as well, need impetus to write. To me, the ticking of the clock was my drive to an essay.

With the endorsement of Honoré de Balzac, whose "fun fact" was invoked in this confession of a procrastinating writer, Bohan attempted to rationalize his lackadaisical approach to writing "academic papers" while trying to reconcile the tension here by claiming that he enjoyed expressing feelings through writing shorter pieces. To Bohan, writing academically was a dreadful, if not excruciating, task that he had to get over with and that he had better downplay to prioritize other tasks. The activity of writing was also entangled with affect: Bohan's emotions and feelings gave rise to his desire to express through writing and also react to his expressive writing. Without getting emotionally charged about a certain rhetorical exigency, Bohan would find writing unnecessary and painful. Obviously, academic writing or, more narrowly, writing tasks assigned in courses in which Bohan did not expect writing components would not easily affectively engage him. The parodied title that alludes to slavery tellingly shows Bohan's self-mockery as a demotivated writer caught up in the academy where writing is mandatory.

Yet just as Bohan rightfully complained, writing haunted him wherever he went. Although the genre conventions required to complete the writing tasks became more static in his major studies, the rhetorical situations less complicated, and the quantity much less, Bohan still needed to go through the emotional ordeal before settling down to write. Thankfully, the course syllabus provided clear scaffolding and instructions in terms of what the genre of lab report entailed and what the expectations were for the particular course.

For example, the fall 2018 syllabus of ECE 20700 laid out the components and structures of the lab notes:

1. What are you doing (Objective)
2. How are you doing it (Procedure)
3. What are the facts (Results)
4. What can we take away from this experiment (Conclusions)
5. What is a summary of what was done? (Abstract)

As straightforward as it seemed, the instruction did not go beyond the components and structures to provide additional support in terms of the tone and style of the report, its intended audience, and the general purpose. Bohan and his classmates were left in the dark, striving to decipher the disciplinary genre code by studying a sample report offered by the instructor.

> We've all read reports of some sort, and to me, they mostly look very dull but clear, are written in simple plain language, and are very formal. And thanks to the syllabus and the sample report, I know what to write about at least, but the most difficult part is how to actually explain the procedures and results in accurate yet simple English. I can describe what I did in plain Chinese without any problem; but there seems to be a set of English words that I have to use to cue my readers that I'm studying the same major, otherwise the readers would simply not get it. For example, if I describe the tool we use to do experiments, I'd simply say 工具 [tools], not "instruments." I need more exposure to the vocabulary of my major to write these reports.

Bohan expressed frustration at his lack of disciplinary genre practice and, at the same time, excitement at successfully orienting himself in a new rhetorical and disciplinary playground.

The first lab report was due the second week of the new semester. To complete the report, Bohan needed to conduct a series of experiments in the lab collaboratively with his lab partner, record the procedures and results, and analyze the results and write up the report individually. He didn't think twice before choosing his lab partner that he would collaborate with for the remaining semester: another international student from China.

> I know having an American partner would save me a lot of time when it comes to writing, because, you know, they naturally know how to write reports using more accurate words. But the thing is, for this lab course, we collaborate on experiments, not on writing! We still need to write our own reports. So working with a Chinese partner actually makes it much easier and more

efficient, because we can communicate in Chinese during the experiments. Plus, I got the impression that American students can be sloppy sometimes. They tend to procrastinate and postpone everything till the deadline.

Bohan successfully submitted his first lab report an hour prior to the deadline during the second week of class. It is an eleven-page document saturated with texts, tables of results, figures of circuits and coordinate systems, and screenshots of computer program codes. To complete this document, Bohan spent approximately 15 hours of the previous week on it. Working with his lab partner was a fairly pleasant experience, not only because they were able to communicate efficiently and accurately about the procedures described in the manual and solve problems quickly whenever they arose, but also because they developed an efficient labor-distribution system: Bohan's partner was responsible for writing the software codes, whereas Bohan himself read and interpreted the manual while executing the procedures.

> I would say for the most part our first collaboration on the experiment was a success. But my partner is not a very detail-oriented person, so he made quite a few mistakes in his coding, which slowed down our process. I call myself a perfectionist, and I don't allow any mistakes. I'm glad that we worked out the problems in time and recorded all the results that we would use to write our individual reports. Actually, I was relieved that we write our individual reports in this class instead of writing together. Writing together sounds like it could save you a lot of time, but my previous experiences taught me that there always will be issues and conflicts.

In addition to the 3 hours spent in the lab conducting the experiment, Bohan pulled two all-nighters in response to the imminent deadline.

> I was on the verge of giving it up when I realized I had two days left. I never thought I'd freak out about a paper. I wrote five big papers in your writing class, and I didn't feel overwhelmed like this. I knew I sort of procrastinated again this time, but I just didn't know where to start.

Bohan recounted the moment he finally decided to sit down and begin drafting: after revisiting the sample lab report and the instructions provided on the syllabus, he typed up the headings for the four small tasks, and then listed the four sections under each task: objective, procedures, results, and conclusion.

> Some of my friends told me they write from the beginning to the end. But I happen to like putting down everything I can think of at the moment and worry about everything else that's still somewhere in my head later.

FIGURE 5.1. Bohan's writing's room.

Once Bohan outlined the entire report by putting down the section headings, he began to fill in the information collected during the experiments. The sample lab report was open and placed on the right-hand side of his laptop screen, the software used to analyze data on the left, whereas his own outlined draft was in the middle. The objective and procedure sections did not seem to allow much rhetorical flexibility since Bohan simply copied the sentence structure from the corresponding section in the sample report and plugged in the correct information:

> Objective: Task 1 involves setting the DC supply to various outputs to energize a circuit. As the first task in ECE 207, its purpose is to familiarize students with the Power Supply Unit. Purpose: To get output from the Power Supply Unit, one must first choose between the 6 and 25 v maximum supply. DMM and VOM were used to measure the voltages.

Bohan explained his rationale:

> I played it safe. I have to say I'm not a big fan of this type of formulaic report. But I also admit that they simply work. Since I'm not so familiar yet with this genre and some of the vocabulary that people use in this field, I'd better learn by mimicking.

The results section was not as straightforward, as Bohan soon realized. Given the different orientations of the assigned experiments, what should be included in the results may be drastically different across tasks: some may include bullet points of observations in support of a hypothesis or established theory, some may include tables of measurements shown in numbers, and some may also include graphs displaying the relationship between current and voltage or images of the tested circuits. Bohan had to rely on his own judgment to discern what particular results were meaningful to certain experiments according to the objectives and deliver the results in a concise and clear manner. Although the sample report was not of much help here, Bohan did manage to borrow a few syntactic structures to shorten his statements so that they would appear more succinct. For example, Bohan stated one of the results in the following manner: "When not connected, the resistance is measured be [sic] 17.08 Ω." He explained,

> Initially, I wrote 'when the circuit is not connected.' Then I checked out the sample report, and found that the subject in a similar sentence was simply removed and the sentence still made sense to me. So I thought it must be acceptable in lab reports, so I copied it in my report.

In another instance, Bohan's experiment results were in accordance with Ohm's law.

> If not for the sample report, I would have written something like "The results of the experiment proved Ohm's Law." Just as I was about to make that statement, I skimmed through some of the results shown in the sample, and learned a very simple way of conveying the same message, which is something "still holds true." How brilliant and clean this is! So I cleaned up the messy sentence in my head and wrote "Ohm's Law still holds true." Cool, right?

Bohan was content with his rhetorical move.

Not until Bohan completed the write-up of the four experiments he conducted during the first lab session did he shift his attention back to the abstract at the beginning of the report. As he learned from the course instructor's brief introduction to lab reports, an abstract serves as a summary of the major arguments or points made in the main text. "It sounds so easy, right? But it turned out to be more complicated than it's supposed to be, because I wrote quite a lot in the report, and I didn't know which part should be highlighted." Baffled by the genre of an abstract, Bohan immediately decided to consult Google. The first search page showing the results of the entry "abstract" directed him to the writing center at the University of North Carolina at Chapel Hill. This writing center page offered introductions to abstracts and tips on writing abstracts. Bohan quickly scrolled down, skipped the sections on the definition of abstracts, and focused on the section titled "All Abstracts Include." Bohan reflected on his use of this online resource,

After reading this section, I realized that the audience of this page may not be exclusive to people in mechanical engineering, and certainly not limited to people like me who write lab reports. But when I looked further down, I found the strategy the page introduced to be helpful, which is called "cut and paste." I just needed to cut and paste some key sentences from the body text to start with.

To implement the strategy, Bohan selected the objective and the conclusion from each experiment task, and copied and pasted them in a blank page, which resulted in a single-spaced page of text.

Then what I did was . . . I tried to get rid of some of the modifiers and only keep the meaningful words, and changed the verb tense to past tense, since I finished all the experiments already, and also, I made sure to turn every sentence into passive voice.

Abstract

In this report, experiments done in the laboratory was documented and explained. A Power Supply Unit was used to energize a circuit which was analyzed with the help of VOM and DMM measurements via SCPI. The relationship between current and voltage was determined with calculation as well as MATLAB plots. Measurements were taken by naked eye as well as SCPI commands. Clearly, the advantage of recording the numbers with digital instruments is that it gives a more accurate value. With the analysis, it was found that the current and voltage are linearly related. In addition, it was determined that the resistance of an LDR increases if it is put in a darker environment.

The evidence of Bohan forcefully piecing together sentences from each experiment is salient, as the abstract lacks logical transitions and appears to be a simple juxtaposition of the description of each experiment and their results. Yet on the other hand, Bohan indeed managed to provide a concise overview of the lab session and the results yielded within around 100 words, fulfilling the instructor's requirements. In Bohan's words, "It got the job done. That's what matters." Despite the pragmatic approach to completing the lab report in time, Bohan did attend to a defining disciplinary writing convention pertaining to engineering fields: the absence of personal pronouns and the strategic deployment of, if not reliance on, passive voice. Each individual sentence in the abstract took on a passive voice, some even affectedly so, rendering the actors who conducted the experiments utterly invisible.

Our instructor explicitly told us to not use first person pronouns in our lab reports, because the experiment itself is more important—what has been done and what happens—but who did it or does it doesn't matter. This is how we maintain objectivity. And he said it's a convention that everybody conforms to in mechanical engineering. It's true. All the materials we read in class were written in passive voice. So if that's what our instructor wants, there's no reason I don't give it to him. He's been in the field for a long time, so I trust him and I believe his experiences will lead us to becoming a true member of the field.

Although Bohan's pragmatism drove him to be compliant with the rules and conventions in an attempt to maximize efficiency, he was not completely uncritical about it. To him, passive voice may sometimes be unnecessary and redundant and sometimes even unclear and confusing.

> When I first started reading the sample lab reports as well as some journal articles in my classes, I felt awkward, to be honest. I remember we had a discussion in your first-year writing class that when we don't know who the doer is, we can use passive voice. Passive voice also takes more cognitive effort to process. One or two sentences in passive voice is fine, but reading a paragraph full of passive voice makes me uncomfortable at first, especially when we know who did those things. It's like we are intentionally hiding them. I found it especially weird when I had to report the results in passive voice, for example, I wrote in the abstract "it was found that the current and voltage are linearly related." It sounds like some invisible superpower found the results. And sometimes who found the results might make a difference. For example, sometimes my lab partner disagrees with me on the results. And we ended up reporting our own different results. Plus, I used to believe that Americans value individualism and always make sure to take credit for things they do. So I don't understand why they pretend when they write lab reports.

The first lab report writing experience paved the way for the ensuing ones. Bohan had not only internalized the genre conventions of lab reports, such as the structure and rhetorical style, but also created his idiosyncratic toolkit that helped him strategize report writing. The second lab report took Bohan significantly less time to complete. However, the quickly produced lab reports look as if they were coming off the same assembly line, exhibiting the same rhetorical moves, opening, transitions, and closing. The only visible differences are the numbers in the results sections, objectives and procedures, and instruments used. Bohan also acknowledged he was more at ease when using the reoccurring "academic discourse markers," such as "measure," "document," "investigate," "hold true," among others.

> If I didn't learn how to properly write lab reports, I wouldn't have used these terms. I'd probably use words like calculate, record, examine, proves to be true. These terms are not wrong in the context, but they are just . . . a bit imprecise.

Bohan also noted that the instructor would encourage him to visit the writing center and have his reports proofread during the first several weeks. After two rounds of tutoring sessions, Bohan fine-tuned his report template by addressing issues such as dangling modifiers and the confusing use of the pronoun "it" that frequently appeared in his reports. Eventually, after about a month and half, Bohan was confident enough to claim that he had become a report master.

Upon reflection, Bohan seemed to have made peace with the formulaic and constraining genre of lab reports and recognized how the typified ways of responding to recurring social constructions (Miller, 1984) facilitated his transition from a disciplinary outsider to a disciplinary apprentice.

> I still don't really like writing lab reports, but I feel like I have learned a lot of useful stuff by following the procedures and sticking to the rules. For example, the way reports are organized helped me to develop a 清晰的思路 [effective heuristic] to conduct the experiments and share the results. If I hadn't written reports by following this recipe, or even if I only wrote one or two, I might have done a good job reporting on the one or two experiments, but I probably wouldn't have been able to go out there and do experiments on my own, not to mention designing experiments. Also, I'm now more sensitive to the subtle differences between the words we use in speaking and those used in writing reports. When I see those words again in our readings, I can immediately relate it to the reports I've written. So I think to some extent writing lab reports helped me to get to know the field of engineering better, and I feel I belong to the community now. Speaking or writing perfect English? It doesn't really matter to me. I can do just as well as my American classmates.

A critical thinker and yet a pragmatist, Bohan was critically aware of his limited resources as a disciplinary outsider attempting to write his way into the community as well as the affordances and constraints of the disciplinary culture, yet he was also cognizant of the rhetorical exigency—what needed to be done at the moment, and what would land him the place he desired to be—and acted accordingly. The ecology of conducting lab experiments and writing reports afforded Bohan the structures (the course syllabus, procedures, sample lab report), social connections (instructor and lab partner), materials (experiment instruments, Internet search engine, computer software), semiosis (discourse markers, circuit graphs), and experiences (conducting experiments and writing in different genres) that he needed to complete the lab report assignments and, more importantly, mark the construction of his emerging and evolving disciplinary identity. The assemblage of interconnected affordances enabled Bohan to cultivate a rhetorical sensibility to the conventions of composing lab reports in his disciplinary field—despite the fact that he was not immediately convinced of the value of the conventions—and develop structure- and tool-mediated strategies to become adept at composing in this particular genre. Through this literate activity, Bohan marked his differences in language and disciplinarity and redefined them through gaining disciplinary cultural capital.

Re-selfing in Social Spaces: A RoboMaster Dwelling "outside" the Chinese Community

Shuttling between courses that seamlessly occupied his entire calendar from 8:00 a.m. to 5:00 p.m., Monday through Friday, Bohan managed to venture out into quite distinct social spaces to claim his multiple selves. These spaces are not restricted to physical ones, such as a course professor's office, Chinese friends' dinner table, RoboMasters student club, and classrooms; they also include digital spaces, such as the instant messaging/social media smartphone application WeChat and the comment sections of viral articles. These physical and virtual spaces present distinct boundaries and material affordances yet are also entangled and networked and ultimately condition Bohan's literate activities. Known as a man of few words, Bohan was, contrary to his title, quite socially active and well-recognized across multiple communities. As he confidently and thoughtfully justified the seeming contradiction,

> I know I'm sort of shy and quiet, but that doesn't mean I can't mingle with people. I believe it's a myth that you have to be vocal to be social. Whether or not your words and actions are meaningful is what ultimately determines your value in your community.

As Bohan traverses and dwells in multiple socioacademic communities, his perception of what it means to be himself as well as what he could potentially accomplish underwent constant shifts. In response to his ambivalent identity, Bohan consciously adopts and recontextualizes the rhetorical analysis strategies we explored together in the first-year writing course 2 years ago to deconstruct his social communities and rhetorical exigencies in order to craft personas that would help to maximize his desired gains. In other words, Bohan needs to re-self as he moves in, out of, and across different social spaces. Although he has, through trial and error, become quite adept at shuttling between community discourses, there were inevitable moments of disruption and uncertainty, some of which may cost him his membership yet afford him new solidarity.

The social community Bohan devoted the majority of his free time to building ties with and maintaining membership in is the student organization RoboMasters—a term adopted from the annual DJI (a technological company based in Shenzhen, China) robotics competition to refer to robot enthusiasts who are also capable of designing and assembling robots to serve different purposes. Bohan was among the few initially recruited undergraduate student members. When he heard about this opportunity to be involved from his course professor, Bohan jumped on board without much hesitation.

> I can't think of a better opportunity than this. I get to be part of a community where everybody does things that I'm interested in and may lead me to a better future, because, you know, RoboMasters is like a playground where I can apply what I learn in the mechanical engineering classrooms directly to making something new and fun, for example, robot dogs that can walk. This would make a great résumé line as well.

Bohan also noted that the founders of RoboMasters were a group of graduate students and mechanical engineering professors, all of whom came from China. "Naturally I felt a sense of belonging, not only because we study similar subjects but also because we speak the same language," Bohan explained.

The organization is structured around a series of creative collaborative projects, which entail the design, modification, and maintenance of a robot fleet and other managerial and promotional activities related to these projects, such as recruitment, advertising, sponsorship, and publication. Their collective goal is to represent Wabash's effort in the DJI competition—an annually held robotics competition in Shenzhen, China. The team grew substantially larger within a short period of time, currently proudly marketing themselves as a cross-disciplinary team of around 80 members from six different countries. Although Bohan was cognizant of the material benefits that his involvement in the organization would bring him, such as accumulating teamwork experiences, learning through hands-on practices, and having opportunities to travel to China and compete with other experienced designers and operators, he began to feel somewhat unimportant—or, worse yet, irrelevant—among organization members, especially during organizational decision making.

> The organization was founded by grad students, so they are the people who ultimately decided where the organization is headed. Plus, we have a few faculty consultants who can provide advice when we need it. I'm on the mechanical team, which is one of the six teams. And everybody is so talented and competitive. I sometimes feel the peer pressure, because what I do could be easily covered by any undergraduate student in mechanical engineering. Although they wouldn't seriously kick me out, but I wish I had some expertise that could make me stand out or at least irreplaceable.

As the organization continued to grow in size and transition into a student-led enterprise, club members needed to rethink the division of labor to maintain its sustainability and efficiency. The club members were reorganized into six designated groups based on each individual's interests and expertise. Bohan volunteered to join the team with the most members, the mechanical team, which focuses on designing, prototyping, and manufacturing robots used in the competition. The team of over 30 members provides Bohan with various opportunities to collaborate with friends and classmates who are equally passionate about designing functional robots. As novice practitioner in the field of mechanical engineering, Bohan benefits a great deal from this collaboration and apprenticeship. However, just as he reflected on his experiences collaborating with the gigantic team, Bohan constantly feels the pressure to justify his knowledge, expertise, or simply usefulness, not because he needs to do so to maintain his membership but because he desires recognition from his peers.

> Learning how to build robots is really really fun. And I became more humble knowing that there's so much out there to learn. I have also made some good friends who have helped me a lot in designing CAD and writing codes. The best thing is most of my team members are Chinese, and we can speak Chinese most of the time, which makes communication so much more efficient than having to speak English. And we sometimes grab late night snacks together after we finish a big task. But still, because I'm usually quiet when I focus on my work, so I tend to give my teammates the impression that I'm not approachable, and not willing to share my ideas. And that's not the type of person I want my teammates to think of me, because I tend to be neglected that way.

Having realized that it would be rather difficult to transform his personality overnight, Bohan made a strategic decision to assume the role of a boundary-crosser and simultaneously a bridge-builder by serving as the team liaison and being responsible for maintaining communication with other teams. For example, Bohan composed and sent weekly emails to the five team leaders reporting on the progress the mechanical team made while requesting updates from the other teams. For the sake of efficiency in communication, Bohan also created a message group on WeChat that included the team leaders. In case of an emergency, WeChat provided a faster means of reaching out to the team leaders responsible for it. He would also sometimes remediate the recruitment advertising materials that other teams prepared and share the information in his social network through WeChat Moments. For instance, during one email exchange with the business team in October 2018, Bohan learned that the team had begun actively recruiting members to share the responsibility of securing sponsorship to compensate for the necessary hardware expenses. Knowing the power of his WeChat network that had helped him to connect with hundreds of people, Bohan personalized the recruitment advertisement and posted it on his WeChat Moments.

Bohan carefully composed the text of the advertisement and inserted three pictures to attract attention. The text, which was composed in Chinese and mixed with English words and which I have translated, reads:

> *Robomasters Business Team* cordially invite the responsible you to contribute your talents and expertise with us. The only credential we are looking for is your excellent interpersonal communication skills and enthusiasm in seeking sponsorship that can turn the foul and rotten into *money*. We provide the most cutting-edge technological platform, communicate and collaborate with robotics teams from top-notch universities around the globe, and talk cheerfully and freely with business tycoons from influential cooperation.

The first picture was taken at the previous year's RoboMasters robotics competition when the Wabash team was competing against another team from a university in Hong Kong. The second picture presents the (almost) entire RoboMasters crew, while the third one shows an organization T-shirt with the major sponsors' logos printed on the back. The text and pictures complement each other to showcase a lively, diverse, and inviting organizational culture and the potential social capital the organization would generate. In merely three compact sentences, Bohan articulated the purpose of the recruitment, required credentials, and the benefits of the membership. Interestingly, Bohan artfully code-meshed an idiom in Chinese, which originally reads "化腐朽为神奇" ("Turn the foul and rotten into the rare and ethereal"),

Robomasters Business Team 诚邀有责任心的你和我们一起贡献你的才华

我们只需要你有良好的人际沟通能力和拉赞助的热情来化腐朽为money

我们提供最前沿的科技平台，和世界各大牛校的机器人队伍交流合作，与各大公司和各类商界大佬谈笑风生

Collapse

1 hour ago

FIGURE 5.2. Bohan's WeChat status.

and modified it as "化腐朽为 money" ("Turn the foul and rotten into *money*"). Using a two-syllable English term, "money," as opposed to its one-syllable Chinese translation "钱" (qián, money) follows the rhythmic convention of a five-syllable Chinese idiom (AABCC) and, meanwhile, shuns the explicit mention of the term "钱" (money), which is often seen as an immoral and distasteful pursuit in Chinese cultural traditions. Bohan reflected on his decision to post this advertisement and the rationale behind his composition:

> The second I knew the business team was recruiting, I thought of helping them to spread the words, because I have many friends on WeChat who study business management and want to work for tech companies in the future. So I thought this may be a good opportunity for them to gain some experience. Because almost all of my WeChat friends are Chinese, I would be thought of as a weird person if I use English to advertise it. But like we just discussed, I particularly used the English term "money" to avoid directly talking about the Chinese term for "money," which sounds so tacky, but ironically, everybody in China always wants more of it. Of course,

helping the business team to get qualified members is the priority here, but I'm also representing the culture of my club through this post, plus, I want my audience to know that I'm not just a novice mechanic in the club, but I'm also someone who cares about the well-being of our club. This is why a lot of thinking went into this post.

Despite the fact that promotional posts in WeChat Moments are usually immediately dismissed, Bohan's recruitment advertisement received over 100 "likes" and dozens of comments requesting additional information. Although it is not clear if anybody from Bohan's social network did apply for the job and successfully became a member, his proactive effort in building cross-disciplinary ties with other teams was recognized and appreciated. By doing so, Bohan further expanded his social network within and outside the RoboMasters community, crafted his ethos as a leader in strengthening intra- and inter-team bonds, and found his niche as an otherwise invisible apprentice in this large organization. More importantly, Bohan's initially utilitarian and somewhat parochial outlook toward community engagement—taking advantage of the resources pertaining to his professional development—also underwent a positive transformation, as he now began to value the vitality of the community that recognized his contribution and afforded him an additional identity.

However, re-selfing in a new social space may sometimes give rise to an ambivalent view of other selves, even when those other selves entail institutionalized identities such as nationality. The Wabash University Chinese Students and Scholars Association (WUCSSA) and Undergraduate Chinese Association (UCA) strive to represent Chinese students and scholars on campus, provide service to meet the needs of Chinese students and scholars, and host regular cultural events to promote Chinese cultural legacies. They are usually the first community in which incoming students from China can claim membership. Bohan was no exception. He had received a great deal of help from the Chinese community in settling down and getting around during the first year and established long-term friendships along the way. The nationality-based, as opposed to interest-based or activity-based, community reinforced Bohan's national identity and meanwhile perpetuated his perception of himself as a cultural outsider.

> It feels like home when you are surrounded by thousands of people who come from the same country. And it gives me a sense of security when I know no matter what I'd go through, there are thousands of others who would understand me and support me. But it's strange that I feel more Chinese

when I'm in a foreign country. They are great resources of course, whenever I need help or just company, they are there in my classrooms and in my phone contacts. But as I dive more deeply into my major studies and get involved in new communities such as RoboMasters, I feel a bit alienated from the Chinese community. What's worse, I started to criticize things they [the Chinese community] do and value that I used to do and value as well.

These things that Bohan frowned upon include some organization members' utilitarian, if not self-serving, desire to hold highly sought-after officer positions just to add a résumé line and feel superior among peers, and the increasingly strengthened bond between the nonprofit student organization and local businesses. To Bohan, the organization almost resembled a corporation and had become a platform to nurture entrepreneurship rather than foster a sense of community and national pride. Due to the impact of the two Chinese organizations in the college town, a number of local small businesses that target Chinese international student customers, such as Chinese restaurants and karaoke rooms, willingly sponsor any cultural events the two organizations promote in exchange for advertisements in the form of recognitions and social media posts. Bohan expressed his concerns with the corporatization of the student organization:

> I know no student organizations can operate without money, and it's better to get external funding than paying out of our pockets. But I think there should be some ethical guidelines, like, you can't excessively advertise on your channel [WeChat public page, etc.]. Speaking of advertisement, the channel used to post useful information, for example, tips for career fairs. But later on, advertisements started to take over, and now basically all the posts are click baits: you think a particular piece of article is useful, but as soon as you start reading, you would realize it's just another piece of 软文 ["soft advertisement," advertorial]. Don't get me wrong, they are still doing meaningful things and providing great resources and service, but I wish they focus more on serving the Chinese community rather than doing business. Also, our [Chinese] community is a bit too conservative. Although the organizations organize cultural events every now and then, compared to some other communities, like the Japanese association, what we are doing is like 自己的狂欢 [party with ourselves]. We should be more open to other cultures on campus.

Bohan didn't deny that his national pride was sometimes at odds with his emerging cosmopolitan ideas and that he was more than occasionally torn between his Chinese nationality and his desire to belong to a community that values positive changes and inclusivity. As a first-year student in 2016, Bohan possessed extremely limited social capital in the new context. However, his nationality and linguistic background enabled him to identify with a social community that would provide him with a sense of belonging during that particular period of time. As he continued to assemble social capital in his major studies and interest-based organizations, and as the cosmopolitan ideas planted in his ideology that can be traced back to his teenage years continued to mature in an even more diverse and complex social ecology, Bohan adopted a critical lens through which he reexamined the fundamental value upon which the communities he had settled in were established. This critical reflexivity allowed Bohan to negotiate his persona in different social communities to be recognized and respected and reinvent the communities for the greater good at the same time. In other words, Bohan reconciled his ambivalent and sometimes conflicting selves that represent his national identity, cosmopolitan ideals, disciplinary apprenticeship, and emergent community leadership.

Conclusion: Bohan's Literacy Affordances

Bohan's extensive exposure to and engagement with tourists and professionals from various linguistic and cultural backgrounds at a young age afforded him a general structure of cosmopolitanism, which then translated into his critical approach to the cultural assimilation course offered at the university, and later reflected in his cynical outlook toward the exclusivity of nationality-based student communities. When it comes to demystifying the genre of lab reports and wading through the laborious and tedious task of composing lab reports, however, Bohan was able to capitalize on the genre awareness developed partly in the first-year writing course and invent his personal structural foundation based on the specific guidelines provided within the rhetorical exigency of the course. Bohan's strategic deployment of "rhetorical absence"—making a strong case by purposefully concealing the warrants—that enabled him to silently express his criticisms regarding cultural essentialization and exclusiveness, translingually and transmodally composed social media posts that helped him more effectively connect with his social resources, and sensitivity to disciplinary discourse markers that allowed him to mimic and eventually internalize the rhetorical style of lab reports, all contributed to constructing his literate world and his multiple personas inhabiting the world.

Bohan's bodily and material affordances are also an indispensable part of his ecology. His physical appearance and clothing style are encoded biopolitical information that granted him certain privileges while depriving him of others. He was automatically considered a member of the Chinese student organizations and received accommodations during the transitional year simply because of his nationality tied to his bodily affordance. The very bodily affordance, too, entangled him with complex and oftentimes conflicting identities and community memberships. Bohan's affective bonds with his complex and conflicting identities and community memberships, as a result, triggered his emotional reactions to the value represented by certain social groups. His body is bound up with material experiences as well: the trips to New York, Miami, Japan, and Shenzhen, his technological tools—laptop and smartphone—that enabled him to connect with people through multimodal texts, and the very texts that he produced with the tools. His bodily and material affordances are further entangled with the structural and semiotic ones, suggesting that his literate world is conditioned by a sociomaterial ecology as opposed to merely his activities. This ecologically afforded literate world, in turn, empowered Bohan to articulate and negotiate his rhetorical differences in response to the changing rhetorical exigencies. Bohan's own words best conclude this chapter:

> I used to be just another Chinese student, now I'm a world traveler, a RoboMaster, a mechanical engineer, an introvert, and a global citizen. I'm comfortable being a world traveler among Chinese students, and a Chinese student among engineers. I learned to make peace with my different selves.

6
Doing Difference Differently

Toward the end of my field work, having spent a total of more than 2 years participating in the four Chinese international students' literate lives, I eventually came to some wisdom in hindsight: I should have approached my writing course a little differently; I should have conceptualized my writing classroom as a space for doing difference rather than seeking agreement. If I had discovered Wentao's or Yang's multilingual and multimodal creativity early on, I would have prompted them to tap into their literate invention process. If I had been curious enough to explore Manna's involvement in the hip hop dance community, I would have encouraged her to translate her verbal expressions into bodily movements or vice versa. Yet, as a teacher-researcher, I can only remorsefully talk about should haves and would haves because I, along with other passionate teacher-researchers, find it impossible to overcome the research latency; also, I, akin to my multilingual students, am caught up in a myriad of constraints, be it institutional, pedagogical, or material. A more constructive revisit of the narratives presented in this book, thus, is to weave the stories together and identify meaningful patterns as to how the four individuals do difference differently and what enables them to do so. As sociologist and ethnographer Paul Atkinson (2015) stresses, "The goal of ethnographic fieldwork is not to amass an inchoate array of personalised impressions and experiences (however illuminating they might be), but to collect and analyse data in the interests of developing systematic conceptual frameworks" (p. 6). We can't anticipate having Wentao, Manna, Bohan, or Yang in our writing classroom again, nor can we bet all of our hope on a forlorn attempt to design a magical one-size-fits-all course that allows every single individual to do difference. What we *can* possibly manage, however, is to be a little better prepared or show a little bit more compassion as we discover our students' emerging differences.

Literacy practices are, as Xiqiao Wang (2019) characterizes, following Prior and Shipka (2003), "inherently heterogeneous, particular, and complex" (p. 567), as they are entangled in "the dispersed, fluid chains of places, times, people, and artifacts that come to be tied together in trajectories of literate action" (Prior & Shipka, 2003, p. 181). As the four writers' reconstructed literate worlds demonstrate, their literacy practices are not only heterogeneous, particular, and complex, but also constantly emerging and shifting, caught up in symbolic and material ecologies, and shaped by agents' histories and expectations. It is how they engage with the literacy practices that define and redefine their differences. In other words, what they do constitutes who they are as in their socially and self-perceived emerging identity and their performance of that emerging identity. Doing difference is coming to terms with our becoming and being (Hall, 1990). It is, as the four stories compellingly illustrate, embracing, leveraging, resisting, negotiating, and redefining "the names we give to the different ways we are positioned by, and position ourselves within, the narratives of the past" (Hall, 1990, p. 225).

Although the notion of doing difference offers an alternative analytical lens through which we re-see the four individuals' positionalities as making rhetorical decisions through literacy practices, we need to acknowledge its conceptual and logical limitations. Taken to its logical extreme, the notion of doing difference may risk forgoing its definitional power and losing its meaning altogether: every individual can be seen as doing their own difference to the extent that difference ceases to mean what we think it means. Taken further, difference risks becoming a conceptual vacuum and nihilistic construct that ceases to matter in our educational practices and public discourse. Difference does matter; certain differences matter more than others in a certain structure of asymmetrical power relations. Considering the conceptual conundrum, what I aim to do in this chapter is sort out ways of doing difference that matter particularly to the four Chinese international students. As such, what I hope you will take away from this chapter is not so much the idiosyncratic difference doing that the four individuals are engaged in but rather a critical awareness of our students and our own difference doing.

Now that you have come this far in the book, I hope it would not be a disappointment to claim that you will be unlikely to see similar differences, oxymoronically, in other Chinese international students. Does this mean the stories of the four individuals that we have hopefully empathized with cannot tell us anything useful in a pragmatic sense? I don't think so. Reading (many) stories like this is an act of and commitment to rhetorically attuning ourselves to our students' literate worlds, listening to their aspirations, feeling their pains, and participating in their difference doing. As we reflect on the stories together in this chapter, I share my reading of the four individuals' difference doing through literacy practices that will hopefully tie the different acts of difference doing together with a touch of coherence and insight. In what follows, I will unpack five forms of doing difference that characterize all four students' literacy practices: embracing difference, leveraging difference, resisting difference, negotiating difference, and redefining difference. Although the four students demonstrated the possibility of an infinite number of ways of doing difference, they more or less uniformly engaged in these forms of difference doing.

Embracing Difference

Embracing difference suggests a voluntary and affectionate acceptance of one's perceived difference, coming to terms with the social implications of the difference, and acknowledging the difference as an essential part of their being and becoming. The perceived difference may be an institutionalized identity marker, such as "international student" or "nonnative English speaker"; it may also be an emerging differential relation that one experiences, such as one's perceived sociocultural distance from the dominant discourse in a student organization. Embracing difference is not passive concession to the uncertainty and arbitrariness of one's self-perceived or socially defined difference; rather, it embodies the agent's attempts to reconcile with the difference and accept it as a part of who they are. Neither is "embracing" equal to uncritically celebrating; it is an agential decision to *be* and *become*. Most importantly, embracing difference, along with other forms of doing difference, is exercised and manifested through the four students' rhetorical decisions that constitute their literacy practices, as opposed to being broadcast as a declaration, although the latter may certainly be an option.

EMBRACING MULTILINGUALITY AND TRANSLINGUALITY

Following a host of scholars who have theorized multilingualism and multilinguality in their respective fields of study, I define *multilinguality* as the linguistic competence of and disposition toward using multiple linguistic systems to achieve communicative objectives (Li, 2011; Tsui & Tollefson, 2007). On the other hand, I define *translinguality* as the linguistic competence of and disposition toward using semiotic and ecological resources that transcend bounded linguistic systems (Bou Ayash, 2019; Canagarajah, 2013c; Horner & Alvarez, 2019). The two concepts seem ontologically divergent from one another given how language and language practice are conceptualized. For example, multilinguality implies an understanding of languages as discrete and compartmentalized linguistic systems, while translinguality stresses the hybridity of the semiotic and ecological resources that a communicator draws from. As I characterize the four students' literacy practices of difference, I use both terms simultaneously but not interchangeably, since the ethnographic data suggest that their conceptualization of their own language practice corresponds to both concepts.

First, although Manna, Wentao, Yang, and Bohan are somewhat ambivalent about their status as English leaners in a predominantly English-speaking environment, they nonetheless acknowledge the cultural capital that their multilinguality and translinguality bring. Their means of embracing multilinguality and translinguality are quite subtle: we are not likely to see them walking around and openly bragging about their ability to shuttle between Mandarin, Shanghainese, English, and Japanese, or shuttle between hip hop choreography, lab reports, lyrics, poems, and social media posts; yet the very fact that they are actively engaged in these multilingual and translingual literacy practices is the most powerful testament to their affectionate acceptance. Manna, for example, was consciously aware of the cultural capital that the universal "language" of dancing brings her. While she admitted that her colloquial English was not yet adequately sophisticated and culturally sensitive for her to easily mingle with her peers, Manna opted for the bodily expression of hip hop dance, which is culturally rooted in the US and internationally popular. In the space of the writing center, Manna meticulously wove her understanding of Chinese students' linguistic and rhetorical struggle and her empathy into the design of the infographic on plagiarism, while courageously confronting her self-perceived "broken English" as a writing consultant. Embracing her multimodal multilinguality provided Manna with access to university spaces that are traditionally deemed inaccessible to students who are linguistically and culturally distant from the so-called "mainstream"; for example, in Manna's case, the writing center and local dance competitions. Wentao's positive attitude toward multilinguality and translinguality, on the other hand, helped him bridge what the general public tends to see as two distinct cultural communities on campus: the Chinese student community and the "rest." Thanks to his ingenuity in crafting English essays and skillful command of lexical resources, Wentao earned a reputation in his social circle made up of peer Chinese students. In a "mainstream" community where Chinese international students typically shy away from, namely, the student performance club, Wentao refused to play it safe by being overly self-conscious about the linguistic accuracy of his promotional message. Instead, he focused on the rhetorical effectiveness and outcome by meshing colloquial English, emoticons, and doodles into an otherwise dull or cheesy message.

Second, the four students see multilinguality and translinguality as an indispensable and defining aspect of who they are. This is embracing multilinguality and translinguality at a more profound level because it transcends the view of language difference as resources and capital, or in other words, cultural utility, and implies that the four students have internalized this difference as part and parcel of their identity construction. For Manna, Wentao, Yang, and Bohan, multilinguality and translinguality are not two remote discursively constructed concepts but an everyday reality that they *do*. They breathe multilinguality and translinguality. For example, although being placed into a first-year writing class designed for international students, Yang did not take this placement decision as a stigma of linguistic "inferiority," as some of her Chinese peers would think. Rather, Yang used this supportive space to explore her multilingual and translingual creativity that characterized her lyrical composition in Japanese. Granted, her vocabulary and fluency in both English and Japanese were still growing at the time of this research (and the growth will probably continue for quite some time). Yet she had long left behind the "growing pain" of feeling self-conscious about her language use and moved on to *do* language—exploring the possibilities that her multilinguality and translinguality enabled, such as composing original pop lyrics in Japanese and navigating/critiquing the transnational pop music industry. In contrast, Bohan's acceptance of his multilinguality and translinguality found manifestation in mobilizing and meshing various linguistic and multimodal resources to create promotional posts for the student organization in which he was involved. While Wentao embraced his translinguality in establishing a communicative channel with a wider English-speaking community through his promotional message, Bohan's translingual creation aimed at a more targeted audience, that is, the Chinese international student community on campus, which suggests that truly embracing multilinguality and translinguality is independent of linguistic context. That is, embracing multilinguality and translinguality is not a performative display of coming to terms with one's relative positionality toward a socially valorized language but a critical acknowledgment of one's full range of semiotic resources in any communicative situation.

EMBRACING IN-BETWEENNESS

Anthropologist Victor Turner (1982) describes *in-betweenness* as liminality: "That time and space betwixt and between one context of meaning and action and another" (p. 113). He continues to characterize this liminality as showing "the appearance of marked ambiguity and inconsistency of meaning" (p. 113). When entering an intense contact zone (Pratt, 1991) such as a university campus, international students find themselves inescapably caught up in various forms of in-betweenness: linguistic, cultural, social, and academic, to name a few. They scramble to carve a path out of the woods, only to find themselves caught up in between other ambiguous or even conflicting meanings. The university campus is a cultural labyrinth for every student, domestic and international alike. Yet the liminality is more strongly felt by international students, because the very compass that students use to navigate this labyrinth—language, or more specifically, a particular variety of English as the dominant language in a US university—is itself a labyrinth marked by ambiguity. Indeed, despite the fact that the four students embraced their multilinguality and translinguality as a salient "difference-as-norm" of their emerging identity, they, every now and then, found themselves baffled by a sense of distance, alienation, and confusion that was invariably tied to their relationship with English. They needed to be constantly on the lookout for a space of recognition and affirmation of who they are regardless of their perceived English proficiency. These "linguistic mental shackles" in the guise of in-betweenness resulted in, for example, Yang and Bohan's conflicting attitudes toward the Chinese student association, Bohan's ambivalence toward working with "American" peers, and Yang's evolving understanding of the roles rhetoric plays in "the West" and China. They also needed to be constantly making sense of the "mainstream" community on campus, the "minority" community of Chinese international students, various other organizational structures, and their own relationship with all of these fluid communities that embody drastically different values and beliefs.

As mentally and emotionally laborious as inhabiting liminal spaces may seem, and although they may not have the vocabulary to articulate the ambiguous state of mind, Manna, Wentao, Yang, and Bohan embraced their in-betweenness with an occasional touch of reluctance but overall an unflinching determination. After all, a liminal space is marked by ambivalence and inconsistency, yet it is also marked by "moments of communion, spontaneity, and insight" (Rosaldo et al., 1993, p. 3). It is a space where they are entitled to do difference on their own terms while reconciling their differences with those of others. And it is a space where they learn how to *be* themselves and *be with* others, namely, be together in difference (Ang, 2001). In-betweenness is a hallmark of Manna's writing center adventure. Writing centers as physical spaces are liminal spaces for everyone who comes in contact with them (Sunstein, 1998), and they are all the more ambiguous and sometimes alienating for those who perpetually dwell in a liminal psychological and emotional state like Manna. Initially feeling "out of place" due to her disciplinary training in a non-humanities field, lack of confidence in writing in standardized English, lack of experience in teaching and tutoring, and her "Chineseness" in a predominantly white space, Manna gradually accepted this space as what it was: a cultural, linguistic, disciplinary, and experiential contact zone where everybody and everything is in a constant state of encountering, clashing, connecting, and becoming. She began to embrace her unique but not singular in-betweenness in this fundamentally ambiguous place: reflecting on her tutorial practices and self-positionality through writing, contrasting Western and Chinese rhetorical devices, crafting an infographic for Chinese students, and eventually coming to terms with her *own* English in a tutorial session. Yang's liminality stood out as a salient theme in her literacy practices of difference, too. The pop music community is borderless; its transnational accessibility empowers anyone wanting to express their lyrical creativity to participate. Yang explored this liberating space to its fullest extent as she composed lyrics in Japanese, recorded her performance, and disseminated her work in transnational digital communities. Yet she felt a sense of in-betweenness professionally, linguistically, and culturally. For example, Yang had high aspirations of making a name in the J-pop community in China, yet she felt constrained by her professional training; she took pride in her translingual competence in lyrical composition, yet her lyrical style still seemed somewhat affected; she needed to simultaneously navigate cautiously and find commonplaces among multiple cultural communities: music creation and production communities, Chinese pop music market, US creators' communities, and Japanese pop culture, among many others. Challenging as it sounded, traversing these liminal spaces as a growing creator afforded Yang the rare cultural mobility that not many of her Chinese peers had the privilege to enjoy. This cultural mobility à la in-betweenness in turn cultivated in Yang a rhetorical sensibility to the operations of the music industry and an aesthetic taste for what she took to be meaningful lyrical expressions.

Leveraging Difference

Leveraging difference suggests purposeful employment of self-perceived emerging differential relations as resources to gain certain material and social advantage. My use of the word "leverage" here, a key concept theorized in finance and business, adds a pragmatic, if not utilitarian, dimension to the four students' difference doing. It is worth noting that leveraging difference does not necessarily imply embracing difference. As the stories demonstrate, the four resourceful individuals were capable of "trading" their differences for a desired outcome without accepting the differences as real or important. In other words, viewed from a somewhat cynical perspective, the four students were more or less engaged in learning how to play the neoliberal "game of difference" to blend in, get ahead, and stay ahead. I am by no means trying to portray the four students as shrewd, calculating, and manipulative pragmatists who are devoted to cracking the code of playing their marginalized identity markers to their own advantage; this would be a gross misrepresentation of the students' motivations. The four students learned how to leverage difference simply because they had to. As Yang said during one of our conversations, "I didn't choose how I look to them [her white US-born peers] or speak English. Everybody wants to stand out and be unique in this culture, so I need to learn how to be different to survive." Yang's perspective here seems rather passive, yet it reveals how the value placed upon individual competitiveness and institutionalized diversity in a neoliberal institutional climate has insidiously shaped the students' literacy practices within their communities. While there are numerous ways of reading the four students' leveraging difference depending on how the notion of "difference" is contextualized, I choose to unpack their leveraging cosmopolitan sensibility and multimodal creativity in this section, given the simultaneous salience of these differences in the data and relative silence of these differences in the current scholarly and public discourses.

LEVERAGING COSMOPOLITAN SENSIBILITY

Cosmopolitan sensibility refers to the acknowledgment of, appreciation for, and responsible reaction to diverse cultural values and modes of life. A cosmopolitan sensibility respects human differences and rejects exclusionary community affiliation on the basis of any particular value. As philosopher Kwame Anthony Appiah (2006) reasons, "Because there are so many human possibilities worth exploring, we neither expect nor desire that every person or every society should converge on a single mode of life" (xv). Make no mistake, a cosmopolitan sensibility is *not* a nod to cultural relativism; it highlights individual responsibilities to each other that transcends group affiliations. As Appiah (2006) continues to argue, "The one thought that cosmopolitans share is that no local loyalty can ever justify forgetting that each human being has responsibilities to every other" (xvi). *Leveraging* such sensibility, for Manna, Yang, Wentao, and Bohan, implies recognizing, and sometimes dismissing, cultural differences as the norm in order to blend in and be recognized as a legitimate member. It does not mean that they actively conceal their self-perceived differences; rather, it means that they are consciously aware of and act according to what they think their differences may imply. Not surprisingly, none of the four students were able to articulate their cosmopolitan sensibility with Appiah's theoretical framework. In fact, their ability to articulate such sensibility is beside the point; their purposeful performing of such sensibility is all that matters.

Bohan, for example, effectively leveraged his cosmopolitan sensibility to claim his legitimate membership and recognition in the student-run RoboMasters club. Compared with Wentao's experience in the performance club, Bohan's enculturation efforts were considerably less because the club's founding members shared similar national and linguistic affinities with Bohan. Yet Bohan's cosmopolitan sensibility was activated when he realized his differences at the level of a small culture (Holliday, 1999), namely, disciplinary community. Bohan was self-conscious about his juniority as a mechanical engineering apprentice among graduate students and professors in the community. He was just beginning to develop an awareness of his peripheral status and the distance to the "center" of the discourse community. In other words, he knew he was a newcomer, if not still an outsider, trying to find his way in. Needless to say, being aware is one thing, but knowing how to leverage that awareness of difference to achieve his goal is all the more important. Bohan strategically downplayed what he perceived as his difference—peripheral status in the small cultural community—while highlighting his affinities by, for example, promoting the organization within his Chinese social circle. It seems that Bohan did not value cultural group affiliation as much as he did the new connections that got made and work that got done.

On the other hand, Yang's cosmopolitan sensibility is reflected in her critical insights into the business and market operations of the transnational pop music industry. She plays the game as an experienced cultural insider while critiquing the game from above: she writes and produces pop songs in Japanese all by herself yet refuses to cater to what she takes to be the vulgar taste of the uniformed public. To Yang, how well her own creative work thrives in any particular music market is less important than how the pop music industry as a whole is perceived and received. For example, Yang noted that creators of original Japanese pop music are faced with a fairly obscure market in mainland China; if she had been determined to make a splash in the pop culture scene in China, she would have opted to write songs that appealed to the general public, for example, Mandopop (Mandarin pop), which Yang utterly dismissed as "triply vulgar" yet also acknowledged as "equally valuable" to the diversity of the global pop music industry. Naturally, Yang also expressed grave concern about the status quo of music education in China, especially over such issues as copyright infringement and plagiarism. The self-serving and materialistic orientation under the "law of the jungle" that was instilled into the next generation of music creators in China, as Yang lamented, was doing the global music industry a disservice. Yang's cosmopolitan sensibility was leveraged to justify her moral outrage, which provoked her to conduct research inquiry into music education in China and make bold, broad-stroke suggestions to educational policy makers and administrators of higher-ed institutions.

LEVERAGING MULTIMODAL CREATIVITY

Literacy practice is multimodal in nature, as scholars have long argued (Canagarajah, 2013c; Fraiberg, 2010; Gonzales, 2015, among others). Writers always consciously or subconsciously employ a range of modalities in meaning making and negotiation, including, for example, spoken or written language, visual, aural, gestural, and spatial. Multilingual students may be more attuned to multimodal composing compared with their monolingual counterparts who mostly rely on English to make meaning, sometimes out of necessity but more often as a purposeful strategy. In her focus group study, Laura Gonzales spotlighted multilingual writers' rhetorical sensitivity and advanced expertise in a multimodal rhetorical context. She found that "L2 students were keenly aware of how to leverage and layer these semiotic resources through their work, reflecting their extensive translanguaging or moving purposely between languages, media, and contexts" (p. 1). Similarly, translingual practices have been conceptualized alongside multimodal writing, since translingual is essentially trans-semiotic and calls for the writer's mobilization of a variety of modes of meaning making and meaning negotiation.

By "multimodal creativity" I refer to the capability and awareness of incorporating various means of meaning making and communication to create new rhetorical spaces. It could mean switching between different modalities and semiotic resources in a single communicative episode. It could also mean weaving together different modalities and semiotic resources across different contexts. Regardless of how multimodality is manifested, the four students in this study are able to leverage their multimodal creativity to blend in, mark their own differences, and confront institutionalized difference markers and associated structures of power. It is fair to claim that we all employ multimodal means to make sense of the world and create new meanings in our everyday literate lives; yet I do want to highlight the four international students' distinctive multimodal creativity in doing difference. Manna's multimodal creativity was uniquely expressed through her bodily performance. Choreographing a hip-hop dance performance is not simply incorporating bodily moves to create a rhetorical narrative that would otherwise be composed through language or other representational means; rather, Manna's multimodal performance is a profound reconceptualization of storytelling in the sense that it creates an alternative rhetorical space for her audience to make sense of who Manna is. Apparently, Manna understood how to leverage her bodily expression to connect with her audience in that alternative rhetorical space. Not only did Manna strategically create an affective bond between herself and her audience through thoughtfully designed and carefully executed dance moves, but she also cultivated a metacognitive ability to transfer her multimodal creativity on the stage to other literate spaces. For example, Manna leveraged her visceral experience of communicating in the "borderless and worldly" language of dancing to negotiate her translingual identity in the writing center. In a sense, Manna's multimodal creativity, in addition to empowering her to practice difference through alternative means, also afforded her the vocabulary to reflect on and negotiate her literate identity in different rhetorical contexts.

Leveraging multimodal creativity played out differently on Wentao's end. Apparently, Wentao was not as interested in creating affective bonds with his community through a bodily modality as Manna was. Quite differently, Wentao was adept at leveraging multimodal creativity in responding to everyday rhetorical exigencies in academic settings or organizational, personal spaces. For example, Wentao capitalized on the iCloud-enabled continuity across Apple devices and platforms to analyze the assignment prompt and craft multiple drafts in an aviation management course. He annotated the assignment prompt with a stylus on his iPad, meshing Chinese phrases and English keywords. He also took class notes and recorded his paper ideas in a notepad application on his iPad for the sake of portability before switching to his MacBook laptop to continue drafting his paper for the sake of productivity. In addition to employing multimodal means of composing texts, Wentao also created texts that are multimodal in nature to appeal to his intended audience on campus as well as in his social media community. Examples can be found in Wentao's deployment of doodling in his promotional message on behalf of his student club and his distinctive poetic style in the construction of his social media presence. Multimodal creativity has been internalized as an integral part of Manna, Wentao, and other international multilingual students' everyday literacy practices of meaning making and difference doing.

Resisting Difference

Acts of resistance are rarely discursively associated with Chinese international students; perhaps it is no exaggeration to say that they have almost never existed in the collective imaginary of the "West." Words that do tend to appear in the public's characterization of this particular cultural group are, for example, "polite," "submissive," "obedient," "modest," "altruistic," and "restrained." More insidiously, East Asian students as a cultural whole are habitually constructed in the "Western" individual psyches as passive recipients of cultural profiling and Othering who are always ready to forgo their rhetorical agency to save "face" and maintain social harmony. "Please be the different you that you are. We appreciate your difference and we celebrate your difference. We love you for who you are!" This ostensibly innocuous compliment, quite unfortunately, reflects the perpetuated collective understanding that our students do and should wholeheartedly embrace their culturally and institutionally constructed identities in our so-called multicultural society. The stories of the four focal Chinese students in this book, however, subtly yet powerfully debunk the myth of the obedient Chinese student, demonstrating that Chinese students do question and resist the public and institutional perceptions of their differences; they do question and resist how power operates through these perceived differences in a Foucauldian sense and take charge of their own narratives, although they have yet to articulate what it means to resist. In unpacking the notion of resisting difference, I zoom in on the four students' resistance to "constructed identity" and "cultural Othering" that seem to bear material implications for their navigating the cultural and institutional space of a US university.

RESISTING CONSTRUCTED IDENTITY

I use the term *constructed identity* to refer to any readily available identity attributes or markers that are purposefully or inadvertently assigned to a rhetorical agent. Identity markers are constructed in an institution or society all the time for various reasons: administration and management, needs analysis, cultural recognition, and socialization, among many others. On the surface, most identity markers are constructed for the sake of social and political expediency; yet one of the natural consequences is, as I discuss at length in Chapter 2, that such identity markers serve to reproduce uneven structures of power that uncritically celebrate certain identities yet in the meantime further marginalize them. Indeed, as Canagarajah (2017) cautions, "Neoliberalism keeps meaning and identity under recognizable uniformity" (p. 50). One particular constructed identity is necessarily tied to one definitive, static meaning; and the meaning necessarily serves those whose constructed identities are valued in a neoliberal institutional environment. As such, resisting constructed identity, first, acknowledges the categorical nature of identity (LeCourt, 2004) and its implications; yet resisting constructed identity goes beyond the categorical nature and highlights the hybridity and contingency of identity (Kerschbaum, 2014). Such an act of resistance rests upon the belief that since identity is socially and institutionally constructed, one has the discursive power and means to deconstruct it in defiance of how one ought to experience their subjectivity.

To the professor of a 150-student calculus class, for example, Yang is perhaps just another Chinese international student who may carry with her some of the stereotypical characteristics of the Chinese students the professor has seen and taught over the years. To the professor, Yang will likely be smart, well-mannered, quiet, diligent, well-off; but Yang will also likely be socially naïve, linguistically incompetent, prone to plagiarism, difficult to assimilate. These are characteristics that are meant to describe individuals yet get discursively attached to the constructed identity of a Chinese international student on a

US campus and then processed and reinforced in people's collective cultural imaginary. Yang, or any other protagonist in this book, attempted to directly and openly challenge this narrative. Yet resisting her constructed identity has been a daily practice for Yang. For example, resisting the identity constructed through a "rhetoric of face"—a cultural association between one's physicality and rhetorical heritage—Yang negotiated the notion of who possessed the authority and cultural capital to teach certain subjects in university. Resisting her constructed identity of a rhetorical outsider, Yang rationalized the differences between her understanding of how the so-called Western rhetoric and Chinese rhetoric play out differently in the political and public realm. Resisting her constructed identity as a struggling language learner, Yang showcased her translingual creativity through composing pop music lyrics in Japanese. Resisting her constructed identity as socially naïve, Yang managed her own music production in a fiercely competitive pop music industry and grew her own fan base. As Yang's stories demonstrate, the constructed identity attributes may not be entirely false: she *is* smart, well-mannered, quiet, diligent, and financially stable; yet she is much more than what the reductive characterization can possibly capture, and she actively rejects the idea of being defined by these terms.

Wentao's means of resisting constructed identity is somewhat ambivalent, which is, paradoxically, more representative of the "Othered" student populations overall. On the one hand, he resisted the institutionally imposed identity of a Chinese student trying to assimilate into the US college culture; yet on the other hand, he actively sought opportunities to claim a sense of belonging within small cultural communities on campus. Viewed from a different angle, Wentao resisted the "public cultural gaze" and defied being recognized only for his perceived "Chineseness;" meanwhile, he embraced his "identity labels" ("the language guy" and "people's poet") affectionately given by his Chinese community. Wentao's ambivalence seems to suggest that the art of resistance is achieved through a balance between destruction and construction: destruction of any form of normalization and construction of one's subjectivity on one's own terms. Although Wentao embraced his in-betweenness, he resisted the constructed narrative that defined him and other Chinese international students as "the homeless" or "passers-by." He did so by, for example, choosing to work with Chinese peers over white American peers, not only for practical reasons but also in defiance of the assimilationist imagination. He did so also by creating a cosmopolitan profile of himself in his Japanese class and in his social media community, which sent out a powerful message: home is nowhere yet everywhere.

RESISTING OTHERING

A decolonial and postcolonial notion (Said, 1978; Spivak, 1985), *Othering* articulates the insidious process of discursively constructing a social boundary between us and "others" and attributing a subordinate status to the latter (Dervin, 2016). Othering is insidious because it appears to objectively describe characteristics of difference without involving value judgments; yet the very act of framing the differences of an essentialized group of Others creates hierarchical power structures (Song, 2020). The Othered is perceived not only as different from the Self, but also as problematic and inferior. As such, Othering is understood as a powerful mechanism by which colonial powers legitimize and rationalize their domination and exploitation of the colonized. For example, when a white, US-born, native-English-speaking instructor asks a student of color coming from a non-US cultural background to introduce "their culture" without critically scrutinizing the lens through which the question is asked, the instructor may unintentionally practice cultural Othering (Kubota, 2004), because the interaction fails to tease out and complicate the power imbalance embedded. Contrary to our conventional wisdom, resisting such practices of Othering in the four focal students' stories does not entail naming the practices of Othering; resistance is what they *do* through everyday literacy practices. Naming the practices of Othering and resisting Othering is what *we* as scholars and students' literacy sponsors do through our analysis and advocacy.

Bohan, through an art of "rhetorical absence," silently resisted the institution-sponsored tacit cultural Othering in the intercultural communication course. Quickly discovering that the course's neoliberal, reductive, and Western-centric interpretation of "intercultural competence," Bohan decided to "play along" rather than call it out, because he understood the purpose of enrolling in the class: (a) learning the basics of intercultural communication, (b) getting the course credits, and (c) making some friends. The personal objectives that Bohan listed at the beginning of the course, for example, mirrored the neoliberal, reductive, and Western-centric interpretation of cultures, or in other words, unintentionally practiced Othering. Yet soon after, Bohan realized that he had been Othered by an Indian-American friend he interviewed for an assignment on the topic of cultural stereotyping. Although Bohan may not have questioned the course curriculum that set him up for being Othered, he eventually silently resisted the Othering by turning in a reflective paper written in a way that he thought the course instructor anticipated. If not for the safe space we co-created for our interview session, Bohan would not have had the opportunity to voice his silent resistance.

In some cases, the rhetoric of Othering is historically entrenched in the public and academic discourses and has long, albeit unwittingly, been internalized by the Othered. The internalized rhetoric of Othering would unjustifiably call attention to constructed differences that the Othered would not otherwise see and convince the Othered to accept the constructed differences as a reality. As such, resisting the force of Othering becomes especially challenging. Yet small everyday resistance continues to play out regardless of the challenges. Manna, for example, has apparently bought into what she believed to be the American romanticization of the smart and hardworking Chinese students, despite the fact that she had not personally been stereotyped by anyone. Manna's way of resisting such internalized Othering is, paradoxically, justifying her "Othered" practices as her choice; that is, her attempting to maintain her straight-A academic status in college is an autonomous choice rather than conforming to anyone's Othering romanticization of Chinese students. In her own words, "I want straight As not because I want to be just another hardworking Chinese, but because I'm determined to prove it to myself that I can do well on anything I want: dance, writing center, and my major courses."

Negotiating and Redefining Difference

Rebecca Lorimer Leonard (2014), quoting her research participant, aptly characterizes the unpredictability and nonlinearity of making sense of language difference as "the 'mess' of multilingual experience" (p. 227). As rhetorical and literacy agents, we constantly attune ourselves to this messiness of difference and multiplicity. She theorizes such rhetorical attunement as "a literate understanding that assumes multiplicity and invites the negotiation of meaning across difference" (p. 228). As we negotiate meaning *across* difference, we negotiate meaning *of* difference, since difference is profoundly constructed and negotiated (Bakhtin, 1981; Goffman, 1981). We also negotiate meaning *with* each other's differences through social and written interactions (Butler, 2017). Negotiating difference is an art of claiming and yielding power; that is, the power to name difference, embrace difference, leverage difference, and define difference and redefine difference. It is redefining what difference matters, to whom, in what rhetorical context, and to what end. If doing difference was too abstract of a notion to capture how the four individuals make sense of themselves in the US university and we had to concretize it with just one action verb, "negotiating" would be the best candidate. In other words, doing difference is essentially negotiating difference. Manna, Wentao, Yang, and Bohan negotiated rhetorics of difference that structure their bodily experiences on campus through embodied literacy practices; and they redefined what it means to be "Chinese international students."

Manna, through her choreographic work, negotiated the institutionally valorized means of meaning making in a university, namely, academic essays written in standardized English. She claimed legitimacy of using her body as a modality of expression and impression to challenge the assumed hierarchy of literacy practices. Through her work in the writing center, Manna negotiated the exclusionary meaning of expertise that is tacitly defined by "the right people." As a multiply marginalized individual in the writing center space—woman in STEM, multilingual, international, and undergraduate—Manna leveraged her insider's perspective on multilingual writers' struggles and her rhetorical sensibility to negotiate a position of expertise and sense of belonging. Manna also negotiated what it means to embrace herself with herself through reading, reflecting, and journaling.

Wentao devoted himself to negotiating his positionality in the ecology of collaborative work in the discipline. Valuing the spirit of "getting it done" when it comes to performing collaborative writing in his major courses, Wentao deliberately assembled a team of Chinese peers for the sake of more efficient communication. However, he did so also for the sake of a more balanced power dynamic within the group that might be more easily achieved when group members share cultural assumptions and values, as he implied but did not articulate. Wentao also negotiated his digitally mediated persona through carefully curating his transcendental understandings of life in the Chinese community, American community, and anywhere in between. In the virtual space where speedy content consumption for instant gratification is the entire purpose by design, Wentao carved out his own salon where "guests" may slow down, take a break, appreciate his poetic aphorisms, and even have a little conversation.

Yang's circumstances called for a more intense negotiation of difference. She shattered the public's imaginaries, or expectations, of a stereotypical Chinese international student on many fronts in a quite transgressive manner: creating pop music in multiple languages, navigating the pop music industry while critiquing it, and mindfully escaping the normalized communicative mores in a US university. In her lyrical and musical world, Yang negotiated her authorial identity as a Japanese language learner located in a US cultural context writing pop songs to be consumed by the Chinese audience. She did so by leveraging her transnational mobility and translinguality as they intertwine in her unique lyrical style. Yang did not readily embrace the pop music industry for what it was. Instead, she negotiated where its aesthetic values should be placed and how newcomers should claim their membership, although such introspective negotiation may only go as far as directing her own engagement. Yang's literacy practices also demonstrate that negotiation of difference does not always succeed. When the curriculum is deeply ingrained in an institutionalized rhetorical tradition, Yang failed to negotiate a place for her own rhetorical practices and decided to withdraw.

Speaking of being withdrawn, Bohan's rhetorical art of negotiation is characterized by his transcendental silence, paradoxically. For example, Bohan needed to negotiate his iteration of cosmopolitanism with an institutional, neoliberal perspective on cultural differences, the incommensurability of which compelled Bohan to resort to his silent resistance. On the other hand, Bohan proactively and strategically negotiated his junior membership of the student club by leveraging his social network in the Chinese community. More saliently, Bohan negotiated his emerging disciplinary voice through imitating, questioning, internalizing, resisting, and eventually reconciling with the conventions of composing a laboratory report in mechanical engineering.

Interestingly and notably, the process of co- and reconstructing the four individuals' literate worlds is also a process of negotiation. They needed to negotiate their presence in their reconstructed literate world in present ecologies by recounting and simultaneously remediating their stories from then ecologies, and all the while anticipating how I, the listener and co-storyteller, would interpret their stories. What will I look like in the book? Who will read the book? What am I (not) comfortable with sharing with Zhaozhe and the future audience? How will the future audience think of me? These are but a few questions that were constantly running through the four students' inquisitive minds during our conversations and prompted them to negotiate their coconstructed, albeit anonymous, identities. As the four students' stories demonstrate, negotiating difference takes place everywhere, all the time, and in multiple cognitive, emotional, and social dimensions. Indeed, negotiating difference is "ultimately negotiating the resonances as well as the dissonances between the full range of our voices" (Roozen, 2009, p. 568).

7
Networked Ecological Affordances

As we critically read the four students' stories of doing difference through literacy practices, we need to be careful not to rush to the conclusion that doing difference is an act of full human rhetorical and literate agency. Prior and Shipka (2003) have long argued that "literate activity as social practices are situated, embodied, mediated and dispersed" (p. 187). The four students' acts of embracing, leveraging, resisting, and negotiating difference are mediated by a complex network of ecological affordances—structural, semiotic, experiential, social, bodily, and material. In this chapter, I would like to revisit the four students' difference doing as embodied in their literacy practices through the lens of networked ecological affordances. Why do we need to attend to the ecological forces at work, you might inquire? Unpacking the four students' literacy practices of doing difference helps us understand this easily stereotyped and unjustifiably marginalized group on campus. Yet only through accounting for the ecological forces that condition and mediate their everyday literate lives can we critically appreciate their "will to difference" and call into question the institutional discourse of difference.

Structural Affordances

When engaged in a certain literate activity within a rhetorical ecology, the participants enter a network of relationships with other individuals and materials. These individuals and materials are governed and organized by an invisible set of customs, rules, and norms. We call these governing and organizing entities structural affordances, as they "shape the opportunities and resources available to individuals" (Cleaver, 2007, p. 226). Structures are de facto generative of power imbalance, as they represent "the inequitable patterning of relations that ensures some individuals (by virtue of their social position) are better placed to deploy resources, to shape rules, to exercise power, than others" (Cleaver, 2007, p. 228). For example, the institutional structure of grading privileges those who are better academically prepared even before matriculating to college. In the same vein, the institutional structure that sponsors English-medium instruction in most US colleges inevitably disadvantages those who learn and use English not as their primary language. However, structures also provide affordances that enable agents to position themselves against the structurally powerful and eventually intervene in the relations of power imbalance. The cultural, social, institutional, academic structures are embedded in and shape multilingual students' practices (Lillis & Scott, 2008). These structures, too, share students' agency along with material things within the ecology (Micciche, 2014). With discursive instruments afforded, the four students negotiate their positions against the dominant structures of the social and academic regime in the university (Canagarajah & Matsumoto, 2017).

For example, the lyrical structure, which embodies the cultural norm of Japanese musical and poetic expression, afforded Yang an alternative discourse to position herself in the dominant structure of English-only academic discourse. Her substantial engagement with the structural affordances—haiku, romaji, imagery, topoi, metaphors, and each individual character, phrase, as well as the connotations embedded—empowered her to carve out a discursive space for her alternative authorial identity as a multilingual creative writer who actively crafts imagination and evokes emotional responses in a language unfamiliar to the audience. The structural affordances of an alternative discourse equipped Yang with confidence, authority, expertise, and a new community membership of both the physical world and online virtual space, with which she negotiated her literate difference with the perpetuated and constantly reinscribed structure of monolingual policy and research-based academic essay. Bohan, on the other hand, appropriated the dominant academic structure to his advantage to gain access to the discourse community representing his academic discipline. Having learned that the particular means of producing, reproducing, and circulating texts in the field of electrical engineering is inextricably intertwined with and indicative of one's membership in the field, Bohan sought to tap into the structural resources in order to eventually gain disciplinary cultural capital. He tried to parse the existing textual materials that embodied the "mysterious" genre of an electrical engineering lab report, such as the guidelines in the syllabus and sample lab reports and major components that he located on the Internet. Although his pragmatism did not help to engage him in further articulation of the genre for future remediation in other rhetorical contexts, Bohan did, during the process of deconstruction, develop his rhetorical sensibility to the discursive conventions that he may carry with him.

Semiotic Affordances

I use the term "semiotic affordance" to mean the multimodal system or process that enable an agent to make and negotiate meaning. Semiotic affordances are, as Canagarajah (2013c) notes, "embedded in a social and physical environment, aligning with contextual features such as participants, objects, the human body, and the setting" (p. 7). Along with other structural and material affordances existing within an agent's ecology, semiotic affordances shape agency (Herndl & Licona, 2007; Miller, 2007). For example, Chinese international students' first language that they carry with them and actively mobilize to negotiate meaning in the predominantly English-only academic environment can be considered the primary semiotic affordance in the case studies. Similarly, their interpretation and appropriation of certain culturally or subculturally conditioned visual material (such as the rainbow flag) or a communicative process (such as learning to give a presentation in public) can also afford them the means of making meaning and constructing their literate identity and authorial voice.

I have recounted extensively in previous sections the participants' practices of embracing and mobilizing their linguistic resources as semiotic affordances to navigate their literate world on and off campus. Here, I will focus on emerging semiotic affordances beyond linguistic resources. The semiotic system and process that to a large extent afforded all four participants is the very act of writing: writing primarily in English but also in other languages, writing primarily for academic purposes but also for other nonacademic purposes. They learn to navigate the cultural contact zone and their own differences and positionalities by engaging in a variety of semiotic activities: seeing, reading, listening, talking, thinking, touching, moving around. Yet it was through writing that they legitimately partake in the socioacademic activity of articulating their differences, claiming community membership, accumulating cultural capital, and ultimately achieving their goals.

Manna's habitual and spontaneous activity of reflective journaling affords her the semiotic resources to document and verbalize her emotional and occasionally intellectual output, with which she engages as a means of securing emotional homeostasis when pressured by external social forces such as peer competition. According to her, the very act of composing, rather than the product of a journal entry, afforded her strengths to combat the socioacademically inflicted stress; for example, acing every single exam, fitting in the small culture of the writing center, or winning a dance competition. Writing introspectively is also a process of semiotically identifying and examining her own ideological position within her literate world that's constructed within the dominant discourse and finding a home for the literature she engaged with in her native language of Chinese. Likewise, Wentao's literate practice of maintaining email correspondence with members of the PPC performing arts club is sponsored by his multimodal semiotic resources beyond his linguistic resources. His emails are imbued with idiosyncratic expressions of hybrid spoken and written registers, colloquialism, contractions and abbreviations, and emoticons. He also boldly incorporated a self-painted doodle to enhance the appeal of the already lively email text. These semiotic affordances are intertwined with his previous interactions with what he understands to be the "American organizational communication conventions" and material encounters with technology and serve to establish his professional ethos as a charismatic and effective communicator.

Writing as a semiotic affordance functions in these participants' literate lives not as an institutionally mandated ticket for academic or professional advancement but as a means of personal fulfillment.

Experiential Affordances

Of course, Manna, Wentao, Yang, and Bohan did not enter the US, the university, classrooms, student organizations, and any other emerging spaces as blank slates. They are who they are as they present themselves and as I perceive them because of their experiences. Here, the notion of experience is understood as one's mentally and physically stored feelings, skills, knowledge, beliefs, and values abstracted from their encounters with certain people, things, and events. It's an assemblage of an individual's connections with a multitude of dots in the world, the dots being anyone or anything with which they meaningfully interact. These new and old connections, as they are already stored and constantly being stored, actively yet tacitly participate in every decision the individual makes and shape their ongoing relationship with their surroundings (Cooper, 2011; Williams, 2018). In other words, experiences afford. The inquiry into the four individuals' experiential affordances adds a temporal dimension to the analysis, which helps us to coconstruct their ongoing literate lives as they are situated in their personal histories.

The material consequences associated with experiential affordances are hardly ever overstated in the scholarship, those concerning the structurally underprivileged students in particular. The institutional discourse is ever so powerful in shaping the public perceptions of others' experiences and oftentimes leaves people unaware of individual experiences and focus on the grand narrative and collective experiences. As LeCourt (2004) rightfully laments, "There is a clear conflict here between how my students explain the world in equity arguments and how they experience it categorically, a conflict that emerges from public rhetorics that attempt to both recognize difference and exceed it simultaneously" (p. 22). We as educators hear stories about, say, our Chinese interactional students' struggles engaging in constructive in-class discussions with domestic peers due to their culturally conditioned lack of interest in confrontational discussion. We buy into the stories because they are discursively narrated and many of them claim to be informed or even confirmed by empirical research. This is why we are easily surprised when we accidentally discover that our students' individual experiential affordances almost always rewrite their record in the grand narrative.

Two salient themes surfaced from my analysis of the participants' experiential affordances. First, contrary to the pervasive discourse of international multilingual students' literacy experiences on a US campus that are fraught with negative or sympathetic terms such as "barrier," "challenges," "struggles," "support," and "more," the four participants all demonstrate their general comfort and ease in navigating college through literate activities. For example, they certainly surpassed my and the writing program's expectation in the first-year writing course, in which they showcased their critical and analytical abilities, reflective ability, and rhetorical sensibility. Wentao and Yang, thanks to their experiences with learning Japanese as a third language and self-motivated participation in Japanese cultural activities, also exhibited their linguistic and rhetorical creativity, while Manna, on the other hand, mobilized her experiences in choreography to enrich her literate composition. Bohan's extensive communicative interactions with "foreigners" in a cosmopolitan metropolitan center (Shanghai) afforded him a "togetherness-in-difference" approach, which later proved to be critical in forming his communicative strategies in his social activities, for example, representing the RoboMasters team.

Second, the four participants' diverse experiences empowered them to engage with and disengage from the dominant discourse and do difference differently. During our interview sessions, Wentao, Bohan, and Yang all explicitly or implicitly revealed their skepticism and cynicism toward their perception of "the mainstream" in US higher education; for example, the widely held belief that they needed language support, that they are unfamiliar with the American academic conventions or values, that they are culturally alien, that multiculturalism and multilingualism are valuable and deserve celebration, and that there is only one way to perform their identities rhetorically to be recognized. Their skepticism and cynicism, along with their well-versed and open discussion of them, are sponsored by their experiences with reading, journaling, traveling, and participating in social organizations. They also disengage from the dominant discourse through their literate activities that do not conform to the prevailing narrative about international, Chinese, and/or multilingual students' experiences, for example, performing rhetorical silence to protest against cultural stereotyping, using Chinese social media platforms to conduct official team recruitment, and carving out a performative space with lyrics composing and music covering in a nondominant language in the target market.

Social Affordances

The term "social," conceived broadly here, denotes any type of relationship established between the agent and the human world through any medium; for example, friendship, membership, authorship, and readership. These relationships afford an individual's participation in their literate life because literacy itself is a social practice and agency that dictates literate lives is exercised in a social world (Brandt & Clinton, 2002; Canagarajah, 2013a; Cleaver, 2007; Lagman, 2018; Prior & Shipka, 2003; Williams, 2018; You, 2016). Following sociologists such as Pierre Bourdieu and Anthony Giddens, scholars and researchers in writing studies and literacy studies have been engaged in a decades-long exploration of the ways in which language and literacy function as resources that elevate an agent's social status and grant social power and that the social status and power in turn shape the way the agent practices literacy. Literate activities, communicative in nature, are a fundamental means of establishing relationships with the human world. They are not, however, free of ideology and value, but are always embedded in complex social relations and structures of power (Barton & Hamilton, 1998; Lillis & Scott, 2008). These literate activities that an individual participates in inevitably determine who they are within a community; and who they are within that very community, in turn, affects how the individual practices literacy.

Manna, Wentao, Yang, and Bohan's literate activities are enmeshed in their social aspirations, participation, and mobility. Their records of reading, writing, thinking, and living revealed to different degrees a strong desire to be a part of multiple social communities and to be able to move between different communities. This desire to belong drove them to proactively connect with others in multiple social contexts through literate practices. These emerging relationships, in turn, were capitalized on to advance or alter their social positioning also through literate practices. Specifically, the participants' relationships with the social world afforded them the motivation to participate in literate activities, the strategies to do so meaningfully, and the mobility to reposition themselves.

First, Wentao, Manna, Bohan, and Yang participate in reading and writing activities on and off campus not merely due to the institutional structure that prescribes this. They do so also, if not *rather*, out of their own desire to claim their social participation. Wentao, for example, demonstrated a wide array of "literate memberships": as a student composing assignment papers for classes, as an organization officer writing emails to recruit new members for the performing arts club, as a Japanese language learner writing essays, as a friend/mentor critiquing and editing papers, and as a small-circle influencer posting social media blogs. The variety of literate activities helped him to earn the reputation within his Chinese social community as a reliable literacy sponsor, which in turn provided impetus for his continued demand for what he took to be excellence in literate activities. Yang's prolific lyrical composing activity was initially driven by her desire to acquire linguistic and cultural capital through practicing literary creation in the target language. However, her increasing involvement in exposing her literary creation to the public and in finding her lyrical voice in a music community soon overshadowed her initial objective to continue motivating her to produce and engage. Similar social motivation as affordance finds their manifestation in Bohan and Yang's cases.

As "authoritative resources" (organization of social time/space, chance for self-development, relationships between people; Giddens, 1984), the participants' social network also proved to be a valuable source of information, one that enabled them to develop strategies to effectively and meaningfully respond to emerging rhetorical situations. Manna's choreographic initiative for the dance competition on campus, for example, was supported by her friend-mentor and co-dancer Daniel as well as her membership in two university dance clubs—they are indispensable social ties that afforded Manna the awareness of audience, morale, advice, collaboration, sense of belonging, and possibility to connect with a wider community.

In addition, the four participants' community engagement is characterized by fluidity and mobility; they belong to multiple social groups simultaneously, which enables them to mobilize resources from a range of networks. Bohan has been strategically managing his online presence via the social media platform WeChat. This constant visibility in his Chinese social circle turned into his social affordance and was later mobilized to assist him in another community to which he was committed—RoboMasters club. Bohan was able to maximize the value of his Chinese social group by requesting collective efforts in circulating the meticulously composed recruitment advertisement so that it would reach a broader audience without compromising its appeal.

Bodily Affordances

The current two major lines of inquiry into the notion of body in literacy and communication are, first, how the body functions as a mode of communication and semiotic resource and how literacy practices are embodied in physical experience (Butler, 2017; Nordquist, 2017; Prior & Shipka, 2003; Rule, 2018; Syverson, 1999); and second, how bodies are discursively categorized in public rhetorics that mediate our physical experiences (LeCourt, 2004). These two lines of inquiry reflect our realization that in addition to language, human body, the corporeal reality, participates in the construction of discourse and practices and is in turn encoded by discourse and practice. The notion of body encoded in the present research refers to both the functional and representational dimensions of the human body, that is, the bodily construction that enables the agent to *do* (think, read, write, touch, perform, move, assemble) and that embodies who the agent *is*. Bodily affordances, then, are those related to the human body that enable the agent to make decisions and participate in practices through both functional and symbolic means. When participants of the research begin to actively partake in literate activities on and off campus, in classrooms and student organizations, their bodies are the first resources that provide functional support, for example, aligning themselves with the writing's room—"the environmental minutiae of where writing takes place" (Rule, 2018, p. 403), operating the writing tools, and moving around to interact with sources, including texts and informants. Some of them also discovered that their body can be employed as an alternative mode of expression, such as in Manna's case. As their literate engagement deepens and socialization into a certain discourse becomes more complicated, they begin to perceive their bodies as not only a functional tool but also a symbol that entails value, be it social or cultural capital.

The most salient and strategic use of bodily affordance lies in Manna's kinesthetic expression of her emerging understanding of power struggles through her choreographic work for the dance competition. Choreography is itself a literate practice of multimodal composing that involves semiotic resources beyond the textual or graphic; it draws largely from the study of kinesthetics and musicology to compose a representational performative work that elicits an audience's multiple sensory reactions. An experienced amateur dancing practitioner, Manna had already begun employing the abstracted theory of kinesphere to reflect on and explain her choreographic practices. As her simulated recall of her kinesthetic composition suggests, Manna was articulate about her strategic invention of bodily motion to provoke her audience's emotions and encourage them to interpret the moves in a way that related to their own bodily and emotional experiences with power struggles. Her capability of coordinating her body parts, thanks to her investment in years of training, also afforded her the rhetorical sensibility to the body's symbolic power. It was this sensibility that enabled Manna to maximize her body's symbolic power to make a performative argument about the shifting power dynamics between people.

The symbolic power of bodily affordances was more clearly manifested in Bohan and Yang's literate socialization, specifically, their interactions with the enormous Chinese community on campus. Bohan and Yang had both benefitted from the networking and informational resources the institutionalized Chinese organization, CSSA, had to offer, while Yang also briefly served the organization as a committee member. They both indicated, too, that their involvement in the community is virtually automatic: their Chinese "faces" simply served as the membership card and granted them access to the services and resources the community provided. Their bodies afforded them easy access to an organization whose primary function is to represent a minority nation-state group on campus yet did not blind them from critically reflecting on their involvement. For example, Bohan was not ignorant about the distinction between a "face"-based and an interest-based community. As his involvement in the latter increased, he began to examine the former with a pair of critical eyes, questioning the organization's strengthening tie with local businesses and student officers' hidden motives to serve the community. Yet Yang, on the other hand, continued to mobilize the social resources transformed from her bodily affordances, namely, the supportive network gained by being identified as a Chinese national, as she sought cultural sanctuary in the community from her minority status on campus.

Material Affordances

To analyze materials that afforded the meaning making of differences and the navigating of literate worlds calls for a reconceptualization of the thing-ontology: things, or nonhuman objects, are "vibrant matters" (Bennett, 2010) and are coconstitutive of the ecology that humans and nonhumans inhabit. New materialist theories posit that agency is distributed across these matters, humans, and structures and always emerging from an entanglement of these actants. When analyzing material affordances, we are not simply looking at how things are being mobilized and used to enable the agent to achieve certain goals. Rather, we should be teasing out the entanglement of human agents and nonhuman actants to understand how agency travels within the entanglement and generates meanings and yields changes. Initially introduced to rhetorical studies to illuminate the rhetorical becoming of things, new materialism has recently begun to exhibit its analytical power in writing studies and literacy studies. For example, Hannah Rule (2018) looked closely at how writing's rooms—the environmental minutiae of where writing takes place—embody writing processes. Fraiberg et al. (2017), in their multiple case studies of Chinese international and transnational students in the US and China, also shed light on material circulations that condition the participants' literacy practices. Yet more research is needed to foreground materials as vital things that coconstitute the literate worlds that individuals inhabit.

Numerous material entities cocreate the physical environment that situates the participants' literate activities. However, certain things surfaced during my observation of and interviews with them as vital to the entanglements. These things may be the participants' private possessions, a public place (physical space with a location), writing tools, technology, financial resources. Due to researchers' excessive, if not exclusive, focus on the constitutive and transformative power of discourses, these material things that are vital components of an individual's literate world are easily downplayed, if not outright neglected, in a narrative of their literate life. As the narratives of the four students show, however, materials that they possess, encounter, utilize, and inhabit exert ultimate forces to connect them with other actors through participation in literacy and position themselves as different in relation to others.

First, technological infrastructure, the Internet, and the virtual world of social media are intertwined with distinct cultural values and expectations and formed the material condition for the four students to display their differences through socioliterate activities. Wentao, Manna, Bohan, and Yang, just like the majority of their Generation Z peers, are tech-savvy and tech-reliant. Technological gadgets and devices have been seamlessly integrated into their literate lives, providing convenience and coherence. For example, Wentao's backpack that he carries around on campus always readies two pieces of technology for him: an iPad with a stylus and a powerful laptop. In any classroom that allows the use of laptop or electronic notepad, Wentao pulls out his iPad and jots down notes with the stylus. The notes are usually code meshed with English, Chinese, and doodles. Sometimes he also records the lectures and uses an audio transcription program to automatically transcribe the recordings into texts. During breaks between classes, while consuming a sandwich or yogurt, Wentao skims through his notes, making annotations, and sometimes leveraging the power of social media on his smartphone to clarify any confusions that arise. Later when he is finally able to thoroughly organize his thoughts and do homework assignments, the notes and scribbled ideas find their way onto his laptop screen. The thoughts generated in his head are materialized, concretized, transformed, and circulated through a series of technologically supported media, and eventually afford him the resources to perform his literacy.

Cultural values and expectations that are embodied in the material circulation of the participants' literate products often convolute the entanglement of the participants and their material environment. For example, among multiple social media or wiki platforms where college students usually seek academic assistance, the four students, Wentao and Bohan in particular, would primarily rely on WeChat, the instant message and social media platform that's the default and nearly exclusive means of communication within the Chinese community, rather than other internationally popular ones such as WhatsApp and Facebook. The first culturally determined factor that affected their choice of destination for peer assistance is convenience; virtually every Chinese international student on campus uses WeChat to connect with other Chinese nationals, as other major international social media platforms (e.g., Facebook, Twitter) are historically blocked within the Great Firewall (a series of legislative actions and technologies enforced by the Chinese government to regulate the Internet domestically; e.g., Wikipedia), which gave rise to domestically developed service platforms. The reliance on this particular technological affordance has been carried over across the national border into transnational spaces. Further, functionalities designed to cater to the needs of privacy for some users transformed the platform into an ideal place to share questions and seek help. Wentao and Bohan, for example, would carefully set a new status post to be viewable to a selected group of people, usually friends within their immediate academic circle. Once the post was up and running and friends began to comment on it, the default setting only allows mutual friends to see each other's comment, unlike comment sections on other social media where sheer transparency is embraced. This particular material affordance that is aligned with the East Asian, and Chinese in particular, cultural value of saving face and losing face are well played out in this technologically mediated social exchange. Wentao and Bohan revealed that they wouldn't have to worry about losing face to peer Chinese international students who may judge them without being helpful, nor feel self-conscious about appearing pretentious or pompous in the face of their Chinese friends in China.

Second, physical place is an integral part of the participants' literate worlds and conditions their literary production and identity projection. In other words, where they are physically affects, if not determines, what discourse they participate in and who they want to be perceived as. The materiality of a place, as opposed to a space (virtual, social, constructed, and emergent), is reflected in its physical and discursive boundaries: walls, gates, cubicles, borders, and so on. For example, the participants' writing's rooms are where most of the writing processes take place and where a diverse set of material things cocreate a piece of text. The four participants have all explicitly or implicitly identified their writing's rooms dispersed on and off campus, such as Wentao's library desk and home workstation, Manna's dance studio, Bohan's dorm room study, and Yang's home music studio. The trends that Rule (2018) summarized in her ethnographic account of the writing's rooms find their manifestation in the participants' physical places, too: "Writers discovered bodily comfort practices, the revealing nature of physical rhythms, and the need to feel connected in their space to the outside world" (p. 419). The particular arrangements of material affordances in their writing's rooms were in line with the tempo of their reading, thinking, writing/performing, directing them to project their own authorial identity in a specific manner. For example, when Yang began to sit down and compose lyrics to a new song her boyfriend wrote, rather than typing them up on her computer or handwriting them in a notebook, she would ritualistically open the note app on her smartphone and type with her thumbs on the touchscreen, with the music she was writing to playing in the background. This is because she found the small screen afforded her the maximum level of focus, despite the possibility of incoming text messages or other notifications. It's also because the smartphone app provided continuity: since she developed a habit of noting down ideas and inspirations whenever she came across them, when other notetaking tools were not readily available, she would simply grab her phone and take notes in the app, which would be compiled into her lyrics later on. Once she completed her composition, she would directly share the note with her boyfriend for review in the note-taking app, or practice performing the song. All of these activities needed to take place in her home studio, where a small part of her bedroom had been transformed into a music creation hub with microphones, speakers, a laptop, an external monitor, and a comfortable chair all neatly arranged. As Yang noted, this is where she felt like a musician even though her work was still immature, and this is where she felt unique as a transnational literacy influencer.

The Network of Affordances and Differences

Close analysis of the participants' literate activities with a focus on affordances offer a nuanced understanding of the discursive and material resources at their disposal that coconstruct their literate worlds, which encompass a complex network of spaces, people, things, structures, and affects. A comparative examination of the institutional discourse of difference and the participants' emerging differences revealed how literate activities serve as a channel through which individual agents position themselves within or against the dominant discursive construction of their experiences and leverage or materialize their differences. Participants' navigating their literate worlds in the academy and extracurricular realm is essentially acquiring the competence of navigating their affordances and coordinating various affordances toward their goals. Through a variety of communicative interactions with the social and material worlds surrounding and enabling them, the four Chinese international students followed distinct growing trajectories of understanding differences, resisting differences, embracing differences, and evaluating and reflecting on differences. Their practices of difference are networked with their affordances; "a pulsating movement of tying, untying, and retying together" whatever is available that enables their literate performance of difference (Engeström et al., 1999, p 346).

First, inquiries into the participants' affordances help to collect ethnographic details about how their practices of difference through literate activities are situated and dispersed within local and transnational ecologies. These activities may be situated within a local context, for example, writing a lab report for a course or mock tutoring a client at the writing center; they may also traverse nation-state borders via virtual as well as physical channels, such as sharing covered Japanese songs on Chinese grassroots music platforms and organizing Chinese cultural events on a US campus. Regardless, what they do, where and when they do it, and with whom they do it all embody who they are, how they perceive themselves as different, and how they desire to be perceived as different.

For example, to offer a counternarrative against the institutional portrayal of Chinese international students as representative of the clearly bounded and discrete "Chinese culture" within a nation-state framework, Yang wrote extensively in her literacy autobiography how she had been practicing lyrics creation in Japanese yet distributing her lyrical works within the Chinese network. Her translingual and transnational literary creation and dissemination were networked into and endorsed by a multitude of interconnected affordances: (a) the structural guidance embedded in the lyrics genre conventions and Japanese linguistic norms; (b) the semiotic resources such as the music her boyfriend wrote and her own linguistic creativity in multiple languages; (c) her experiences of independently learning the Japanese language and studying its cultural artifacts as well as her experiences of engaging in the grassroots music community as a consumer and creator; (d) her social network of likeminded self-made musicians; (e) her bodily affordance that allowed her mobility to migrate from China to the US and identify herself with fellow Chinese peers; and (f) her material possessions and tools that not only enabled but also mediated the messy processes of translating thoughts into words, documenting and synthesizing notes, and inventing coherent passages. No doubt, listing the affordances in broad strokes by no means justifies the interplay between them. Yet it nonetheless shows that the participants' practices of difference through a variety of literate activities are always conditioned by meditational powers beyond what their agency allows.

And that leads to my second point: a deconstructed account of the participants' affordances also enables us to recognize and take stock of the extent to which they agentially mobilize resources to fulfill their goals and the extent to which their practices are discursively and materially constrained. As I discussed at more length in previous chapters, the scholarly field of writing studies has embraced a material turn that expanded and reconfigured the notion of agency, which is understood to be distributed across humans and nonhuman things and structures (Micciche, 2014; Rickert, 2013). As the narratives of the four participants' practices of difference and the subsequent analysis of affordances illustrate, although they generally made informed rhetorical moves in varying situations, their agency was always an emerging relationality to the material and structural ambience. Their cognitive understanding of their differences and literate engagement with the differences were already caught up in the rhetorical and discursive environment. They may have bodily experienced the material consequences of certain discursive conditions with regard to difference, yet more often than not their cognitive ability, experiences, and other affordances have not reached the level where they could agentially make a meaningful change. Most of the time, evidence of the constitutive power of the ambience is nuanced.

For instance, Manna demonstrated her evolving rhetorical sensibility to her unique cultural capital during one of the interview sessions when she attempted to list the rhetorical strategies that seemed commonsensical in Chinese literary works yet lackadaisical in Western writings. Later on, when creating an infographic for the final project in the writing center practicum, Manna leveraged her perceived cultural capital by purposefully appealing to the underrepresented cultural group—the Chinese international student community—which is manifested in her choice of topic and her rhetorical approach to the topic. Yet the rationale for her rhetorical moves, as she revealed in the follow-up reflective essay, seemed well aligned with the widely circulating institutional deficit discourse: "I think for other international students should pay more attention when they write their papers. Also, the audience can also be native speakers who is in business, college, or even high school." In contrast, although Bohan was also developing an idea about his cultural capital in the US, where multiculturalism is celebrated in accordance with a neoliberal discourse, he did not readily conform to the widespread deficit narrative; instead, his instrumentalism came into play and, interestingly, dovetailed with the institutional discourse of cultural diversity, which then shaped his general approach to perceived differences. For example, when laying out his objectives for the intercultural communication course, Bohan did not squander words to discuss what intercultural communication would mean to him in the long run but focused on concrete and tangible benefits this course may bring: to help him with socialization, to facilitate interpersonal relationships in future workplaces, and so on, the presumption being that multiculturalism is a product that possesses use value. Bohan's pragmatic approach to practicing difference, as can be argued, is caught up in the convoluted network of discursive, structural, and material affordances, as is the dispersed agency.

EPILOGUE

Toward a New Understanding of Chinese International Students' Literacy Practices

What does this extensive discussion of differences and affordances all mean to literacy and writing educators or, in fact, anyone who comes in contact with Chinese international students or international students in general? And what does this discussion all mean to our students themselves? How do we renew our sedimented view of who they are; what they do; how, why, where, and when they do it; and with whom they do it when the institutional discourse regarding difference is constructed in neoliberal marketing terms? How do we resist the impulse to frame students' literacy practices in accordance with the reduced, simplified, generalized, and reiterated profiles? Ultimately, what am I advocating through my research and coconstruction of the literate worlds of the four literate agents?

First, regardless of the roles we are in—writing instructors, program administrators, admission staff, academic advisers, organization leaders, or fellow students—we need to cultivate a critical sensibility (Griffin, 2003) to distinguish between institutionalized and discursively framed differences and international multilingual students' emerging differences, acknowledging that differences are not reified attributes but dynamic processes of changing relationality. To do so, it's important to first recognize the constitutive power of the top-down, institutional discourse of cultural diversity and the way in which neoliberal corporatized universities appropriate the discourse to serve marketing purposes. Admittedly, such discourses, as materialized in, for example, universities' statements of diversity and on-campus cultural fests, should undoubtedly take credit for raising public awareness of cultural differences and facilitating cross-cultural communications. Nevertheless, as stakeholders who collectively shape international multilingual students' experiences, we have full responsibility of taking stock of these discourses before uncritically reinscribing them in our pedagogical or programmatic practices to avert essentializing and stereotyping their experiences. Doing critical work entails engaging our "minds, hearts, and bodies" (Shapiro, 2022, p. 65).

As the narratives of Manna, Wentao, Yang, and Bohan suggest, Chinese international students do share certain similar literate experiences; for example, as the very label indicates, they are transnational migrants who embody the precarious student visa status and who usually communicate in English as their second or additional language (Faist et al., 2013; Guerra, 2016a). They do encounter similar linguistic, cultural, and social hurdles and thus need substantial institutional and programmatic support. Yet their similarities do not justify simplicity when it comes to providing equitable educational experiences. The constantly emerging differences that students perform through their literate activities demand adaptable and dynamic approaches and our willingness and skills to observe, listen, and participate.

Second, we ought to recognize and understand that students perceive and practice differences differently, and through various literate activities of reading, writing, learning, living, and interacting with humans and nonhuman things, embody them, feel them, see them, hear them, ponder them, question them, dismiss them, resist them, embrace them, leverage them, showcase them, and eventually live with them. Behind every verb, we can easily find students' lived experiences that embody and endorse it. Difference is something our students do, rather than something that designates or categorizes them. It is not something that can be pinned down and articulated until it is associated with an action. And there is no single way of doing difference: as the four students' lived experiences demonstrate, the differences they practice through literate activities range from the already institutionalized ones such as language and nationality to the emerging ones such as creative expression through bodily movement and the mobilization of social network resources in diverse cultural groups. In any case, the four highly resourceful and astute individuals time and again defied through their engagement in literacy practices the stagnant societal and institutional difference label—international student/ESL student—that define and categorize them, and presented themselves as mobile literate agents that are able to traverse and inhabit multiple sociocultural, linguistic, and disciplinary spaces and adapt their differential relations with their surroundings.

In general, contrary to the resource/deficit discourses that usually accompany the international/ESL label, which depict these students as financially stable but sociopolitically precarious, the four students in my study never, under any circumstances, emphasized the difference marked by their financial wellbeing or display their insecurity toward their unstable immigration or minority status and linguistically and culturally marginalized position. Quite the opposite; the differences that did consistently play out in their literate practices tended to construct the images of four students who were confident, modest, competent, globetrotting, cosmopolitan, sensitive, reflective, critical (sometimes cynical), versatile, adaptive, and overall different from the *imagined differences* we conveniently attributed to them.

Third, students' practices of difference are always situated and dispersed across complex networks of affordances. These tying and untying structural, semiotic, experiential, social, bodily, and material affordances collectively shape one's perceptions of difference and one's approaches to the practice of difference. On the one hand, we acknowledge that students are agentive decision-makers capable of participating in literate activities for a particular purpose in a particular way with particular people or social groups. On the other hand, we also need to be cognizant of, and sensitive and open to, the ecological forces at work that afford or constrain them as they strive to achieve their goals. In other cases, these affordances may also inhibit their meaning making and decision making, resulting in their silencing certain differences and shifting their expectations. When we set out to understand their practices of difference through literate activities, identifying the affordances undergirding their decisions is an essential first step, as affordances may bear significant material consequences on how they make meaning and position themselves.

The six modes of affordance—structural, semiotic, experiential, social, bodily, and material—to varying degrees mediated the participants' practices of difference. As it stands, the holistic framework proves to be important in interrogating the reductive or one-sided view of who the students are, what they do, and how and why they do what they do. This is because the framework fundamentally challenges the assumption that students possess agency as an innate property while conceptualizing agency as a constantly emerging process distributed across various actants and giving rise to students' actions. It situates students' practices of difference in a vibrant ecology and takes into account multiple modes of affordance beyond the social or discursive ones that we find in the current scholarship. When adopting the framework in our everyday interactions with students, we need to resist the temptation to make premature judgment or inference based on students' one salient affordance; for example, attributing Bohan's perceptions of cultural difference only to his experiences of traveling abroad and interacting with Westerners at a young age without factoring in his pragmatism-driven rhetorical approach to college writing.

Ultimately, reconceptualizing difference as an emergent relationality suggests that to understand students' practices of difference through literate activities, we need to start somewhere and examine the relations from a certain perspective and through a certain lens. The question of where, thus, has always been the source of ultimate contention in the field of anthropology. I dare not claim that the present research has moved beyond cultural relativism, the -emic/-etic debate, and perspectivism to establish a new methodological order in studying Chinese international students' practices of difference. At its best, the research fulfills my long-term desire to advocate a particular way of seeing, listening to, feeling, empathizing with, and fighting for and alongside our students, a way that is microscopic, holistic, humane, and just. I hope, too, that the four stories of my students' ever-so-real bodily experiences not only add to but also question the grand narrative of difference; yes, we are different, but we are different *differently*.

Notes

Introduction

1. All but a few names of people, places, and institutions that appear in the book are pseudonyms.
2. See Chapter 2 for a more thorough explanation of the notion of an institutional discourse of cultural diversity.
3. I use the term "difference" to refer to any asymmetrical relations between two actants. "Difference" is seperate from "diversity," which has been appropriated to denote identity categories.
4. While cautious about the reductive and Western-centric nature of the demographic label "Generation Z," along with its implied cultural stereotypes, I repurpose it to characterize Chinese international students who are collectively "different" from those portrayed in the grand narrative yet different in their unique ways.

Chapter 1: Discourse of Cultural Diversity and Ethnographic Case Study of Literacy Practices

1. It's worth noting the total number of nonimmigrant visas issued in 2021 is less than one third of that in 2017, partly due to pandemic-induced travel restrictions and related geopolitical reasons.

Chapter 2: Manna: From the Dance Floor to Writing Tutor's Table

1. The assignment prompt reads as follows: "*Autoethnography* is a research methodology that seeks to systematically analyze situated personal experience in order to understand cultural experience (Ellis et al., 2011). It is a narrative; and yet, it is also a critical reflection. You need to provide a rich narrative account of a critical incident in your life while also analyzing it from a distance. This means you need to not only *recollect* the details of that critical incident but also *collect* material artifacts relevant to it. You may also interview family members, close friends, or previous teachers to help you recall certain events. For this autoethnography assignment, I invite you to focus on your development as a writer in different languages, for example, your native language and/or English. Particularly, I encourage you to reflect on how different language environments influence your writing and how your writing changes who you are over time. Other areas you might want to consider include: people who have influenced your writing, your memories of successes and failures in writing, your feelings about writing, and your strengths and weaknesses in writing. Feel free to incorporate languages other than English into your autoethnography *when it is necessary* and provide translation. Length: 1500 words."
2. Blair is a pseudonym.

Chapter 3: Wentao: A Structuralist Poet in Disguise

1. "Performing Arts" is a pseudonym.

Chapter 5: Bohan: A Cosmopolitan "Robot Master"

1. Pseudonym.

References

Alexander, J., & Rhodes, J. (2014). Flattening effects: Composition's multicultural imperative and the problem of narrative coherence. *College Composition and Communication*, 65(3), 430–454.

Alexis, C. (2017). The symbolic life of the Moleskine notebook: Material goods as a tableau for writing identity performance. *Composition Studies*, 45(2), 32–54.

American Council on Education & American Association of University Professors. (2000). *Does diversity make a difference? Three research studies on diversity in college classrooms*. American Council on Education & American Association of University Professors.

Ang, I. (2001). *On not speaking Chinese: Living between Asia and the West*. Routledge.

Appadurai, A. (1996). *Modernity at large*. University of Minnesota Press.

Appadurai, A. (2013). *The future as cultural fact: Essays on the global condition*. Verso.

Appiah, K. A. (2006). *Cosmopolitanism: Ethics in a world of strangers*. W. W. Norton & Company.

Atkinson, D. (2014). Language learning in mindbodyworld: A sociocognitive approach to second language acquisition. *Language Teaching*, 47(4), 467–483.

Atkinson, D., Churchill, E., Nishino, T., & Okada, H. (2007). Alignment and interaction in a sociocognitive approach to second language acquisition. *Modern Language Journal*, 91(2), 169–188.

Atkinson, D., Churchill, E., Nishino, T., & Okada, H. (2018). Language learning great and small: Environmental support structures and learning opportunities in a sociocognitive approach to second language acquisition/teaching. *Modern Language Journal*, 102(3), 471–493.

Atkinson, P. (2015). *For ethnography*. Sage.

Bakhtin, M. (1981). Discourse in the novel. In M. Holquist (Ed.), *The Dialogic Imagination* (M. Holquist & C. Emerson, Trans.) (pp. 259–422). University of Texas Press.

Barlow, D. (2016). Composing post-multiculturalism. *College Composition and Communication*, 67(3), 411–436.

Barton, D., & Hamilton, M. (1998). *Local literacies*. Routledge.

Bateson, G. (1972). *Steps to an ecology of mind*. University of Chicago Press.

Bennett, J. (2010). *Vibrant matter: A political ecology of things*. Duke University Press.

Bhabha, H. K. (1990a). The third space. In J. Rutherford (Ed.), *Identity: Community, culture, difference* (pp. 207–221). Lawrence.

Bhabha, H. K. (1990b). *Nation and narration*. Routledge.

Bou Ayash, N. (2019). *Toward translingual realities in composition: (Re)working local language representations and practices*. Utah State University Press.

Bourdieu, P. (1977). The economics of linguistic exchanges. *Social Science Information*, 16(6), 645–668.

Brandt, D., & Clinton, K. (2002). Limits of the local: Expanding perspectives on literacy as a social practice. *Journal of Literacy Research*, 34(3), 337–356.

Butler, J. (2017). Bodies in composition: Teaching writing through kinesthetic performance. *Composition Studies*, 45(2), 73–90.

Canagarajah, A. S. (Ed.). (2013a). *Literacy as translingual practice: Between communities and classrooms*. Routledge.

Canagarajah, A. S. (2013b). Negotiating translingual literacy: An enactment. *Research in the Teaching of English*, 48(1), 40–67.

Canagarajah, A. S. (2013c). *Translingual practice: Global Englishes and cosmopolitan relations*. Routledge.

Canagarajah, A. S. (2017). *Translingual practices and neoliberal policies: Attitudes and strategies of African skilled migrants in anglophone workplaces*. Springer.

Canagarajah, A. S. (2019). Weaving the text: Changing literacy practices and orientations. *College English*, 82(1), 7–28.

Canagarajah, A. S., & Matsumoto, Y. (2017). Negotiating voice in translingual literacies: From literacy regimes to contact zones. *Journal of Multilingual and Multicultural Development*, 38(5), 390–406.

Center for the Study of Education Policy. (2018). *Annual Grapevine compilation of state fiscal support for higher education results for fiscal year 2017-2018*.

Chiseri-Strater, E. (2012). "What goes on here?" The uses of ethnography in composition studies. In K. Ritter & P. K. Matsuda (Eds.), *Exploring composition studies: Sites, issues, perspectives* (pp. 199–210). Utah State University Press.

Choi, J. (2013). *Constructing a multivocal self: A critical autoethnography* [Unpublished dissertation]. University of Technology, Sydney.

Cleaver, F. (2007). Understanding agency in collective action. *Journal of Human Development*, 8(2), 223–244.

Cooper, M. M. (1986). The ecology of writing. *College English*, 48(4), 364–375.

Cooper, M. M. (2011). Rhetorical agency as emergent and enacted. *College Composition and Communication*, 62(3), 420–449.

Costino, K. A., & Hyon, S. (2007). "A class for students like me": Reconsidering relationships among identity labels, residency status, and students' preferences for mainstream or multilingual composition. *Journal of Second Language Writing*, 16, 63–81.

Creswell, J. W. (2013). *Qualitative inquiry and research design: Choosing among five approaches*. Sage.

Daniel, J. R., Malcolm, K., & Rai, C. (Eds.). (2022). *Writing across difference: Theory and intervention*. Utah State University Press.

De Costa, P. I., Li, W., & Lee, J. (Eds.). (2022). *International students' multilingual literacy practices: An asset-based approach to understanding academic discourse socialization*. Multilingual Matters.

Deleuze, G., & Guattari, F. (1987). *A thousand plateaus: Capitalism and schizophrenia*. University of Minnesota Press.

Dervin, F. (2016). *Intercultruality in education: A theoretical and methodological toolbox*. Palgrave Macmillan.

Division of Diversity and Inclusion. (n.d.). *What we do*. "Wabash College." Retrieved April 2023.

Douglas-Gabriel, D. (2017, April 27). Wabash acquires for-profit Lawson University. *The Washington Post*. https://www.washingtonpost.com/news/grade-point/wp/2017/04/27/Wabash-acquires-for-profit-Lawson-university/

Engeström, Y., Engeström, R., & Vahaaho, T. (1999). When the center does not hold: The importance of networking. In S. Chaiklin, M. Hedegaard, & J. Uffe (Eds.), *Activity theory and social practice: Cultural-historical approaches* (pp. 345–374). Aarhus University Press.

Faist, T., Fauser, M., & Reisenauer, E. (2013). *Transnational migration*. Polity Press.

Fetterman, D. M. (2010). *Ethnography: Step-by-step*. Sage.

Fraiberg, S. (2010). Composition 2.0: Toward a multilingual and multimodal framework. *College Composition and Communication*, 62(1), 100–126.

Fraiberg, S., Wang, X., & You, X. (2017). *Inventing the world grant university: Chinese international students' mobilities, literacies, and identities*. Utah State University Press.

Gibson, J. J. (1979). *The ecological approach to visual perception*. Houghton Mifflin.

Giddens, A. (1984). *The constitution of society: Outline of the theory of structuration*. University of California Press.

Gilroy, P. (1993). *The black Atlantic: Modernity and double-consciousness*. Harvard University Press.

Gilyard, K. (2016). The rhetoric of translingualism. *College English*, 78(3), 284–289.

Giroux, H. A. (2002). Neoliberalism, corporate culture, and the promise of higher education: The university as a democratic public sphere. *Harvard Education Review*, 72(4), 425–463.

Goffman, E. (1981). *Forms of talk*. University of Pennsylvania Press.

Gonzales, L. (2015). Multimodality, translingualism, and rhetorical genre studies. *Composition Forum*, 31.

Gries, L. E. (2015). *Still life with rhetoric: A new materialist approach for visual rhetorics*. Utah State University Press.

Griffin, E. A. (2003). *A first look at communication theory*. Boston: McGraw Hill.

Guerra, J. C. (2016a). *Language, culture, identity and citizenship in college classrooms and communities*. Routledge; NCTE.

Guerra, J. C. (2016b). Cultivating a rhetorical sensibility in the translingual writing classroom. *College English, 78*(3), 228–233.

Gurin, P., Dey, E. L., Hurtado, S., & Gurin, G. (2002). Diversity and higher education: Theory and impact on educational outcomes. *Harvard Educational Review, 72*(3), 330–366.

Hall, S. (1990). Cultural identity and diaspora. In J. Rutherford (Ed.), *Identity: Community, culture, difference* (pp. 222–237). Lawrence & Wishart.

Hammersley, M., & Atkinson, P. (1995). *Ethnography: Principles in practice* (2nd ed.). Routledge.

Harris, M. (1968). *The rise of anthropological theory: A history of theories of culture*. T. Y. Crowell.

Harvey, D. (2005). *A brief history of neoliberalism*. Oxford University Press.

Hasler tapped to communicate Wabash's promise. (2018, September 5). Wabash University News. https://www.Wabash.edu/newsroom/releases/2018/Q3/hasler-tapped-to-communicate-Wabashs-promise.html

Heath, S. B. (1982). Ethnography in education: Defining the essentials. In P. Gilmore and A. A. Glatthorn (Eds.), *Children in and out of school: Ethnography and education* (pp. 33–55). Center for Applied Linguistics.

Heath, S. B., & Street, B. V. (2008). *Ethnography: Approaches to language and literacy research*. Teachers College Press.

Herndl, C. G., & Licona, A. C. (2007). Shifting agency: Agency, kairos, and the possibilities of social action. In M. Zachary & C. Thralls (Eds.), *Communicative practices in the workplace and professions: Cultural perspectives on the regulation of discourse and organizations* (pp. 133–153). Baywood Publishing Company.

Holliday, A. (1999). Small cultures. *Applied Linguistics, 20*(2), 237–264.

Horner, B., & Alvarez, S. P. (2019). Defining translinguality. *Literacy in Composition Studies, 7*(2).

Horner, B., Lu, M.-Z., Royster, J. J., & Trimbur, J. (2011). Language difference in writing: Toward a translingual approach. *College English, 73*(3), 303–321.

Institute of International Education. (2020). *Open doors report on international educational exchange*.

Jordan, J. (2015). Material translingual ecologies. *College English, 77*(4), 364–382.

Kerschbaum, S. L. (2014). *Toward a new rhetoric of difference*. NCTE.

Kubota, R. (2004). Critical multiculturalism and second language education. In B. Norton & K. Toohey (Eds.), *Critical pedagogies and language learning* (pp. 30–52). Cambridge University Press.

Laban, R. (1966). *Choreutics*. Dance Books Limited.

Lagman, E. (2018). Literacy remains: Loss and affects in transnational literacies. *College English, 81*(1), 27–49.

Latour, B. (1993). *We have never been modern*. Harvard University Press.

LeCourt, D. (2004). *Identity matters: Schooling the student body in academic discourse*. State University of New York Press.

Leki, I. (2007). *Undergraduates in a second language: Challenges and complexities of academic literacy development*. Lawrence Erlbaum Associates.

Li, W. (2011). Multilinguality, multimodality, and multicompetence: Code- and modeswitching by minority ethnic children in complementary schools. *The Modern Language Journal*, 95(iii), 370–384.

Lillis, T., & Scott, M. (2008). Defining academic literacies research: Issues of epistemology, ideology and strategy. *Journal of Applied Linguistics*, 4(1), 5–32.

Lorimer Leonard, R. (2013). Traveling literacies: Multilingual writing on the move. *Research in the Teaching of English*, 48(1), 13–39.

Lorimer Leonard, R. (2014). Multilingual writing as rhetorical attunement. *College English*, 76(3), 227–247.

Madison, D. S. (2005). *Critical ethnography: Methods, ethics, and performance*. Sage.

Makoni, S., & Pennycook, A. D. (2006). Disinventing and reconstituting languages. In S. Makoni & A. Pennycook (Eds.), *Disinventing and reconstituting languages* (pp. 1–41). Multilingual Matters.

Mao, L. (2005). Rhetorical borderlands: Chinese American rhetoric in the making. *College Composition and Communication*, 56(3), 426–469.

Marston, S. A., Jones, J. P., & Woodward, K. (2005). Human geography without scale. *Transactions of the Institute of British Geographers, New Series*, 30(4), 416–432.

Matsuda, P. K., Saenkhum, T., & Accardi, S. (2013). Writing teachers' perceptions of the presence and needs of second language writers: An institutional case study. *Journal of Second Language Writing*, 22, 68–86.

Micciche, L. R. (2014). Writing material. *College English*, 76(6), 488–505.

Miles, M. B., & Huberman, A. M. (1994). *Qualitative data analysis: A sourcebook of new methods* (2nd ed.). Sage.

Miller, C. R. (2007). What can automation tell us about agency? *Rhetoric Society Quarterly*, 37(2), 137–157.

Miyoshi, M. (2000). Ivory tower in escrow. *Boundary 2*, 27(1), 7–50.

Nordquist, B. (2017). *Literacy and mobility: Complexity, uncertainty, and agency at the nexus of high school and college*. Routledge.

Office of Diversity & Inclusion. (n.d.). *A vision for our campus*. The University of Arizona. Retrieved October 2018, from https://diversity.arizona.edu/vision-our-campus.

Office of Institutional Diversity and Inclusion. (n.d.). *About*. Northwestern University. Retrieved October 2018, from https://www.northwestern.edu/diversity/about/office-diversity-inclusion.html

Office of International Students and Scholars. (2019). *Enrollment & Statistical Report*. Wabash University.

Paige, R. M., et al. (2002). *Maximizing study abroad: A students' guide to strategies for language and culture learning and use*. Center for Advanced Research on Language Acquisition, University of Minnesota.

Papacharissi, Z. (2015). *Affective publics: Sentiment, technology, and politics*. Oxford University Press.

Pennycook, A. (2018). *Posthuman applied linguistics*. Routledge.

Philipsen, G. (1991). The forum: Writing ethnographies. *Quarterly Journal of Speech, 77*, 327–329.

Pratt, M. L. (1991). Arts of the contact zone. *Profession 91*, 33–40.

Prior, P. (2004). Tracing process: How texts come into being. In C. Bazerman & P. Prior (Eds.), *What writing does and how it does it* (pp. 167–200). Lawrence Erlbaum.

Prior, P., & Shipka, J. (2003). Chronotopic lamination: Tracing the contours of literate activity. In C. Bazerman & D. R. Russell (Eds.), *Writing selves/writing societies: Research from activity perspectives* (pp. 180–238). The WAC Clearinghouse.

Ramanathan, V., & Atkinson, D. (1999). Ethnographic approaches and methods in L2 writing research: A critical guide and review. *Applied Linguistics, 20*(1), 44–70.

Readings, B. (1996). *The university in ruins*. Harvard University Press.

Rickert, T. J. (2013). *Ambient rhetoric: The attunements of rhetorical being*. University of Pittsburgh Press.

Roozen, K. (2009). From journal to journalism: Tracing trajectories of literate development. *College Composition and Communication, 60*(3), 541–572.

Roozen, K. (2010). Tracing trajectories of practice: Repurposing in one student's developing disciplinary writing processes. *Written Communication, 27*(3), 318–354.

Rosaldo, R., Lavie, S., & Narayan, K. (1993). Introduction: Creativity in anthropology. In S. Lavie., K. Narayan, & R. Rosaldo (Eds.), *Creativity/anthropology* (pp. 1–8). Cornell University Press.

Rule, H. J. (2018). Writing's rooms. *College Composition and Communication, 69*(3), 402–432.

Said, E. W. (1978). *Orientalism*. Vintage Books.

Said, E. W. (1999). *Out of place: A memoir*. Vintage Books.

Shapiro, S. (2022). *Cultivating critical language awareness in the writing classroom*. Routledge.

Silva, T. (1997). On the ethical treatment of ESL writers. *TESOL Quarterly, 31*(2), 359–363.

Silva, T., & Wang, Z. (Eds.). (2021). *Reconciling translingualism and second language writing*. Routledge.

Song, J. (2020). Contesting and negotiating othering from within: A Saudi Arabian female student's gendered experiences in the U.S. *Journal of Language, Identity & Education, 19*(3), 149–162.

Spivak, G. C. (1985). Can the subaltern speak? *Wedge, 7*(8), 120–130.

Spradley, J. P. (1980). *Participant observation*. Holt, Rinehart & Winston.

Stake, R. E. (2000). Case studies. In N. K. Denzin & Y. S. Lincoln (Eds.), *Handbook of qualitative research* (2nd ed., pp. 435–454). Sage.

Streeck, J. (2015). Embodiment in human communication. *Annual Review of Anthropology, 44*, 419–438.

Street, B. (1993). *Culture is a verb: Anthropological aspects of language and cultural process*. British Association for Applied Linguistics.

Sunstein, B. S. (1998). Moveable feasts, liminal spaces: Writing centers and the state of in-betweenness. *Writing Center Journal*, 18(2), 7–26.

Syverson, M. A. (1999). *The wealth of reality: An ecology of composition*. Southern Illinois University Press.

Thomas, J. (1993). *Doing critical ethnography*. Sage.

Tsui, A. B. M., & Tollefson, J. W. (Eds.). (2007). *Language policy, culture, and identity in Asian contexts*. Routledge.

Turner, V. (1982). *From ritual to theatre: The human seriousness of play*. PAJ Publications.

United States Department of State-Bureau of Consular Affairs. (2021). *Nonimmigrant visas issued by classification and nationality (including border crossing cards): Fiscal year 2021. Report of the Visa Office 2021*.

University of California Regents v. Bakke, 438 U.S. 265 (1978).

van Lier, L. (2004). *The ecology and semiotics of language learning: A sociocultural perspective*. Kluwer Academic Publishers.

Vertovec, S. (2007). Super-diversity and its implications. *Ethnic and Racial Studies*, 30(6), 1024–1054.

Wang, X. (2019). Tracing connections and disconnections: Reading, writing, and digital literacies across contexts. *College Composition and Communication*, 70(4), 560–589.

Wang, Z. (2019). Relive differences through a material flashback. *College Composition and Communication*, 70(3), 380–412.

Wang, Z. (2022). Auto-ethnographic performance of differences as anti-racist pedagogy. In B. Schreiber, E. Lee, J. Johnson, & N. Fahim (Eds.), *Linguistic Justice on Campus: Pedagogy and Advocacy for Multilingual Students* (pp. 41–57). Multilingual Matters.

Wargo, J. M., & De Costa, P. I. (2017). Tracing academic literacies across contemporary literacy sponsorscapes: Mobilities, ideologies, identities, and technologies. *London Review of Education*, 15(1), 101–114.

Weedon, C. (1987). *Feminist practice & poststructuralist theory*. Blackwell Publishing.

West, C., & Fenstermaker, S. (1995). Doing difference. *Gender and Society*, 9(1), 8–37.

West, C., & Zimmerman, D. H. (1987). Doing gender. *Gender and Society*, 1(2), 125–151.

West, J. T. (1993). Ethnography and ideology: The politics of cultural representation. *Western Journal of Communication*, 57(2), 209–220.

Willard-Traub, M. K. (2018). Writing programs and a new ethos for globalization. In S. K. Rose & I. Weiser (Eds.), *The internationalization of US writing programs* (pp. 44–59). Utah State University Press.

Williams, B. T. (2018). *Literacy practices and perceptions of agency: Composing identities*. Routledge.

You, X. (2016). *Cosmopolitan English and transliteracy*. Southern Illinois University Press.

You, X. (Ed.). (2018). *Transnational writing education*. Routledge.

Zhang, J. (2013). 从你的全世界路过. Hunan Literature and Art Publishing House.

Zhang-Wu, Q. (2022). *Language myths and realities: Journeys of Chinese international students*. Multilingual Matters.

Index

Page numbers followed by n indicate notes.

affective experiences/bonds, 42, 50; with complex and conflicting identities and community memberships, 147; lyrics writing and, 99, 101–2; making translingual and transmodal, 84–89; to social and material surroundings, 60

affordances: complexly networked affordances, 101, 178–81; differences and, 178–81; transformation of, 72

agency, 18, 30–32, 59, 159; material affordances and, 175; network of affordances and differences and, 180–81; semiotic affordance and, 168; social affordances and, 171; structural affordances and, 167

Alexander, J., 23

ambivalence, 91, 139–40, 144, 146, 153, 161

Ang, I., 21, 106

Appadurai, A., 20–21

appearance, 113–14, 129, 146

Appiah, K. A., 156

appropriations, 5, 6, 9, 24–27, 168

Atkinson, D., 31, 32

Atkinson, P., 148–49

authorial identity, 49, 164, 167, 178

authorial voice, 168

autoethnography, 187–88n1

awareness: audience, 42, 60; conscious, 53, 59; cultural, 125, 156; of cultural differences, raising, 182–85; genre, 77, 146; rhetorical, 112, 116–17; situational, 71

Barlow, D., 22
Bateson, G., 31
Bhabha, H., 21, 23
bias, 14, 34, 108

bodily affordances, 29, 36–42, 173–75; of Bohan, 127, 132–33, 174–75; of Manna, 42, 58–59, 174; of Yang, 109–17, 174–75, 179

Bohan, literacy affordances of: bodily affordances of, 127, 132–33, 174–75; cosmopolitan sensibility, 156–57; cultural stereotyping, views on, 126–29; disciplinary identity through writing to learn, 130–39; embracing in-betweenness, 153–55; embracing multilinguality and translinguality, 142, 152, 153; experiential affordances of, 171; intercultural communication by, 181; introduction, 11, 16, 119–21; material affordances of, 127–28, 134, 176–77; negotiating rhetorics of difference, 165; reflecting on cross-cultural experiences, 121–29; re-selfing in social spaces, 139–46; resisting cultural Othering, 162; rhetorical sensibility to cultural differences, 122–23; social affordances of, 173; structural affordances of, 125, 168; transnational affordance of, 129

Canagarajah, A. S., 22, 31, 160, 168
Chiseri-Strater, E., 34
Choi, J., 21–22
code meshing, 142, 176
collaborative writing, 68, 77, 164
communicative competences, 69, 72, 79
community engagement, 144, 173
competing identities, forming, 43–52
Cooper, M., 29
cosmopolitan sensibility, 78–84, 93–102, 156–57
critical reflective ability, 114–15
cross-cultural rhetorical awareness, 115–17

cultural boundaries, redrawing, 121–29
cultural capital: dancing talent as, 36, 151, 180; disciplinary, 139, 168; of linguistic resources, 48, 84, 139, 151, 172
cultural differences, representations of, 124–25
cultural diversity, institutional discourse of, 23–27
cultural experiences through language learning, 99. *See also* language learning
cultural insider, 157
culturally conditioned visual material, 168
culturally constructed identities, 159; resisting, 160–61
cultural mobility, 155. *See also* transnational mobility, leveraging
cultural Othering, 159–60; resisting, 162–63
cultural profiling, 159
cultural repertoires, 17
cultural representation, 34, 99
cultural sensibility, 48, 60, 83, 105–6; difference and, 43–52, 60, 83, 105
cultural stereotyping, 125–29, 162, 171
cultural utility, 152
cultural values and material environment, 176–77

dancing, to articulate rhetorical difference, 36–42
data collection, 12, 37, 43, 112
Deleuze, G., 30
developing friendship, 39–40. *See also* community engagement; social networking
difference(s): acknowledging, 43–52, 65; negotiating meaning of, 163; network of affordances and, 178–81; perception of, 77; rhetorical, 36–42. *See also* Bohan, literacy affordances of; Manna, literacy affordances of; resisting difference; Wentao, literacy affordances of; Yang, literacy affordances of
differences, embracing, 150; in-betweenness, 153–55; multilinguality and translinguality, 151–53
disciplinary identity through writing to learn, 130–39
discursive construction of notion, 114
dominant affordances, 72

ecological affordances, 17–18, 27–31, 41, 70–71. *See also* bodily affordances; experiential affordances; material affordances; semiotic affordances; social affordances; structural affordances

The Ecological Approach to Visual Perception (Gibson), 28
educational goals, 123
emotional homeostasis, 55, 59, 60, 169
ethnographic case study, 31–34
ethnographic fieldwork goals, 148–49
experiential affordances, 29, 169–71; Bohan, 139–46, 170–71; Manna, 52, 171; Wentao, 65, 170–71; Yang, 93–102, 170–71

Fenstermaker, S., 14
Fenstermaker, W., 14
Fraiberg, S., 175

gaze, public cultural, 161
gender, reconceptualizing, 14
Gibson, J. J., 28
Gilyard, K., 22–23
global corporatization in academia, 26
Gonzales, L., 157–58
Guattari, F., 30

Heath, S. B., 33
Horner, B., 22

identity construction: institutionally constructed identities, resisting, 160–62; through community engagement, 144; through language learning, 78–84, 93–102; through social media, 84–89
identity labels, 7–9, 161
identity markers, 28, 155, 160; institutionalized, 7, 16, 150
in-betweenness, 21, 83, 153–55, 161
individual competitiveness in neoliberal institutional climate, 155
institutional discourse of cultural diversity, 6–7, 15, 23–27
institutionalized difference markers, 13, 25, 158
institutionalized diversity in neoliberal institutional climate, 155
institutionalized identity marker, 7, 16, 150
institutionally constructed identities, 24, 160–62
institutional rhetorics, 115. *See also* Yang, literacy affordances of
intercultural communication, 123, 127, 130, 162, 181
intercultural competence, 16, 123, 128, 162
intercultural learning, 123–24. *See also* language learning
interviews, 10, 12–13, 58, 176

Japanese language learning, 78–84, 93–102
Jordan, J., 31

kinesphere, extending, 36–42, 174

language learning, 28; ecological affordances in, 31; identity construction through, 78–84, 93–102
Latour, B., 30
LeCourt, D., 170
leveraging difference, 155; cosmopolitan sensibility, 156–57; multimodal creativity, 157–59
liminal space, 60, 117, 153–55
linguistic capital, gaining. *See* Japanese language learning
linguistic creativity, 62–72, 89–90, 179
linguistic ingenuity, 62, 65, 68, 72
linguistic legacies, 99
linguistic repertoire, 28–29, 42, 82, 89, 110–11, 129
linguistic representation, 99
linguistic resources, 101; learning new language as, 78–84, 93–102; limitations on, 82–83
linguistic sensibility, 83. *See also* language learning
literate activities: Bohan's, 129, 130, 139, 166; doing difference through, 12, 13, 17, 27, 33; language and, 9–10; Manna's, 36, 43, 60; network of affordances and differences and, 178–80; on social media, 86–89; Wentao's, 63, 84, 86, 88; Yang's, 101
literate socialization, 84, 92, 174–75
Lorimer Leonard, R., 27, 163
Lu, M.-Z., 22
lyrics writing in Japanese, 93–102

Makoni, S., 22
Manna, literacy affordances of: approaching writing center with differences, 43–52; articulating rhetorical difference through dancing, 36–42; bodily affordances of, 42, 58–59, 174; ecological affordances of, 43–52; embracing in-betweenness, 153–55; embracing multilinguality, 43–52, 151–52; experiential affordances, 52, 171; introduction, 10–11, 15–16, 35–36; material affordances of, 41, 177; multimodal creativity, 158–59; negotiating rhetorics of difference, 164; performing the introspective self through reading and journaling, 52–59; resisting cultural Othering, 163; rhetorical sensibility of, 180; semio-material affordances of, 59; semiotic affordances of, 48–49, 169; social affordances of, 42, 173; structural affordances of, 41
marketization of diversity, 25–27
material affordances, 29, 175–78; agency and, 175; of Bohan, 127–28, 134, 176–77; of Manna, 41, 177; social media as, 176–77; technological infrastructure as, 176–77; of Wentao, 63, 69–71, 176–77; of Yang, 177–78, 179
material goals, 84
Maximizing Study Abroad: A Students' Guide to Strategies for Language and Culture Learning and Use (Paige), 125
meaning: making, 13, 27, 31, 69, 157–59, 164, 175; negotiation, 158, 168
metacognitive ability, 158
Micciche, L. R., 30
Miyoshi, M., 26
Modernity at Large: Cultural Dimensions of Globalization (Appadurai), 20–21
multicultural pedagogy, 23
multilinguality, 151–53; Bohan embracing, 142; Manna embracing, 43–52; Wentao embracing, 73–78; Yang embracing, 93–102
multimodal artifacts, 13
multimodal creativity, 148, 155, 157–59
multimodal forms of expression, 77–78
multimodal semiotic resources, 169

negotiate meaning of difference, 163
neoliberalism, 25, 160
new materialism, 30, 175
nonverbal communicative information, 112, 113–14

Othering. *See* cultural Othering

Paige, R. M., 125
peer group, 11, 36, 62, 83, 119, 141, 145
Pennycook, A., 22
perception of difference, 77
performative identity, creating, 101–2
physical place, 177–78
positionality, negotiating, 7, 15, 72, 88, 153, 154, 164
Prior, P., 149, 166
professional development, 124, 144
proxy cultural experience, 123
public cultural gaze, 161

Regents of the University of California v. Bakke, 6
religious legacies, 99

research methodologies, 32, 33, 109
resisting difference, 159; constructed identity, 160–61; negotiating and redefining difference, 163–65; othering, 162–63
rhetorical difference, articulating through dancing, 36–42
rhetorical education, 109, 117
rhetorical escape, 116
rhetorical exigencies, 126, 129, 131, 138–39, 140–41, 159
rhetorical goals, 84
rhetorical sensibility to cultural differences, 99, 174, 180; of Bohan, 122–23; of Manna, 180; of Yang, 109–17
rhetorical sensitivity, 16, 27, 89, 112, 114–17, 122–23, 139, 155
rhetorical versatility, 109–15
rhetoric of face, 114–15, 161. See also bodily affordances
Rhodes, J., 23
Rickert, T., 30–31
Rule, H., 175, 177–78

Said, E., 21
self-sponsored literate activities, 9
semio-material affordance, 59
semiotic affordances, 28, 174, 179; agency and, 168; concept of, 168–69; of Manna, 48–49, 169; multimodality and, 158; of Wentao, 63, 65, 67–71, 169; writing as, 169; of Yang, 101
sense of self, 21, 49
Shipka, J., 149, 166
social affordances, 29, 36–42, 171–73; agency and, 171; of Bohan, 173; of Manna, 42, 173; of Wentao, 65, 172–73; of Yang, 102–9, 179
social capital, 15–16, 142, 146
social media: content, 86; ecological affordances in, 87–88; identity construction through, 84–89; as material affordance, 176–77; posting, timing of, 85–86
social motivation as affordance, 173
social networking, 126–27, 144; avoiding, 92–93. See also developing friendship
social participation, 172. See also community engagement
social resources, 42, 65, 72, 78, 146, 175
sociocultural integration, 61–62
spatiotemporal specifics, 70
Stake, R., 33
storytelling, 18, 158
Street, B., 31–32
structural affordances, 28, 41–42, 167–68; agency and, 167; of Bohan, 125, 168; of Manna, 41; of Wentao, 63–64; of Yang, 93–102, 167–68
student club, affordances through participating in, 72–78
Syverson, M., 29–30

technological infrastructure as material affordance, 176–77
togetherness-in-difference, 89, 106–7, 109, 171
transcultural competence, 84
translingual creativity, 16, 93–102, 152, 161
translingual identity, negotiating, 158
translinguality: Bohan embracing, 142; leveraging, 164–65; Manna embracing, 43–52; Wentao embracing, 73–78; Yang embracing, 93–102
translingual lyrics writing and affordances, 93–101
translingual practices, 9, 158
transnational affordance, 129
transnational mobility, leveraging, 7, 164–65
Turner, V., 153

Undergraduate Chinese Association (UCA), 8
US universities, marketing campaigns of, 5–6

van Lier, L., 28

Wabash Performance Collaborative (WPC), 73
Wabash University Chinese Students and Scholars Association (WUCSSA), 8
Wang, X., 149
WeChat as Chinese identity, 64, 85, 89, 128, 139, 142
Weibo (a popular Chinese Twitter-like microblogging site), 53
Wentao, literacy affordances of: ecological affordances of, 87–88; embracing in-betweenness, 153–55, 161; embracing multilinguality and translinguality, 73–78, 152–53; experiential affordances of, 65, 170–71; introduction, 11, 16, 61–62; involvement in student organization, 72–78; Japanese learning as a gateway to a transcultural and cosmopolitan self, 78–84; linguistic ingenuity and teamwork, 62–72; making translingual and transmodal affective connections, 84–89; material affordances of, 63, 69–71, 176–77; multimodal creativity of, 158–59; negotiating rhetorics of difference, 163–64; resisting constructed identity, 161; semiotic affordances of, 63, 65, 67–71, 169;

social affordances of, 65, 172–73; structural affordances of, 63–64; working for the Performing Arts club, 72–78
West, C., 14
West, J., 34
Willard-Traub, M., 25
writing: collaborative, 68, 77, 164; disciplinary identity through, 130–39; lyrics writing in Japanese, 93–102; as semiotic affordance, 169; as a simile, 37–38, 40
writing centers, 154; approaching with differences, 43–52

Yang, literacy affordances of: an onlooker/player's insights into the game of pop music industry, 102–9; bodily affordances of, 109–17; cosmopolitan sensibility, 93–102, 157; ecological affordances of, 95–97, 116–17; embracing in-betweenness, 153–55; embracing multilinguality and translinguality, 93–102, 152, 154; experiential affordances of, 93–102, 170–71; introduction, 11, 16, 91–93; liminality, 154; lyrics writing, 93–102; material affordances of, 177–78, 179; negotiating rhetorics of difference, 164–65; resisting constructed identity, 160–61; rhetorical sensibility, 109–17; semiotic resources of, 101; social affordances of, 102–9, 179; structural affordances of, 93–102, 167–68; symbolic bodily affordances of, 174–75, 179

Zhang-Wu, Q., 9
Zimmerman, D. H., 14

www.ingramcontent.com/pod-product-compliance
Lightning Source LLC
Chambersburg PA
CBHW022221090526
44585CB00013BB/659